COMPLETE

Charleston

A GUIDE TO THE ARCHITECTURE, HISTORY, GARDENS AND FOOD OF CHARLESTON AND THE LOWCOUNTRY

By Margaret H. Moore
Photographs By Truman Moore

•

Introduction by Robert Russell
Addlestone Professor of Architectural History
College of Charleston

This book was made possible by a grant from Furthermore, the publication program of the J. M. Kaplan Fund and was sponsored by the Preservation Society of Charleston

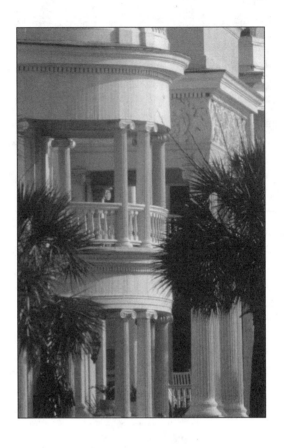

ISBN 978-0-9660144-3-3
Fourth Edition

Published by TM Photography, Inc., P.O. Box 351,
Charleston, SC 29402 • 843-577-3237

Cover and design by Janet Vicario
Layout Dan Peschio, Rachel Brown, and Fireball Media

TABLE OF CONTENTS

THE TOURS

EXPLORING THE LOWCOUNTRY

RESTAURANT GUIDE

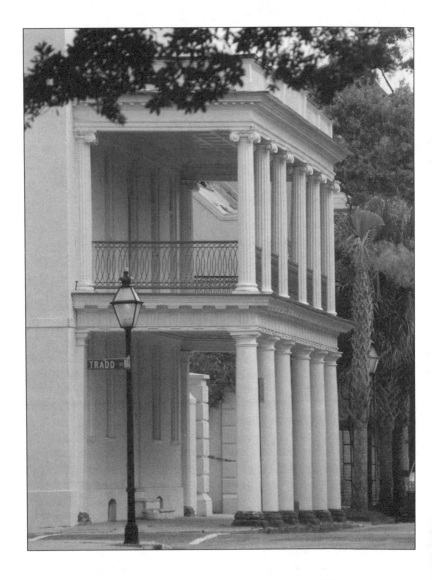

PREFACE

Welcome to Charleston, America's most historic city and also the most walkable, not just because the city is small, but because the scale is small. When you walk down a street, there is plenty to look at. On Broad Street, for example, there are 35 ornate historic buildings between East Bay and Church. One block of King has 22 shops and two restaurants. Even on the Battery, and in the antebellum planter neighborhoods, such as the Mazyck Wraggborough Garden District, the large mansions are surprisingly close together.

You can easily stroll from the Visitors center to the Battery — it's only 1.3 miles. The very compact central business district includes several hundred shops and over 130 RESTAURANTS. Charleston is a serious culinary city. The presence of so many nationally-acclaimed chefs, as well as its geographic location, makes Charleston a logical base for an extended stay for exploring the Lowcountry. The culinary tourist might settle in for a week for the food alone. See our updated RESTAURANT GUIDE on Page 270. It is always wise to make reservations for dinner.

You can explore all of the Old and Historic District with Complete Charleston — in your armchair at home and step by step while you are here. We also guide you on Lowcountry SIDE TRIPS to PLANTATIONS, BEAUFORT, BROOKGREEN GARDENS, GEORGETOWN and SAVANNAH.

The incredible beauty which exists on a single block of Charleston is due to the remarkable intactness of the city's streetscapes. In 1931, Charleston was the first city in the world to pass a preservation ordinance protecting entire neighborhoods rather than just individual landmarks. An assemblage of historic buildings, both grand and modest, presents a compelling representation of a city's heritage.

It is a dreadful mistake to try and see Charleston from a car or a tour bus. Or to think the Battery is the main sight. Grand mansions of the planter aristocracy are located in Radcliffeborough, Harleston Village and Mazyck Wraggborough Garden District. The Victorian district is centered around Colonial Lake in Harleston Village. Ansonborough has the largest concentration of Greek Revival buildings in America. All the neighborhood walks include buildings significant to AFRICAN-AMERICAN HISTORY (See index).

Strolling slowly is the only way to savor the sensuous fragrances of tea olive and jasmine and experience the serendipitous pleasure of discovering the many beautiful byways, gardens, intricate doorways, lacy iron gates, ornaments and the compelling urbanism.

The architecture and urbanism of Charleston have been a major inspiration for hundreds of "New Urbanist" communities being built in America today. Andres Duany, the founder of that movement, spoke in Charleston recently, extolling Charleston as an "incredibly unique place"—he tells Europeans that Charleston is the best America has.

A mere decade ago the center of town was at Broad and Meeting, and the misconception was that the "historic district" was all south of Broad. Today the center has moved up to Marion Square. On Saturday morning, the farmers market here is not to be missed — it is a weekly festival featuring local produce and organic veggies for serious foodies, crafts, pony rides, music and highly coveted café tables where locals and visitors meet for breakfast and lunch.

You may well be overcome by the Palladian grandeur of a city that surely has more columns than any city built since the Renaissance. Palladian

Randolph Hall

details have prevailed in Charleston through the centuries. The tiers of colonnaded piazzas (Charleston's word for porches) and elevated basements are ideal for Charleston's climate just as they were for the villas Palladio designed for the Lowcountry of the Veneto. The temple portico of Randolph Hall at the College of Charleston reminds one of the Villa Malcontenta by Palladio in Italy. Stucco over brick and scored to resemble stone is another practical Palladian detail.

The city's unique single house (see Introduction) has been a major factor in continuing the presence of Palladian colonnades for 250 years. By historian Gene Waddell's count, nearly 3000 single houses survive and more are being built.

Although sidewalk loggias (as on page IV) have been around since the first century AD and can be found all over Europe, they are rare in the United States. They are perfect for Charleston's climate, giving protection from the intense sunshine and frequent showers in the spring and summer. Historically they were found throughout Charleston's central business district, especially on Meeting Street. The sidewalk loggia/portico is making a comeback today and can be seen in a number of New Urbanistic communities. The contemporary classical architect Jaquelin Robertson included a sidewalk portico on Broad Street in his design for Charleston's new Judicial Center, which is mostly behind historic buildings on Broad Street, between King and Meeting.

During the Renaissance, Palladio's works were noted for their chiaroscuro (light and shade) effects. Charleston is enriched with chiaroscuro as well. Ornate small-scale ornamental details create a special texture on the city's streetscapes, which is constantly changing as the sun changes. Notice the variety of columns and capitals. More elegant buildings have fluted columns and ornate Corinthian capitals. The Tower of the Winds motif was popular in

Chiaroscuro on King Street

Charleston. A measure of architectural sophistication can be seen in piazzas where there is a progression of the orders with Doric on the first level, then Ionic and Corinthian on the third story (such as 24 Meeting Street, see page 289).

You may have thought of Charleston as a thoroughly colonial city, like Williamsburg. Stylistically, Charleston is a textbook of many classical styles. The city streetscapes illustrate the incredible variety that can be achieved by creative builders and architects, who combined elements from such pattern books as James Gibb's *Book of Architecture* (1728) and Palladio's *Four Books of Architecture* (1580).

As you explore the eleven neighborhoods in the Old and Historic District, we urge you to pause along the way to experience another of Charleston's pleasures—its charming small restaurants and cafes, which abound on the edges of the residential neighborhoods. We've included convenient COFFEE BREAK suggestions in each chapter, some where you might have a cool drink or some for a complete meal. See our expanded RESTAURANT GUIDE, page 270, for dinner ideas as well.

Between feasts, we urge you to explore the Lowcountry. This expanded edition of Complete Charleston now includes SIDE TRIPS to Savannah, Brookgreen Gardens, the plantations, Georgetown and Beaufort, complete with walking-tour maps, photographs and restaurants, plus a historical overview by Professor Robert Russell.

Many people made *Complete Charleston* possible. Professor Russell shaped many of our ideas and supplied us with a host of observations you will find woven through the text. He and Dr. Alexander Moore read the manuscript, but what errors remain are entirely ours. Anthony Tung gave us the idea of a book that would take the visitor on foot though the whole Old and Historic District, not just the well-trod paths of the Battery. Anthony Wood walked the first walks and kindly pointed out our follies. Janet Vicario in New York, aided by fax, phone and FedEx, designed the book, the maps and the cover. The staffs of the Charleston County Library, The Library Society, The College of Charleston Library, The Avery Research Center for African-American History and Culture, The South Carolina Historical Society and City Planning could not have been more helpful, unfailingly guiding us though the labyrinths of historical research. Information for Guides of Historic Charleston was invaluable as were the articles of Robert Stockton and W. H. J. Thomas in the *News & Courier*.

In various ways, we were aided and encouraged by Joanie Lucas Harth, Dr. Jack Simmons, Annelise Simmons, Lynn McBride, Mary Moore Jacoby, Marjorie Pearson, Suzannah Simmons, Elise Pinckney, Barbara Vaughn, Jane Lucas Thornhill, Elizabeth Jenkins Young, Carol Tiernan, Sarah Bradford Landau, Randolph Martz, Ethel S. Nepveux, Kay Townsend, Rose Tomlin, Helen Jacobs, Chilton Simmons, Carol Power, Don Tomlin, John Townsend, John Markham, Gene Waddell, Charles Duell, Lois Reamy, Selden Hill, William Kinney and Cynthia Cole Jenkins, Electra Yourke for her merciless editing of our wandering style, and Seabrook Wilkinson for copyediting the expanded restaurant guide.

We would especially like to thank Joan K. Davidson of Furthermore, the publication program of the J. M. Kaplan Fund, for a timely grant, and the Preservation Society of Charleston for sponsoring the book.

During the summer months, Charleston is quite hot. We urge you to have a nice long lunch and do your walking in the morning and the evening. Wear comfortable shoes.

For further insights into Charleston as a living historic city, visit the web site of The Committee To Save the City, Inc., of which we were among the founding members. www.savethecity.org.

We hope our book will enrich your trip and help you plan your next visit.

Margaret and Truman Moore

INTRODUCTION

Charleston single house

Charleston is a small scale city and needs to be seen on foot. The neighborhoods you will see with this book will bring you in close contact with the buildings, the people and the history that made this unique place.

Charleston is a town unlike any other, and its architecture contributes significantly to its uniqueness. The history of the city and the history of its architecture are more closely intertwined than is true of perhaps any other North American city, if for no other reason than that Charleston invented its own unique form of domestic dwelling: the famous Charleston single house.

But the single house was not created simultaneously with the city, and the early architectural history of Charleston is the history of colonial development, from the earliest roof-over-your head structures (convincingly recreated across the Ashley river at Charles Towne Landing State Historic Site) to the already-substantial brick buildings of a generation or so later (Old St. Andrew's parish church, west of the Ashley of c. 1706 or St. James', Goose Creek, of 1715), to the unabashedly high style of mid-eighteenth century Drayton Hall, also west of the Ashley river (1738-43), St. Michael's church (1750s) and the old Exchange building and the Miles Brewton house (both from the late 1760s). In itself, this early history is not surprising. What is surprising is the speed at which it occurred, and the very high quality of what was built. Evidently, the colonial citizens of Charles Town were much more interested in (and were more able to afford) top-drawer architecture for their town, almost from the very beginning.

Old Exchange Building

Miles Brewton House

St. Michael's Church

Colonial architecture ended, of course, with the transformation of colonial America into the United States, and the next great period of Charleston architecture corresponds to this political shift. What is frequently called the 'Federal Period' in American architecture — the curious mutation of a political designation into a stylistic one — was called in Charleston the 'Adam Period' or 'Adamesque.' While less generally well-known than 'Federal Style' as a style name, it actually makes more sense to call late 18th and early 19th-century American architecture by this name, since so much of it derived from the architectural work of the Scottish brothers James and Robert Adam (active in the mid-eighteenth century). Robert Adam in particular was heavily influenced by the recently rediscovered Roman towns of Herculaneum and Pompeii, and his architecture, particularly his interiors, was characterized by the use of classical Roman decoration of the most attenuated and delicate sort.

Professional architects were scarce in this period in America, and the most important name in Charleston architecture around 1800 is undoubtedly Gabriel Manigault, member of an important Charleston Huguenot family and a dedicated and talented gentleman architect along the lines of America's most famous amateur builder: Thomas Jefferson. Manigault, who had made his Grand Tour (not at all unusual for the sons of Charleston's elite), might well have had first-hand knowledge of contemporary European architectural practice. He certainly made his mark on his native city, building the South Carolina Society Hall on lower Meeting Street, his brother

City Hall

Fireproof Building

First Baptist Church

Joseph's house on upper Meeting Street, probably the present-day City Hall at the corner of Meeting and Broad, and a whole host of other buildings which have either been demolished, or not securely attributed to him.

Manigault moved from Charleston to Philadelphia early in the nineteenth century, leaving something of an architectural vacuum in the city. Robert Mills, another native son, attempted to fill it, beginning in 1804 with his design for the Circular Congregational Church on Meeting Street (destroyed in the fire of 1861). Although he designed several important buildings in Charleston, and many more elsewhere in South Carolina, for reasons that remain unclear, Mills was never enthusiastically embraced by his fellow citizens, and the architect of the two most famous Washington Monuments in the nation remains more of a national figure than a local one.

While understandably proud of his First Baptist Church (1819-22, lower Church Street) and the superb Fireproof Building (1822-26, Meeting and Chalmers Streets), Mills may have been a little austere for Charleston's taste. Mills proclaimed himself to be the first to introduce 'correct' Greek architecture to the city with his design for the Baptist Church (proving that intention is about 9/10s of the rule for Greek Revival). He was not to be the one to make it popular.

It was actually one of Charleston's periodic disasters that set the stage for the large-scale introduction of Greek Revival architecture into the city. The fire of 1838 destroyed a large part of what is now Ansonborough, including a number of religious buildings, and Antebellum Charleston proved itself *au courant* with national taste by rebuilding almost all of these structures in the then-fashionable Greek style, characterized by simple Greek-temple rectangular shapes, low pediments, recognizable Greek orders, particularly the Doric, and the color white. Ranging from

Hibernian Hall

elegant and archaeologically correct examples by nationally-known architects (T.U. Walter's Hiberian Society Hall, for example, on Meeting Street), to the homespun Greek of St. Mary's Roman Catholic Church on Hasell Street, Charlestonians carried on a love affair with this style of architecture for nearly fifteen years, giving it up only in the face of local and national ridicule in the persons of William Gilmore Simms, Charleston poet and literary figure and the New York landscape architect and mid-century arbiter of national architectural taste, Andrew Jackson Downing.

It was Downing, famous as a proponent of almost any style except the Greek, who is probably the key figure standing behind the architectural transformation in Charleston in the late 1840s and 1850s. The important architectural personalities of this period are E.B. White in the 1840s, and E.C. Jones and F.D. Lee, the dynamic duo of Charleston's architectural scene in the 1850s. White, who had begun as Charleston's most accomplished practitioner of the Greek Revival in the early 1840s, had by the middle of the decade become Charleston's most adept Gothic Revival designer. By 1850, he had moved beyond Gothic Revival to an elegant and impressive manner of Roman-Renaissance classicism. By the early 1850s, White seems to have traded his concern for stylistic innovation for a steady paycheck, becoming the supervising architect of the new Federal Custom House at the foot of Market Street.

Jones and Lee, both together and separately (they were in partnership from 1852 until 1857), carried the torch of stylistic eclecticism through the decade of the 1850s. Edward Jones, the older of the two, strongly favored the Italianate, or 'bracketed' style so dear to the heart of A.J.Downing, with such picturesque works as Magolia Cemetery (1850), 1 Broad Street (1853), and the J.A.S. Ashe house at 26 South Battery (by 1853). Francis Lee appears to have been even more stylistically adventurous than Jones, equally at home with the Moorish exoticism of the Farmers' and Exchange Bank (1853), and the late English Perpendicular Gothic of the interior of the Unitarian Church. Jones and Lee were also responsible for what must have been one of Charleston's most exotic examples of Mid-century Eclecticism, the 'Moorish' fish market

Ashe House

which stood at the foot of the Market, about where the Custom House stands now, and has, alas, disappeared without a trace.

Jones and Lee's fish market was remarkable in its day not only for its exotic style, but also for its technical innovation. It was constructed with quantities of cast iron, which was a new innovation in architecture. The row of cast iron store fronts along the west side of Meeting Street, from Hasell to Market, give still some indication of what many of the commercial districts of the city must have looked like around the middle of the century. Charleston was mentioned in the advertisements of James Bogardus of New York City in the mid-1850s as a place where his cast iron architectural elements were in use.

The great advantage of cast iron as a new architectural material in the middle of the nineteenth century was that it was not tied to any particular historical style. This made it a perfect material for the time, since the middle of the century saw the rise of an approach to architecture that was much less concerned with stylistic rigor or purity than it was with overt picturesque effects, which could be created by any means necessary. Whereas eighteenth-century colonial Georgian architecture, or the Greek Revival of the earlier part of the nineteenth century, had specific and overt political and social connotations, the approach taken by mid-century architects was one that was essentially eclectic — that is, characterized by a

Cast Iron Store Fronts

mixture of various (and sometimes competing) styles — rather than stylistically rigorous. No longer was it particularly important to get all the details right; it was much more necessary to create a memorable and effective piece of architecture. Thus the Moorish markets and banks of Charleston, the Persian houses and Venetian society halls and Norman churches all reflect the mid-century opening of the city's taste to national (not to mention international) influences.

But it was an opening of the taste of Charleston's mercantile middle class, not of the aristocratic elite that had for so long controlled the city. The taste of this upper crust seems not to have been mightily changed by what was happening in the larger architectural world, perhaps because this stratum of Charleston society was already well provided for with earlier examples of high-style architecture, both domestic and institutional.

There is no doubt but that the most typical, the most characteristic, and the most curious sort of Charleston architecture ever developed has nothing to do with the stylistic transformations that have been mentioned above. What is known as the Charleston single house is an architectural form, only peripherally, if at all, affected by stylistic change. There are

Greek Revival single houses and Adamesque single houses. There are Italianate single houses. There could be Gothic Revival single houses (but there aren't). Whatever the particular style used, this most effective definer of the Charleston streetscape remains essentially the same, and it is therefore imperative, for one who wishes to understand how Charleston works as a city, to understand the make-up and functioning of the single house.

The most immediately distinguishable characteristic of the single house is that it is turned perpendicular to the street so that one of its short sides faces — and generally buts up against — the sidewalk. The house itself is a single room wide, hence the designation 'single house.' It is two principal rooms deep, though there was generally a third small office or work room behind the rear room. In the classic single house, the entrance is not directly into the house itself, but rather onto a porch that can be generally found either on the south or the west side of the building, depending on which way the street goes. This porch is known in Charleston as a 'piazza,' pronounced in the soft English way, rather than with a break at the 'zz' as the Italians would have it. The piazza is separated from the street by a solid wall pierced by the piazza door. Entry into a single house is thus a two-staged affair: first passing from the street to the piazza, and then from the piazza into the house proper by means of a true front door, generally symmetrically set between the two main rooms on the floor and opening into a stairhall for circulation. Upper floors followed the pattern of the principal floor, with two rooms per floor, one front and one back. Kitchen and laundry facilities were located in an outbuilding (locally called a dependency) behind the main house. In the twentieth century the small back room of the primary floor has frequently been converted into a kitchen, and the originally free-standing dependency has very often been connected to the main house to form an exceedingly long, narrow dwelling.

Except for the Italian Renaissance palazzo, the Charleston single house is the only architectural form that maintains the same number of rooms (per floor) no matter how large or small the dwelling. A three-story single house will have essentially six rooms; a two-story one, four. Grand single houses have big rooms, but still the same number per floor. Though not intended as such, an argument could be made that the single house is the closest thing yet to truly democratic architecture.

The single house: block and attached piazzas, does not stand alone. It is invariably connected to a yard that extends the open space of the piazza over to the next house. In the surviving blocks of Charleston singles, the ensuing rhythm is immediately apparent: house, piazza, yard, house, piazza, yard. It is the Charleston rhythm, found nowhere else.

As might be expected, not all single houses conform exactly to the classic description, given above. The most common variant is known as the side-hall plan house. In this modified single house, the entrance to the house is on the side away from the piazza, and leads into a hall that runs down the length of the house. The rooms are still lined up behind one another, but they now open directly into each other, rather than into the central circulation hall.

They still open onto the piazzas, the site of so much Charleston living.

The genesis of the single house is, surprisingly enough, still the subject of a great deal of debate. The frequently repeated story that Charlestonians were taxed by their street frontage, and thus minimized it with this house form, while attractive as a hypothesis, unfortunately lacks any supporting historical evidence. It does not seem to be the case that recognizable single houses appeared much before the middle of the eighteenth century. What is true is that it is a house form that is inextricably bound up with Charleston, present and past.

The other great early house form in the city is called the Double House, referring to the fact that it was two rooms wide and two rooms deep. This type of house faced the street squarely, typically being entered by a grand staircase from the sidewalk. It was a house that meant to impress, and generally did a good job. Surviving examples can be seen in the Blacklock House (18 Bull Street), the William Blake House (321 East Bay) and the Elliott house (58 George Street).

Double House, 321 East Bay

As the Blake and Elliott houses make abundantly clear, the materials used for construction of Charleston structures do not always conform to a strict hierarchy. A clapboard sided double house is still generally grander than a brick single house. The city was built with what was available, which was, for the most part, wood and brick. Wood rots in the Charleston climate. Brick conducts damp from the ground into the house. And, as the earthquake of 1886 demonstrated, rigid brick structures did not survive the rolling of the earth as well as the more flexible frame ones. That any houses survive at all on the peninsula is remarkable, and is a tribute to the many people for whom their upkeep is a labor of love. Frequently the effect is created by printed or spoken word that important Charleston architecture ended with the Civil War, and that the twentieth century is a period in the city's history about which the less said the better. Neither of these views adequately expresses the reality of the city and its architecture. In 1865 Charleston was prostrate. Her younger architects of the antebellum days left for greener pastures: E.C. Jones to Memphis, where he continued to practice until 1902, and F.D. Lee to St. Louis until he died in 1885. Both contributed substantially to their new cities, and it must be thought that had Charleston offered equivalent work they would not have strayed.

The later part of the nineteenth century — frequently referred to as the Victorian period — was not a great time for new building in the city. Many more structures were remodeled than were built from the ground up. Nevertheless, under Mayor Courtenay in the early 1880s, Charleston

Colonial Lake

began a concerted city beautification project which saw the landscaping of Washington (City Hall) Park, the long-delayed creation of Marion Square north of Boundary (Calhoun) Street and in front of the Old Citadel, and the creation of Colonial Lake (the Rutledge Street Pond) from the marshes of the Ashley river. One need only look briefly at the substantial residential blocks surrounding the Pond to recognize that by the end of the nineteenth century the city was getting back on track.

The twentieth century has been hard for Charleston, but not as devastating as was generally the case elsewhere. The single most disruptive and destructive event the city has ever confronted is the brainchild of Henry Ford: the affordable private automobile. It has been more destructive of the urban fabric than all the fires, hurricanes and earthquakes together have been. It led directly to the establishment of the first citizen preservation organization: the Society for the Preservation of Old Dwellings, in 1920, and it has led in our own time to what some see as Charleston's greatest threat: its success as a tourist town.

As you explore the Charleston of this moment, you may be seeing it at its peak. In all its long history, it has probably never looked better. Even after its long saga of catastrophe, Charleston has never been safer, cleaner, more sanitary, more accommodating to travelers and more rewarding to all its citizens. There have been times of greater wealth, power and prestige, but those were times for the enjoyment of the few. Never has the city offered so much to so many. In the years ahead, Charleston will either become that rare, cherished place that maintains its integrity and sense of place or it will succumb to the pressures of mass tourism and all its horrors. If you take a quiet stroll down these lovely streets, you and Charleston will be the better for it.

Robert Russell
Addlestone Professor of Architectural History
College of Charleston
June, 1997

COMPLETE

Charleston

South Battery

The Waterfront

Charleston began here on the waterfront. After a brief first settlement at Charles Town on the Ashley River in 1670, relocation to the peninsula was decreed at the end of 1679, and the city moved in 1680. Charles Town, named in honor of King Charles II, was governed by eight Lords Proprietors, politically powerful Englishmen who had been granted a charter from the Crown to own and rule the area of the Carolinas. It was they who devised a baroque town plan known as the Grand Modell.

In just a few decades the tiny settlement along the bay was transformed from a raw frontier town to a cultivated city. As early as 1700, a visitor to Charles Town wrote of the "genteel sort of People" that were "well-acquainted with Trade" and were "raising themselves to great Estates." By 1715, the port was booming. Deerskins, furs and rice were early exports, joined later by indigo and cotton. Within 20 years, the city boasted a weekly newspaper, concerts, theater and dancing assemblies.

THE WALLED CITY VERSUS THE GRAND MODELL

The Lords Proprietors' plan for Charles Town called for a tidy grid of streets "in broad and straight lines" with a large square at the intersection of Broad and Meeting Streets. Proprietor Lord Anthony Ashley Cooper envisioned "beautiful buildings." One of the colonists noted that the town was carefully laid out so as to avoid the "irregularities" of other English colonies. Much of that 17th century Grand Modell survives in the essentially gridded—but narrower and denser—pattern of Charleston's streets. What are today known as Queen, Broad, Tradd, East Bay, Meeting, Church, King, Legare and Archdale appear on the earliest maps of Charles Town. To these have been added a number of streets and alleys to reduce the size of the blocks. The early colonists completely ignored the plan for a central square at Broad and Meeting Streets and focused instead on the waterfront. Here they built their homes, shops and warehouses near the wharfs and ships that would make them rich. The waterfront focus was reinforced further in 1704 when a wall was constructed around the city to give protection from the Spanish settlement in St. Augustine and the French. Indeed in 1706, a French and Spanish fleet entered the harbor, but withdrew without attacking upon seeing the fortress. On this tour, you will pass the Granville Bastion site at East Bay and Water Street, which marks the SE corner of the walled city. The SW bastion was on Meeting Street by First Scots Presbyterian Church. The wall continued up the middle of Meeting Street to Cumberland Street (where the French Quarter neighborhood is now) and across to the site of the Custom House at East Bay. The wall was taken down in 1717, and the center of town was eventually established at Broad and Meeting in the form of four important public buildings on the site of the originally proposed square.

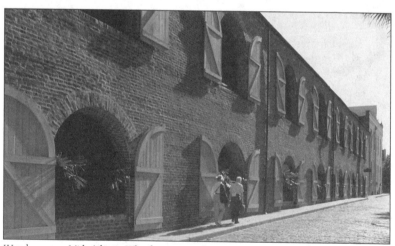

Warehouses on Mid Atlantic Wharf

By mid-century, Charles Town was the 4th largest city in Colonial America (after Boston, Philadelphia and New York) and the third largest port. However, it was wealthier and outshone all the colonial cities in its beauty. When Josiah Quincy, Jr., a Boston lawyer, visited Charles Town, he noted that in "grandeur, splendor of buildings, decorations, equipages, numbers, commerce, shipping and indeed in almost every thing," the town surpassed all he had ever seen or expected to see in America.

Visitors from abroad were equally impressed. A London magazine would report, "the merchants are opulent and well-bred" and that the town was the most polite as well as the richest in America. A French visitor noted that there were public buildings here that "would pass for beautiful even in Europe...the inhabitants live with luxury and magnificence." The commercial life here along the waterfront generated that prosperity. The city was cosmopolitan, with English settlers joined by Scotch, Irish, French Huguenots, Germans, Dutch, Sephardic Jews and Creoles from San Domingo. Influences from these diverse cultures and from Africa and the West Indies, combined to give Charleston a unique flavor of its own.

ELIZA LUCAS, THE INDIGO QUEEN

The Lucas family came to Charleston from Antigua, where George Lucas, Eliza's father, was governor. The climate here was more favorable to the fragile health of Eliza's mother. Thus when Gov. Lucas returned to Antigua, Eliza, at 16, found herself in charge of three plantations, her younger siblings and ailing mother. Lucas sent seeds of indigo from Antigua, and from 1741 until 1744 Eliza worked on perfecting the crop. The leaves of Indigofera suffruticosa, a native plant of the West Indies, produced a dark blue dye so valuable to the British textile industry that Parliament granted it a bounty. Indigo came to rival rice as a major export of Charleston. Eliza also collaborated with Dr. Alexander Garden in collecting plant specimens for identification and experimented in growing cotton, corn, ginger and alfalfa. Like many Charleston gardeners of the era, she exchanged seeds and plants with friends abroad. Educated in England, Eliza once wrote to a friend that she had a "little library well furnished in which I spend part of my time. My music and the garden, which I am very fond of, take up the rest of my time that is not employed in business." In 1744, Eliza married Charles Pinckney, Chief Justice of South Carolina. They had two sons, Charles Cotesworth and Thomas. In 1791, George Washington was the guest of Eliza Lucas Pinckney at Hampton Plantation on the Santee, north of Charleston, now a state park. The plantation is open to the public. (see page 240 for information.)

The merchant families who became wealthy trading here at the waterfront sought to emulate the life style of London society. As you stroll through the city today, you may notice that a tradition of formality and urbanity continues. Even in the heat of August, proper Charlestonian gentlemen wear coats and ties and ladies, skirts and stockings.

The serendipitous pleasures of Charleston's streetscapes have also survived. The city's preservation ordinance protects the architecture, but it is the Charlestonians themselves who provide the embellishments: fragrant jasmine vines near the sidewalk which perfume the whole city during the spring; classical statuary, pineapple finials, urns with formally clipped topiary, ornamental ironwork, the correct mortar for their brickwork. They sweep their own sidewalks, keep the brass polished and tend miniature gardens in niches by the curb. While some European towns may be noted for window boxes all lush with ivy geraniums, Charleston planters tend to have a cottage garden exuberance.

William O. Stevens is one of the many 20th century visitors who have been charmed by the city. He writes in *Charleston, Historic City of Gardens*, in 1939, "Lady Charleston, keep your pride in the past...we like your love of privacy as expressed by those homes standing endwise to the street and those high walls and iron gateways. How little privacy there is to most American homes! You are not the only old town...but you are one of those with the strongest individual character in a nation standardized to boredom."

Charlestonians persevere to protect their heritage, and today's visitors come from all over the world to step back in time. Tourism has become the major industry of the city, but by no means the only one. Industry continues to grow, and the port seems well positioned for the new generation of container ships. Charleston is a living, historic city.

In very few cities can you see the historical record so well preserved as in Charleston. Reading that record is not easily done without some knowledge of the city's history. (Fraser and Rosen have written excellent readable histories available in paperback in any good local bookstore like Waldenbooks on Meeting Street and the Preservation Society's Resource Center on King Street at Queen Street.) The record is there nonetheless, preserved through the early preservation efforts of individual citizens in the 1920's, the preservation groups they formed and by the action of city government in passing the zoning ordinance of 1931. The preservation effort continues to this day and will continue far into the future.

White Point Gardens. Monument to the Confederate defenders of the city.

A VISIONARY PRESERVATION ORDINANCE

During the 1920's, big city museums and wealthy collectors were carting off entire rooms from Charleston's historic mansions. In 1929, the Heyward-Washington House's drawing room was threatened with being acquired by

Henry Francis du Pont for Winterthur Museum. Preservationists began to press the city for an ordinance. Fortunately Mayor Thomas P. Stoney and his successor, Burnet Rhett Maybank, shared their concern and vision. Mayor Stoney pushed through City Council an ordinance setting up a temporary City Planning and Zoning Commission in 1929. Two years later, in October 1931, Charleston passed a zoning ordinance that was unique in its comprehensive, non-elitist protection of the entire fabric of an historic neighborhood. Communities all over the world have looked to Charleston's ordinance as a guide to protecting their own heritage. It was one of the most significant events in the city's history and was cited by Robert Kohn of the AIA as the "most progressive ordinance ever adopted in America." Today it is widely recognized that individual landmarks lose their value in an unsympathetic context and that the "tout ensemble" is crucial to a community's heritage and sense of place.

A good example of buildings as historic record is Rainbow Row on East Bay, perhaps the most photographed and painted street in Charleston. These row houses were built by merchants in the early 1700's who wanted a place close to where the ships came in and cargo was unloaded. The first floor was where the merchant stored his goods. And he lived on the upper level to keep an eye on his valuable imports. With time and prosperity, the children took over the business and moved out of the teeming, cramped area around the docks to grander and

East Bay, just south of Rainbow Row

pleasanter neighborhoods. The dockside became a less desirable place to live, declining into an outright slum as sailing ships gave way to the era of steam locomotives. When preservationists bought and restored the houses in Rainbow Row, the houses rose in respectability to achieve their present eminence which is, ironically, far above their station at any time in the past. The process in New York was essentially the same, except that in New York, the old neighborhoods were leveled for skyscrapers, and the record was erased.

In order to follow the story in Charleston, it is necessary to visit other neighborhoods further uptown to see some of the grander houses built by the newly prosperous merchants and planters. In the mistaken belief that everything worth seeing is "South of Broad" and on the Battery, where much of the residential area is landfill, with houses of fairly recent construction, many visitors miss the splendors of such neighborhoods as Harleston Village and Mazyck Wraggborough Garden District.

→ Begin the walk at East Bay and Vendue Range. Walk east toward the river.

1 VENDUE RANGE: Named for the vendue masters (auctioneers) of the 18th and 19th centuries who had their businesses here. The warehouse buildings survive from a time when Charleston was rather like a city-state, the center of trade, law, education, social life and transportation to Europe for the whole colony.

Vendue Range

→ As you cross Prioleau Street, look right at the warehouses on the nearby streets. Charleston has used historic preservation to benefit the economy. Rehabilitated 18th and 19th century warehouses have been transformed into offices, hotels, restaurants and homes. New infill buildings are mindful of the older traditions of design and scale. As you enter the Park, look east across the Cooper River to the Yorktown, the World War II aircraft carrier, moored at Patriot's Point Naval and Maritme Museum (884-2727).Walk south through Waterfront Park until you reach Adger's Wharf at the far end.

WATERFRONT PARK & THE "BEST GRAVEL PATH IN AMERICA."

The old port where the early wharfs were, has been transformed into a thirteen-acre park. After a decade of planning it opened in 1990, featuring the popular Vendue Fountain and the Pineapple Fountain. As you walk, notice the gravel. Charleston's Mayor Joseph P. Riley, Jr. believes it to be the "best gravel path in America." He has been a very hands-on mayor in regard to architecture and urban design in the city. When the park was being planned, the right sort of gravel to work well for wheelchairs and high heels and to have a softer feel than slate or bluestone, was not easy to find. Whenever he traveled, the Mayor would scoop up samples of gravel to bring home. Robert Behre reported in the Post *and* Courier *that city planners analyzed some fifty samples, resulting in a gravel with a soft pinkish hue that is a custom mix of Texas and South Carolina granites. Smell the pluff mud. For many Charlestonians, it is a cherished aroma of home.*

Pineapple Fountain, Waterfront Park

2 **ADGER'S WHARF** has been incorporated into Waterfront Park. It was named for James Adger and became the southern terminus of the first steamship line between New York and Charleston. Adger was reputed to be the wealthiest man in South Carolina in mid-19th century. His cotton warehouse survives on North Adger Street.

Waterfront Park from Adger's Wharf

→ Go west to Concord Street and walk right (north) along Concord Street, turning left on Exchange Street to the rear of the Old Exchange Building.

3 **OLD EXCHANGE BUILDING:** (122 E. Bay Street) This was originally the front entrance, facing out to the sea. When George Washington visited Charleston in 1791, his barge docked at Prioleau's wharf where he was met by Charles Pinckney, Intendant (mayor) Arnoldus Vanderhorst and other dignitaries and escorted here. Charles Fraser, the great Charleston painter of miniatures in the 19th century, was a small boy at the time. He recalled that "one of the civilities" which Washington received was a "splendid concert and ball" at the Exchange. "The ladies wore fillets, or bandeaus of white riband, interwoven in their head-dress with the head of Washington painted on them and words 'Long Live the President' in gilt letters."

→ As you walk around the north side of the Old Exchange Building to East Bay, notice the small cobbled Gillon Street.

GILLON STREET is named for Alexander Gillon, who during the British blockade of Charleston in 1777-78, captured three British vessels, two without firing a shot. After the war, Gillon served as state senator and attended the convention considering the Constitution. In a debate with Charles Pinckney, the latter used a lengthy Latin phrase to clarify a point. Gillon thanked him for his erudition and concluded his remarks in High Dutch. There was no more Latin quoted during the debate.

Old Exchange Building

3 **122 EAST BAY:** (The Old Exchange Building of 1771.) Designed by W. Rigby Naylor, it has been cited as one of the most sophisticated buildings in America from the 18th century. The builders, Peter and John Adams Horlbeck, imported shiploads of cut, dressed and beveled Portland stone for the facade. The Exchange was the birthplace of the South Carolina state government, which was formed following a protest of the tea tax in 1773. In 1776, the Declaration of Independence was read here, and South Carolina declared its independence. During the war, the British imprisoned such notable citizens as Arthur Middleton, Christopher Gadsden, the Sarrazin sisters and Edward Rutledge in the prison in the cellar. In 1783, it housed City Hall as well as customs offices. When the U. S. Constitution was ratified here in 1788, some of the delegates included patriots who had been imprisoned in the dungeons below. In 1818, the building became a U. S. Post Office. In 1912, the U. S. government was about to sell the building to a developer who planned to demolish it for a gasoline station. In one of the city's first preservation efforts, the Rebecca Motte Chapter of the Daughters of the American Revolution persuaded the federal government to convey this national treasure to them instead. The Old Exchange Building is a memorable example of what seems to be the lost art of creating vistas by concluding a street with a striking building.

Coffee Break: *Jake's, 19 Broad Street. Blind Tiger, 38 Broad. Opens at 11am. Salads, mussels, burgers.*

→ Walk south on East Bay

4 **109 EAST BAY:** Built in 1909 as the printing plant for Walker, Evans and Cogswell, publishers who had been printers of Confederate bonds and currency. It has been converted into condominium apartments and has lush and colorful window boxes and plantings.

5 **114-120 EAST BAY:** Picturesque Coates' Row. The northern building in the row is believed to have been built sometime between 1740 and 1788 and to have been Harris' Tavern. Later the tavern became the property of Catherine Coates and was known as "Mrs. Coates's on the Bay." When coffee houses began to surpass taverns in popularity at the end of the 18th century, Mrs. Coates kept up with the times, opening the Carolina Coffee House on Tradd Street, which became "one of the most important in the city." The house with the cupola was once known as the "French Coffee House" and was a popular meeting place, according to historian Samuel Gaillard Stoney.

Coates Row

79-107 East Bay

THE TAVERN—CHARLESTON SOCIAL CENTER

Colonial taverns were so much more than merely places to eat and drink. Businessmen gathered there to do business, read, receive mail. Public meetings and entertainments were held there. According to News and Courier reporter W. H. J. Thomas, such taverns began to operate in Charleston as early as 1732. A 1734 issue of the Gazette advertised a performance of a "Tragedy called The Orphan or the Unhappy Marriage" which was to be held at Shepheard's Tavern at Broad and Church Streets. That same year Charles Town's court of Sessions was held in the same tavern. In 1797, another such notice read: "At Mrs. Coates's Tavern on the Bay, Moulthrop and Street are showing...the best collection of wax figures ever exhibited in America—32 figures as large as life." Other surviving 18th century taverns are McCrady's on Unity Alley and the Pink House on Chalmers Street, both in the French Quarter.

6 **79-107 EAST BAY:** Rainbow Row is one of the most famous blocks in Charleston, so named in the 1930's when the block was restored and painted in early colonial colors. The Row is architecturally significant for its intactness and as surviving evidence of the early to mid-18th century merchant housing of "English" type, meaning that it has a ground floor store with a dwelling above. It is believed to be the longest such Georgian row in America. This part of East Bay was the city's commercial center in early colonial days, and settlers built in the area as early as 1680. The block is said to have inspired DuBose Heyward's "Catfish Row" in *Porgy*. The neighborhood had deteriorated and was being eyed for demolition in 1931, when Judge and Mrs. Lionel K. Legge bought one of the decaying buildings, restored it, and bought another. Others followed their example. Mrs. Legge was one of the founders, in 1920, of what became the Preservation Society of Charleston.

101 East Bay *51 East Bay*

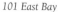 **101 EAST BAY:** The Col. Othniel Beale House, c. 1740, was restored by the Legges in 1931. Two crumbling stores became garages and a trash-strewn yard was transformed into a garden.

7 **71 EAST BAY:** Another early preservationist in the area was Mrs. N. L. Roosevelt, a relative of F.D.R. Simons and Lapham added a third story and remodeled the building in the Charleston single house tradition.

8 **76-80 EAST BAY:** America's oldest apartment house, built in 1800 by Gen. Arnoldus Vanderhorst, Governor of South Carolina (1792-1794), and Intendant (mayor) of Charleston when Washington visited in 1791. Once abandoned and in ruins, Vanderhorst Row was restored in 1936.

9 **51 EAST BAY:** The Casper Christian Shutt House dates to about 1799 and was built by a wealthy German who had his home and counting house here. In 1821, it became the home of John Fraser, one of the city's most able merchants of the 19th century. Fraser was a partner in his own firm and in Fraser, Trenholm & Co. Both firms became blockade runners during the Civil War. Note the correct progression of orders on the piazzas, with Doric on the bottom, then Ionic and Corinthian.

→ Walk onto the Battery Promenade to the Missroon House where there is a plaque with a map of the 18th century walled city.

10 **40 EAST BATTERY** (Historic Charleston Foundation) The Missroon House of 1789 is named for Captain James Missroon, a maritime trader who bought it in 1808. It was the site of the Granville Bastion when Charleston was a walled city. Like other homes in the area, it fell into disrepair. Rehabilitated in the 1920's, it is now owned by and houses the offices of Historic Charleston Foundation.

The wide sea wall at the southeast corner of the city is known as the High Battery, named for a battery of guns placed along it during the war of 1812. The wall was enlarged in the 1830's to provide protection from hurricane tides. The city filled in the marshes behind the sea wall and sold lots, stipulating that "no house less than three stories shall be erected thereon." The resulting famous antebellum mansions were a skillful blending of the most fashionable architectural styles with features traditional to Charleston homes—raised entrances, ornamental ironwork, piazzas to shade sunny windows and capture cool afternoon breezes.

High Battery

→ Continue along the promenade past Water Street. At the NW corner of Atlantic and East Battery is:

⚑ 29 EAST BATTERY: The Porcher-Simonds House was built c.1856 by Francis J. Porcher, cotton broker and president in the 1870's of the Atlantic Phosphate Co. It was remodeled in the Italian Renaissance Revival style by banker John C. Simonds in 1894.

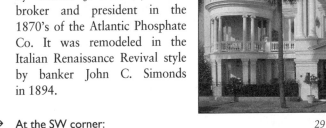

→ At the SW corner:

29 East Battery

12 **25 EAST BATTERY:** (SW corner at Atlantic Street) Charles Drayton's home was considered very modern in 1885—a rare example of the Eastlake Style in Charleston. Victorians loved to borrow and mix styles from the past. Local architect W. B. W. Howe adventurously combined medieval gables, slender columns with Gothic trim with piazza railings derived from Chinese temple design. Although trendy in the design for his city home, Drayton, a rice planter and phosphate miner, carefully preserved his ancestral plantation Drayton Hall.

25 East Battery

21 East Battery

→ Immediately to the south:

13 **21 EAST BATTERY:** The home that Charles Edmonston built in 1825, is considered one of the best examples of Regency style in the city. This style was popular during the brief transitional period between the Adamesque and Greek Revival styles. Edmonston made his fortune as a merchant and wharf owner. Charles Alston, a rice planter, bought the mansion in 1838, adding such Greek Revival details as a piazza with Corinthian columns on the third floor and a balustrade above the cornice. Alston had more than 700 slaves, real estate, racing stables and a library of 250 books. The Edmonston-Alston House, open to the public, has beautiful Neoclassical furnishing and unusual woodwork. Note the balls (instead of dentils) and the rope moldings down the center of the pilasters. General Beauregard watched the bombardment of Fort Sumter in 1861 from the piazza. Later that year, Robert E. Lee took refuge here when the Great Fire threatened the Mills House hotel where he was staying.

14 **17 EAST BATTERY:** (The large pink house) One of the special visual pleasures of Charleston is the city's wide variety of beautiful entrances. Here, wide marble stairs lead to a doorway flanked by Ionic pilasters and a fan window above.

Charleston appears to be a city set in a lush garden. From the earliest times, gardening has been a passion, and this tradition continues not only in public plantings, such as the oleanders lining the Battery, but also privately. Residents fill small curbside plots, urns and window boxes with flowers. Many private gardens are partly visible from the sidewalk. In cities where the rowhouse prevails, gardens are hidden in the rear. It is Charleston's unique architectural mode of houses turned sideways, with piazzas facing side gardens rather than the street, which adds to the garden ambience of the whole city. Thus your stroll will be perfumed by tea olive, wisteria, Confederate jasmine, roses, pittosporum and gardenias. Watch for the astonishing sub-tropical flowers and foliage plants that thrive here—yellow Carolina jessamine, gladiolus byzantinus, parkinsonia, cassia, cestrum, tibouchina, vitex, ginger lilies, palms, crape myrtle, camellias, solanum jasminoides, banana, loquat, tall blue and purple salvias, hibiscus, ruellia, passionflower and trumpet vines, rosemary, amaryllis, canna, nandina and plumbago.

17 East Battery

9 East Battery

→ Immediately to the south is:

15 **13 EAST BATTERY:** Built in 1845 by William Ravenel, a shipping merchant. The grand arcaded, rusticated base once supported a Palladian portico with two-story Corinthian columns and a pediment, which was destroyed by the 1886 earthquake.

16 **9 EAST BATTERY:** Next door, Robert William Roper, a planter and state legislator, clearly wanted to make a fashionable statement. His home was one of the first Charleston mansions in the Greek Revival style. Historians have speculated that it might have been designed by Edward Brickell White, architect of Market Hall, or Charles Reichardt, important Greek Revival architects. Note the rope molding around the door and the traditional Charleston piazza, with *au courant* (in 1838) two-story Greek Revival columns. In 1968, the Roper Mansion was bought by Richard Jenrette of Charleston and New York who is credited with sparking economic growth in the city when he rebuilt the Mills House Hotel the same year.

→   The large pink house is:

17 **5 EAST BATTERY:** This Italianate mansion was built in 1849 by John Ravenel, planter, merchant and leading shipper. The Italianate bracketed cornice, window cornices and arches were added after 1886. Dr. St. Julien Ravenel inherited the house. He was a pioneer in the city's phosphate industry, and his wife was famous as the author of books on Charleston history and architecture.

18 **1 EAST BATTERY:** Built in 1858-1861 by Louis D. DeSaussure, an auctioneer who is said to have sold everything from ships to slaves. The ornate iron balconies date to 1886.

1 East Battery

→   The best way to view the South Battery mansions is to walk along the northern edge of the park. Avid gardeners, however, will want to walk on the sidewalk in order to study a parade of small front gardens, some patterned, some with a cottage garden profusion of vines and blooms. At Church Street, the mansion with the 2-story Corinthian columns is:

19 **4 SOUTH BATTERY:** Completed in 1893 for Andrew Simonds, bank president, this Italian Renaissance Revival Mansion originally had a cupola and balustrades around the roof. The villa was inspired by those seen by Mrs. Simonds while traveling in Italy. According to the News and Courier, when the design was exhibited at the Architects' Union in 1892, it "received more comment than that of any other private building." It was designed by F.P. Dinkelberg of New York who later worked for Daniel Burnham, collaborating on plans for the Flatiron Building, built in New York, 1903. In 1909 the Simonds mansion became the hotel Villa Marguerita. Guests included Henry Ford, Alexander Graham Bell, Presidents Cleveland, Taft and Theodore Roosevelt. Sinclair Lewis finished writing *Main Street* while staying at the Villa.

Between 1830 and 1840, the City bought up land at the tip of Charleston's peninsula, an area known as "Oyster Point" or "White Point." The seawall was extended to King Street, and by 1852, the land had been filled in for a "public pleasure park." The News and Courier reported that New York architect Charles F. Reichardt had prepared a plan for a "public promenade or garden covering an area of three acres...unsurpassed in beauty...by any similar spot in the United States." Monuments commemorate notable people and events in Charleston's history, such as the Civil War, when earthworks were thrown up in the park with guns commanding the Ashley River and the harbor. Near the east end is a Pirate Marker for the death of Stede Bonnet, hanged here in 1718. Forty-nine pirates were hung here that year and are buried nearby. The Williams Music Pavillion dates to 1907 and was donated for Sunday evening concerts by Mrs. Martha W. Carrington as a memorial to her parents, who built the Calhoun Mansion. The Carringtons had convenient seats for the concerts at their house at 2 Meeting Street. Though officially known as White Point Gardens, the park is popularly called "The Battery." It is a good example of self-financing development. The cost of filling the marshes, building the High Battery and creating White Point Gardens was largely covered by the sale of the newly created building lots on the East Bay extension.

→ Next door:

20 **8 SOUTH BATTERY:** The Col. William Washington House was built c. 1768. A Virginian, he was related to George Washington. The garden, in a paisley design, is believed to have been designed about 1830.

→ Next door:

21 **2 MEETING STREET:** Charleston is famous for its Colonial architecture, yet many of its grand buildings are of a much later date, such as this Queen Anne mansion of 1892, which was built by George Williams as a wedding present for his daughter, who married Waring P. Carrington, a King Street jeweler. Williams was well known for building, in 1876, a Victorian mansion at 16 Meeting, now known as the

2 Meeting Street

Calhoun Mansion. The Carrington home has been an inn for many years. Famous guests have included President Warren G. Harding and a woman claiming to be Grand Duchess Anastasia (who, we now know, was killed with her family.)

22 **1 MEETING STREET:** Built in 1849 by a cotton broker, it has a particularly handsome entrance. Notice the double wooden doors with etched glass which front on Meeting Street. Unusual rope molding ornaments the arch of the entrance as well as the arched windows of the first story.

1 Meeting Street

→ Next door:

23 **20 SOUTH BATTERY:** Col. Richard Lathers bought this 1843 mansion in 1870. His architect, John Henry Devereux, who also designed the Federal Post Office at Broad and Meeting, added the Second Empire mansard roof and transformed the interior. Col. Lathers was a cotton broker and businessman who owned nine estates near New York City which produced grain and hay. Col. Lathers gave lavish parties here with leaders from the north and south, hoping for a reconciliation. In April, 1873, the *News & Courier* reported that one of the "most notable events of the Charleston season was the brilliant party last evening" given here in honor of Hon. Horatio Seymour, ex-Governor of New York and Hon. William Cullen Bryant, editor of the New York Evening Post. The early evening hours were occupied with "conversazione in the elegant drawing room of the mansion." In 1920, the mansion became the home of Mr. & Mrs. Ernest Pringle, who bore the financial burden of saving the Joseph Manigault House in Mazyck Wraggborough. It was here that 32 people met to save the Manigualt house and organized the Society for the Preservation of Old Dwellings, which later became the Preservation Society of Charleston.

24 **26 SOUTH BATTERY:** An extremely significant building architecturally, the Col. John Algernon Sydney Ashe House was the first Italianate villa in Charleston. It was designed in 1853 by Edward C. Jones, who sought to become the city's premier architect and who, that same year, introduced the Italianate style to commercial buildings at 1 and 3 Broad Street. The Ashe villa sounded the death knell for the formal symmetry of Greek Revival and paved the way for Mid-Century Eclecticism. The Italianate villa style had been popularized by Andrew Jackson Downing in the 1840's and is characterized by brackets under the cornice, asymmetry, a lavish use of curves and arched windows. The double loggia is a local interpretation, responding to the Charleston tradition of piazzas. Jones was also the architect of Trinity Methodist Church on Meeting Street and is believed to have designed the Isaac Jenkins Mikell mansion at 94 Rutledge Avenue (Harleston Village). Col. Ashe was a bachelor with 30 slaves who lived in the rear dependencies.

25 **32 SOUTH BATTERY:** The father of Col. Ashe built this house with a romantic cupola and front piazzas c.1782.

26 **46 SOUTH BATTERY:** George Gershwin was a guest here in 1934, while immersing himself in the culture of the Lowcountry in order to write the music for Porgy and Bess. One evening, his piano playing brought out the whole neighborhood, as people gathered on their piazzas to better hear the music coming from the drawing room.

27 **48 SOUTH BATTERY:** Built c. 1846, this home is an excellent example of Greek Revival in the Charleston tradition.

28 **58 SOUTH BATTERY:** (NW corner at Legare) John Blake, a revolutionary patriot and state senator, built his home before 1800. Georgian details include the raised doorway, the general proportions and modillioned cornice. An old patterned garden has been restored here. When Hugh and Mary Palmer Dargan were preparing to do a garden for Mrs. Roger Hanahan, they discovered the brick borders of the old garden. It is one of the few extant 18th century gardens in the city.

58 South Battery

THE PATTERNED GARDEN

When Charleston was settled, English gardens were modeled after formal French gardens with decorative parterres, straight walks, statuary and elaborate fountains. However, after 1689, when William III of Holland ascended the throne, the Dutch influenced English gardens. Smaller, more intimate walled gardens with more flowers and ornamental plants became popular. These influences crossed the Atlantic, and having an orchard and a flower garden became a sign of gentility in Charleston. Historian George Rogers noted that *"The gardeners were conspiring, as was almost everyone else, to make Charleston, by the 1790's the most beautiful city in America."* And historian David Ramsey wrote, in 1804, that *"A passion for flowers has of late astonishingly increased...(and) those who cannot command convenient spots of ground have their piazzas, balconies and windows richly adorned with the beauties of nature."* In addition to 58 South Battery, early pattern gardens may be seen at 8 South Battery and 74 Rutledge Avenue in Harleston Village. The Heyward Washington House, open to the public at 87 Church Street, has created an 18th century style garden. During the spring and fall house and garden tours by Historic Charleston Foundation and the The Preservation Society, many of the city's most beautiful private gardens may be visited.

64 South Battery

29 **64 SOUTH BATTERY:** In 1772, William Gibbes, merchant, ship owner and planter, built an 800 foot wharf and began construction of one of the finest Georgian mansions in America. It is modeled after those of England using the classical vocabulary of Palladio—high masonry basement, large crowning pediment with supporting brackets, modillioned cornice, a bull's eye window and symmetry. The Adamesque features—entrance side-lights and the wrought iron railings—were added later. In the 1920's, The house was bought by Mrs. Washington A. Roebling, the widow of the man who, with his father, designed and built built the Brooklyn Bridge.

30 **68 SOUTH BATTERY:** (Harth Middleton House) Built c. 1797 by John Harth, a mill owner and planter. Later it became the home of Henry Middleton, who enlarged it. Note the beautiful Italianate formal garden.

68 South Battery

→ Go left on Lenwood Boulevard and right on Murray Boulevard.

MURRAY BOULEVARD. The area behind Murray Boulevard included 47 acres of mud flats between the original shore and the sea-wall and extended from the west end of White Point Gardens to the west end of Tradd. The land-fill project, begun in 1909, was finished in 1911. The seawall was extended south of White Point Gardens to link Murray Boulevard and East Battery, an idea promoted by Andrew Buist Murray, businessman and philanthropist, who financed much of the project.

31 **46 MURRAY BOULEVARD:** When Dr. & Mrs. R. Barnwell Rhett built their home in 1926, designed by local architects Albert Simons and Samuel Lapham, Jr., it was considered the best new house in Charleston. Albert Simons was among the early preservationists in Charleston who pressed for an ordinance to protect the architectural heritage of Charleston.

32 **52 MURRAY BOULEVARD:** C. Bissel Jenkins was the first person to propose reclaiming land from the Ashley River for the landfill project. In conjunction with the city, he began the project in 1909. Jenkins was the first to build a house on the Boulevard in 1913. It was designed by Walker and Burden in a modified colonial style with a Palladian pedimented portico. The iron fence is laden with yellow Carolina Jessamine which blooms in February, Confederate Jasmine with its

52 Murray Boulevard

heady fragrance in April, and roses which bloom for many months. A Pittosporum hedge has been trimmed to allow a glimpse of flower borders which surround the lawn.

→ Go right on Limehouse Street and cross Lowndes Street. In Colonial days this was the waterfront. Old maps show the Charles Town peninsula ending on the north side of South Battery and the area east of Limehouse Street patterned with creeks and marshes. As you reach 22 Limehouse Street, look for the plaque explaining the system of seawalls which once existed in the city. These walls, constructed of tabby—a mixture of oyster shells, sand and lime based mortar— protected residents from flooding. A remnant of a tabby seawall may be seen just south of the piazza at 20 Limehouse Street running east. Watch for gardens as you walk north.

33 **18 LIMEHOUSE:** Built in 1852, this was originally the last house on the east side of Limehouse street and overlooked the Ashley River. Note the Eastlake brackets under the cornice, applied later.

34 **9 AND 10 LIMEHOUSE:** In antebellum Charleston, fortunes were made and lost by planters and merchants, such as William Pinckney Shingler, who built #9 c. 1856. Shingler was a daring business man and suffered economic reverses which forced him to sell his mansion in 1857. However, by 1858 Shinglers's fortunes had improved and he built #10 across the street. The architect Edward Brickell White designed #9, gracefully adapting the Greek Revival

9 Limehouse

style to the typical Charleston house plan. Fluted Doric columns and classic friezes ornament the piazza and there are classical pediments at the entrance and over the windows. The mansion at #10 is very similar.

35 **7 LIMEHOUSE:** The Robert Limehouse House, c. 1870.

36 **4 LIMEHOUSE:** Another side-yard flower garden.

→ Go right on Tradd Street.

ARCHITECTS' DETOUR: It is well worth the walk, two blocks left to Rutledge Avenue, to see one of the most spectacular examples of Charleston Greek revival—172 Tradd Street. This impressive temple, built c. 1836 for Alexander Hext Chisolm, owner of the nearby rice mill building, uses the Corinthian order from the Choragic Monument of Lysicrates. It is lavishly ornamented with ten of the intricate capitals, which are copies of those designed in BC335 in Athens. Most visitors to Charleston miss this architectural gem as it is rather off the beaten path in a neighborhood that was devastated by the great fire of 1861. When it was built, the Ashley river was just beyond the front wall. The Chisolm Mansion has been attributed to the New York architect Charles F. Reichardt who also designed the Charleston Hotel, the New Theater and Guard House. None of

172 Tradd Street

these grand colonnaded buildings survive. Reichardt, a German, is said to have been a pupil of Karl Friedrich Schinkel.

ARCHITECTS' DETOUR: Walk right on Greenhill Street, a small eclectic street of houses in varying sizes and styles. There is a notable example of New Classicism at 14 Greenhill Street. Designed in 1990 by Jim Strickland of Historical Concepts. This firm is in the forefront of what is being called the Second Renaissance—the novelty architecture of Modernism is being replaced by sophisticated very au courant classicism.

→   To continue the tour, return to Tradd Street and go right.

37   **143 TRADD Street:** When this home was built c. 1797, the property extended to the marshes of the Ashley River. In 1885, it was remodeled and the Greek Revival piazzas—all with Doric colonnades— were added by Solomon Legare, Jr. It is said that a man suffering from yellow fever was nursed back to health in the 4th story of this house, where air was believed to be purer than near the ground. In 1861, when fire raged on Tradd Street, the servants here climbed up on the roof and with a bucket brigade, quenched all the sparks that fell on the roof. A Union bomb tore a hole in the roof during the Civil War, which was patched with a tin can. After the earthquake of 1886, neighbors camped under blankets in the front yard as it was one of the few open spaces in the area. The carriage gate is in a rare arrow design.

38   **129 TRADD STREET:** (With the unusual Dragon Gate) Joseph Winthrop from Massachusetts became a Charleston merchant, building his home here in 1797 when this was a very open area

129 Tradd

on a salty creek which led to the Ashley River.

39 **128 TRADD STREET:** Humphrey Sommers, an English-born builder, was one of the contractors for St. Michael's church. He built his home c.1765 with a modillioned cornice and an intricately designed window on the East facade. The Greek Revival piazzas were added in 1841.

128 Tradd Street

40 **125 TRADD STREET:** John Morrison, formerly a sea captain and later a prosperous merchant, built his home here in 1807. A generously proportioned single house, 4 bays wide, it has a Greek Doric piazza door and Adamesque styling at the main entrance. The site is significant to Charleston's horticultural heritage, as it was here that Robert Squibb had his garden. Squibb owned one of the city's earliest nurseries and was the author of *The Gardener's Calender* in 1787, the second work on gardening to be published in America.

41 **126 TRADD STREET:** Mrs. Peter Fayssoux House, built by a tailor in the 1730's. In 1790 it became the home of the widow of the Surgeon-General in the Continental Army during the Revolution. Later, it became the childhood home of two Confederate Generals, Hamilton Prioleau Bee and Barnard Elliott Bee.

→ Walk left onto Legare Street.

LEGARE STREET (pronounced La-gree in Charleston) is named for Solomon Legare, a prosperous Huguenot silversmith who owned a good deal of real estate in the area. It is one of the most beautiful residential streets in the city. According to Samuel Stoney, "It used to be said that a Charlestonian who went to St. Michael's and the St. Cecilias and lived on Legare Street could go to Heaven if he wanted to, but probably wouldn't want to."

42 **43 LEGARE STREET:** Built c. 1759 and one of the oldest houses on the block, by Charles Elliott, whose daughter married Col. William Washington, the Revolutionary hero. The facade was remodeled in 1911.

43 **38-44 LEGARE STREET:** Much of Charleston's sense of place is derived from its unique single houses, such as the ones here. They often have a piazza on the west or south side to capture the breezes and to shade the interior from the sun. Houses of this style are found all over the city up to Line Street. The piazza is believed to have been introduced

43 Legare Street

to the city in the mid-18th century. Note the Charleston single-house rhythm: side yard-piazza-house-side yard-piazza-house.

→ Continue to Broad Street. The mansions on Broad Street between Legare and King Streets are included in the Broad Street tour.

Coffee Break: *Gaulart & Maliclet, 98 Broad. Also called Fast & French.*

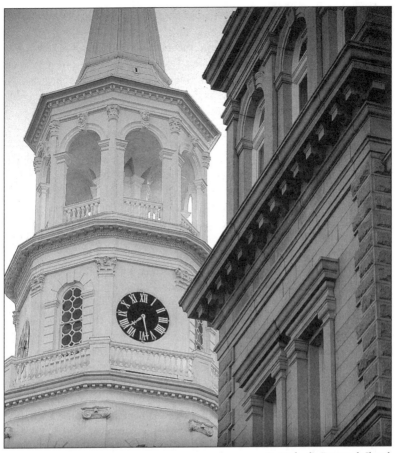

St. Michael's Episcopal Church

Broad Street

There is probably no other downtown street in America where so much of historical importance—both nationally and locally—has occurred and where the physical evidence of that history survives in such an intact streetscape. Broad Street, one of the original streets of the 17th century Grand Modell for Charleston, was intended from the beginning to be a major central thoroughfare.

Charleston is justly famous for its Colonial domestic architecture, however there is also a remarkable assemblage of commercial and civic buildings of a high architectural quality from later periods.

For 300 years Broad Street has been the vital center of Charleston, a street known for its financiers and influential lawyer-politicians. Traditionally, Broad Street has been lined with a mixture of banks, private homes, shops, taverns and offices, as well as the city's oldest church and municipal buildings.

In 1968, property owners and the Historic Charleston Foundation established a Broad Street Beautification Committee which led to repainting and repairing facades, planting trees and removing inappropriate signage and overhead power lines. The views up and down this street are remarkable for an American city—free of neon, gaudy signs and brown aluminum store fronts which have defaced most downtown centers.

The County Judicial Center was the center of a preservation storm in 1997. Originally designed to be five stories tall, it would have loomed inappropriately large in scale over the narrow vertical historic structures of Broad Street. Preservationists were successful in having the height reduced. As designed by Jaquelin Robertson, one of America's most important New Classicists, with NBBJ, the Center restores a sidewalk portico on Broad Street, an amenity that was once common in Charleston. The Center is important in preserving downtown as the County's legal system center.

As you stroll along this beautiful main street, lined with Palmettos, you will see two of the nation's finest high style Colonial buildings, a mansion where the U. S. Constitution was first drafted and buildings where President George Washington had breakfast, danced and attended church.

The visual pleasure of Broad Street is enhanced by a great deal of chiaro-suro, the light and shadow effects popularized during the Renaissance by Caravaggio and Palladio. Chiaroscuso is an important feature of Charleston's architecture throughout the historic district. On commercial streets, such as Broad and King, it is particularly intense because there are so many narrow buildings so close together. The small-scale ornamentation of the buildings in a wide variety of styles is enhanced by Charleston sunshine.

→ Begin the walk at Broad and Legare Streets

1 **122 BROAD STREET:** The Cathedral of St. John the Baptist was rebuilt in 1890-1907 after the fire of 1861 and is nearly identical to the earlier cathedral, designed in 1850 by Patrick Charles Keely, whose work set the style of Roman Catholic Churches in America for the last half of the 19th century. Keely was one of the most prolific architects of the era, designing some 500 churches in New York State, exclusive of those he did in New York City. This Charleston building was his 23rd cathedral. Keely's most outstanding work is

122 Broad Street

said to be the Jesuit church of St. Francis Xavier, 1822, on West 16th Street in Manhattan. He also designed St. Patrick's Church, 1887, on St. Philip Street in Charleston and probably St. Mary's on Hasell Street. Irish born, Keely is believed to have been a pupil of A. W. N. Pugin, the great English Gothic Revivalist. Historian Kenneth Severens cites a model church by Pugin as a major source of inspiration for Charleston's cathedral, a plan which also inspired Richard Upjohn's Trinity Church and James Renwick's Grace Church, both in New York City.

→ Directly across the street is:

2 **125 BROAD STREET:** One of the most unusual Charleston Victorian homes was built in 1886 by Charles Robert Valk, who owned an iron foundry. There were few examples of the Jacobean style in the U. S. before 1890. It is based on the English vernacular architecture of the 16th and 17th centuries.

→ Turn around and walk east on Broad Street.

3 **117 BROAD STREET:** Built c. 1760 by Edward Rutledge, a signer of the Declaration of Independence and a younger brother of John Rutledge. In 1965, the mansion was owned by the Bishop of Charleston and used as a convent.

→ Across the street is:

4 **116 BROAD STREET:** The U. S. Constitution and she-crab soup were born here. Built c. 1763, this was the home of John Rutledge, member of the S. C. Assembly, Stamp Act Congress, Continental Congress and the Constitutional Convention, President of South Carolina after the Revolution and Governor from 1779 to 1789. George Washington had breakfast here in 1791. In 1853, the mansion was remodeled for Thomas Gadsden, a real estate broker and slave trader, by Swedish architect P. H. Hammarskold. The ironwork is attributed to Christopher Werner. When the house was later owned by Mayor Robert Goodwin Rhett, President William Howard Taft visited several times. William Deas, Rhett's butler, (no pun), is said to have created she-crab soup.

116 Broad Street

If ever there were a "power dinner", it was the one held in the spring of 1787, when Charles Pinckney dined with his good friend John Rutledge at 116 Broad Street. The two men talked of the upcoming Constitutional Convention in Philadelphia which they were both attending. That night, they composed what came to be known as the "Pinckney draught" of the Constitution. Most of its key provisions ended up in the final document. Rosen relates the story about deTocqueville who, when told that Thomas Jefferson wrote the Constitution pointed out that Jefferson was in France at the time. "There is no mystery about it," he said. "A man named John Rutledge wrote it."

5 **114 BROAD STREET:** (Next door) Planter Ralph Izard began to build this mansion with an imposing Palladian portico c. 1790, but died before it was finished. His daughter Elizabeth married Thomas Pinckney, who bought the house in 1829 and finished it. Confederate commander General Pierre G. T. Beauregard was headquartered here in 1863 and Confederate president Jefferson Davis was a visitor.

6 **110 BROAD STREET:** Built c. 1728 by William Harvey, a butcher. In 1837, the house was owned by the Poinsetts. Joel Poinsett, a Congressman, U. S. Secretary of War and diplomat, best remembered as a horticulturist who introduced the poinsettia. In the early 19th century he was famous in Charleston for his breakfasts. An invitation to these weekly events was almost as coveted as an invitation to the St. Celcilia Society Ball. Poinsett valued intelligence as much as beauty and charm in a woman and insisted upon agreeableness in both men and women. Next to adventure, Poinsett loved conversation and flowers. He was skilled at inducing each guest to speak about that of which he knew best. The breakfasts were lessons in the art of conversation.

7 **106 BROAD STREET:** The Lining House is one of the oldest houses in Charleston, an important example of Colonial architecture, characterized by a high-pitched gable roof, simple cornice, dormer windows with hipped roofs. It is named for Dr. John Lining who came from Scotland in 1730. He was a close observer of the weather and did the first such scientific reporting in Colonial America. He corresponded with Benjamin

106 Broad Street at right

Franklin and carried out Franklin's famous kite and key experiment in a local thunderstorm. There have been several pharmacies in the building, and an early interior survives in the Charleston Museum. The Preservation Society of Charleston rescued the building from demolition in 1961, restored it and sold it as a private residence.

8 **105 BROAD STREET:** The Bredenberg Building was built in 1880 as a store and residence. In the 1890's August F. Doscher, a grocer, lived and worked here. Today, it contains the retail store of the Historic Charleston Foundation, where handsome reproductions of Charleston antiques are sold.

→ Cross King Street.

102 Broad Street

9 **102 BROAD STREET:** A Greek Revival residence, built in 1844 for Dr. Henry Frost, whose office was at #98.

THE STREET AS AN OUTDOOR ROOM

Modern planners have forgotten that the street is the "preeminent form of public space, and the buildings that define it are expected to embellish it." So wrote James Howard Kunstler in Home From Nowhere, a stirring indictment of urban and suburban sprawl. Small scale buildings with some visual interest, built out to the sidewalk provide a sense of friendly enclosure and encourage pedestrians, just as plain one story buildings set

The Classical Street Wall of Broad Street

back from the road and surrounded by parking lots create a sense of isolation and dehumanization and make walking dangerous, if not impossible. Broad Street is made up of buildings in which people live, work and shop. It has a sense of community. Current zoning laws of many towns and cities require that people live, work and shop in separate, distanced places, connected by the automobile. Kunstler calls these "anti-places", designed to accommodate cars, not people.

Broad Street, just east of King Street, has been altered dramatically by new constsruction. The Federal Couthouse annex, on the south side, is a serious architectural mistake -- too tall, stylistically inappropriate and damaging to the historic integrity of the street. The break in the crucial street wall at #101, once the site of two 3-story buildings identical to #97,needs restoration. On the north side, a gap in the street wall at #96 has been filled by moving an historic building to the site.

10 **95 BROAD STREET:** Built c. 1770 by Peter Bocquet, Jr., a merchant, planter and politician. Bocquet was a member of the Privy Council of Gov. John Rutledge. The iron balcony is believed to be original.

11 **98 BROAD STREET:** This was the office of Dr. Henry Frost who lived in the Greek Revival Building at #102. The rear part is believed to have been the kitchen of Dr. Alexander Garden, for whom the gardenia is named.

Coffee Break: Fast and French, (Gaulart and Maliclet), 98 Broad Street.

12 **92 BROAD STREET:** Dr. David Ramsay, who was a doctor, politician, historian and delegate to the Continental Congress, bought this house in 1783. It was built c. 1740 and is said to have some of the finest Georgian paneling in the city. The portico extending over the street is an interesting feature which used to be more prevalent in Charleston. The lavish use of columms throughout the city creates a classical fabric that is unique in America. Dr. Ramsay was a delegate to the Continental Congress and a member of the South Carolina Senate. He was married to a daughter of Henry Laurens. He is credited with introducing the smallpox vaccine to the colony. When the British captured Charleston in 1780, they considered Dr. Ramsay so important

92 and 90 Broad Street

he was imprisoned for a year. He wrote his books on American history in this house.

NEO-GREC

One of the distinctive architectural features of Broad Street is the high concentration of Neo-Grec ornamentation, much of it adorning older buildings that were updated in the last decades of the 19th century. Neo-Grec originated in France in the 1850's and 1860's. Russell Sturgis credits the style to Viollet-le-Duc, Duban and Labrouste, citing the Biblioteque Ste. Genevieve and Palais de Justice in Paris as

Neo-Grec Details

examples. The style came to America via Richard Morris Hunt, who studied at the Ecole des Beaux Arts and designed a Neo-Grec Studio Building in New York in 1857. Marjorie Pearson, Director of Research at the New York City Landmarks Commission, an authority on Neo-Grec, confirmed the identification of a large collection of Neo-Grec ornament here on Broad Street and on other buildings on King and Meeting. Pearson notes that "The American variation also used abstracted classical forms and ornament to emphasize the structure of the building, but more often for decorative effect. It is the product of an increased use of industrialization...as the ornament was usually created by machine tools and/or castings, rather than being carved by hand."

13 **90 BROAD STREET:** Dates to 1794, to which stylized Neo-Grec lintels and cornice have been added. Its former piazza has been enclosed with an outstanding example in diminutive form of what historian Sarah Bradford Landau called the "bony grid-like wall treatment" typical of Neo-Grec skyscrapers by Hunt and George Post.

14 **85-87 BROAD STREET:** Josiah Smith built this valuable Adamesque double house as a home for his sons in 1796, and his descendants were living here until the middle of the 19th century. Smith was a wealthy merchant, banker, planter and patriot of the Revolution. DuBose Heyward, author of *Porgy*, lived here as a young boy.

→ Set back and just beyond **88 Broad** is:

15 **6-8 COURTHOUSE SQUARE:** The 17th century Grand Modell plan by the Lords Proprietors envisioned a grid of streets with a large square at Broad and Meeting. Court House Square forms one corner of that envisioned square and is the only remnant of it. The 1760 apartment house here is considered to be one of the city's best examples of Georgian architecture, with a low hipped roof, 18th century ironwork and a double string course under the third floor.

FOUR CORNERS OF THE LAW: The intersection of Broad and Meeting Streets was given its name in Ripley's Believe it or Not: St. Michael's represents God's law; City Hall, municipal law; the Court House, state law; and the U. S. Court House and Post Office, federal law.

County Courthouse, 77 Meeting Street

16 **77 MEETING STREET:** (At the NW corner of Broad and Meeting.) The Charleston County Court House, built 1752-1788, is nationally important. The design, which is often credited to Judge William Drayton, is quite similar to plate 54 in *A Book of Architecture*, published by the English architect James Gibbs in 1728, and very influential. It has been theorized by historians William Seale and Kenneth Severens, that James Hoban, who emigrated from Ireland to Charleston in 1787, may have influenced the court house design, as there is a similarity between the Court House and Hoban's prize-winning plans for the White House. In 1997, a new Judicial Center was planned to go behind the historic court house to the dismay of many Charlestonians and also people "from off." New York architect and preservation expert Anthony M. Tung made a special trip to testify against the proposed complex: "You are a unique place in the world...(and) to approve the present design would exacerbate the 'fractured' character of the city center...No other building in the foreseeable future may offer such an important chance to heal or damage the cityscape for the century to come." The design was subsequently altered,

Federal Post Office, 83 Broad Street

however, preservationists failed to get an entrance or shops on the King street facade to make the block more pedestrian friendly.

17 **83 BROAD STREET:** (SW corner Broad and Meeting Streets) The United States Court House and Post Office, 1896, designed by John Henry Devereux, a prolific local architect, in the Renaissance Revival style. Until the 1886 earthquake, this site was occupied by one of Charleston's most monumental colonnaded buildings—the Guard House of 1838, designed by Charles F. Reichardt, believed to have been a pupil of Karl Friedrich Schinkel. Reichardt's building was built as a stoa with a covered Doric colonnade over the sidewalk on Meeting Street and Broad Street. Built about the same time, further north on Meeting Street, was the Charleston Hotel (demolished 1960) by Reichardt with a block-long Corinthian colonnade. The grandeur of Meeting Street's colonnades of the mid-19th century has all but vanished above Broad Street.

SIDEWALK PORTICOS

Sidewalk porticos, such as those on St. Michael's church and on buildings just to the south, were once a more prevalent architectural feature of the center of Charleston, as practical for the city's sub-tropical climate as the colonnaded piazzas. According to Anthony Tung (PRESERVING THE WORLD'S GREAT CITIES) such sidewalk porticos, were also once an important feature of downtown Singapore, but many were demolished in the 20th century, and retail activity fell. The city has mandated their return, and at considerable expense, the sidewalk portico is making a comeback as a public amenity in Singapore.

18 **80 MEETING STREET:** (SE corner Broad and Meeting Streets) St. Michael's Episcopal Church is one of the most important 18th century Colonial Georgian buildings in the nation. It was built by Samuel Cardy. The architect is unknown but the design is very similar to St.-Martin-in-the-Fields, 1726, in London by James Gibbs. Gibbs published a book of plans in 1728 that is known to have been in Charleston when St. Michael's was built in 1752. The windows have the characteristic Gibbs surrounds of small and large blocks. Tiffany windows were installed in 1906. George Washington, the Marquis de Lafayette and Robert E. Lee attended services here.

St. Michael's Church, 80 Meeting Street

City Hall, 80 Broad Street

19 **80 BROAD STREET:** (NE corner Broad and Meeting) City Hall, built in 1801 in the Adamesque-Palladian tradition, is nationally important. The design is attributed to Charleston architect Gabriel Manigault. Originally a bank building, it became City Hall in 1818 and has not only two full length portraits of General Pierre G. T. Beauregard with his sword, but also his ghost which has been heard humming an 18th century tune and rustling paper. The City Council chamber, a handsome late 19th century room on the second floor, is a mini museum of Charleston history, open to visitors.

CITY HALL PARK was officially named Washington Square in 1881 to commemorate the centennial of the surrender of the British at Yorktown. Created in 1824, as part of the construction of Robert Mills's Fireproof Building, it was not landscaped until the 1880's. Around the Confederate monument, there is a colorful octagonal flower border which blooms continually with an array of seasonal flowers, rather than the usual bedded-out displays of red salvia.

City Hall Park

→   Walk north on Meeting Street to Chalmers Street.

20 **100 MEETING STREET:** The Fireproof Building, now the home of the South Carolina Historical Society. A magnificent temple designed by Robert Mills in 1822. He claimed to be the first native-born American who studied to be an architect. Born in Charleston in 1781, Mills may have studied with James Hoban, architect of the White House. He received the bulk of his architectural training with Benjamin Latrobe, an architect of the U. S. Capitol, and with Thomas Jefferson. Mills wrote, "Mr. Jefferson kindly offered me the use of his library, where I found several of these works, all of Roman character, principally Palladio's, of whom Mr. Jefferson was a great admirer. During this period I made some plans and elevations for his Mansion at Monticello, according to his views on interior arrangement...This was in 1801." The Fireproof Building, as Mills designed it, would have been even more impressive with a rusticated base, fluted columns and a graceful curving staircase. The original staircase, built to Mills's design, was lost in the 1886 earthquake. According to Kenneth Severens, Mills was so concerned about

100 Meeting Street

105 Meeting Street

protecting his building from fire, he insisted upon having open space around it, and thus the buildings that once stood on the site of City Hall Park were removed.

This area, the very heart of Charleston, has been fractured by the 20th century out-of-scale buildings. The classical language of the city has been ignored. Mills's dignified Greek Revival Public Records building is a reminder of the vision once held for Charleston's civic center.

21 **105 MEETING STREET:** Hibernian Society Hall, 1840, was designed by Thomas U. Walter, a Philadelphia architect who is best known for adding the great dome to the U. S. Capitol and designing the House and Senate wings. Walter's design for Hibernian Hall won in a competition that also included Robert Mills. The original, more purely Greek, pedimented portico collapsed in the earthquake of 1886 and was rebuilt using the same Ionic order, but with more Roman elements, such as the modillion blocks and bull's eye window in the pediment.

The Hibernian Society was formed in 1801 as an Irish Benevolent society. The panel above the door is of the Irish harp. The ironwork design is attributed to Christopher Werner of Charleston. The St. Cecilia Society balls and other social events are held here.

22 115 MEETING STREET: The Mills House Hotel opened in 1853 and over the years attracted such patrons as Stephen A. Douglass, Robert E. Lee and Theodore Roosevelt. General Lee was a guest in 1861 and watched the great fire from the balcony until it came too close and he took refuge in the Edmonston Alston House.

115 Meeting Street

Confederate General Pierre G. T. Beauregard used the old hotel as his headquarters. It became the St. John Hotel and operated as such until 1967. The building was found to be unsound, and it was razed and rebuilt, adding height, but retaining much of the original design and ornamentation. Terra cotta window lintels were made from the original molds. The balcony is identical to the original.

→ Turn around and return to Broad Street. Go left on Broad.

23 67 BROAD STREET: In 1809 Jehu Jones, a free black entrepreneur and his wife Abigail, opened an inn which catered to travellers on extended visits. After selling the original hotel property to St. Michael's Church (it is now the churchyard), Jones moved his inn to #71 and to this building. Elite white society (e.g. Samuel F. B. Morse, architect William Jay and the English actress Fanny Kemble) highly praised the inn for its comfort and fine food. One visitor wrote, "Every Englishman who visits Charleston will, if he be wise, direct his baggage to Jones' hotel." Jones was also a trustee of the Brown Fellowship Society of fifty "lighter skinned" men who maintained a cemetery and a school and raised money for charity and social functions. Jones died in 1833, leaving an estate of $40,000. His daughter ran the inn for another twelve years. Jones's Georgian style hotel at #71 was demolished in 1928. The second story drawing room (used by the hotel for dining) with a Venetian window, chimney piece and overmantel were later installed at the Henry Francis DuPont Winterthur Museum.

24 65 BROAD STREET: Building dates to the early 18th century, having been built by planter Thomas Fleming. The facade was altered with Neo-Grec elements in the mid 19th century.

25 **68 BROAD STREET:** When Daniel Ravenel built his home c. 1800, the Adamesque style was new to the city. This home continues to be occupied by the Ravenel family.

26 **66 BROAD STREET:** Greek Revival, c. 1844. A whiff of Palladio in miniature.

27 **63 BROAD STREET:** Dates to c. 1834, with a c. 1850 Renaissance Revival facade.

28 **62 BROAD STREET:** The Confederate Home Building (now offices and apartments) was, in 1834, the Carolina Hotel. After the 1886 earthquake, architect E. R. Rutledge of New York remodeled it in the fashionable Neo-Grec. Note the lintels, segmental arches and narrow columns. The *News & Courier* praised the remodeling as being "one of the finest architectural attractions of the city."

62 Broad Street

29 **61 BROAD STREET:** Federal style, c. 1815, built by a tinsmith.

30 **56-58 BROAD STREET:** John Geddes, lawyer and Governor of South Carolina, 1818-1820, once lived at #56. The building was damaged in the earthquake of 1886. Late in the 19th century — note the Neo-Grec lintels — the building was joined with #58. At one time the Freedman's Bank occupied #58.

31 **53 BROAD STREET:** The Clark Mills Studio building dates to 1740 with an 1899 alteration. It was the studio of sculptor Clark Mills, who developed techniques for casting bronze statues. Later it became the law office of Thomas P. Stoney, mayor of Charleston, 1923-1931, and author of the city's pioneering preservation ordinance.

32 **54 BROAD STREET:** Peter and John Adam Horlbeck, who built the Exchange Building, used leftover materials, which had been imported from England, to build this home for the Geiger family in 1771. From 1870-1905, it was the office of Henry Ficken, who became mayor in 1891.

33 **50 BROAD STREET:** The Old Bank Building was built in 1797 for the Bank of South Carolina. White marble was used for the Adamesque lintels, sills and belt course. In 1835, it became the Charleston Library Society, and for much of the 20th century, it was occupied by banks.

34 **49 BROAD STREET:** A merchant shop/residence which dates to 1740 when it was the practice to live and work in the same building. This dual-use building mode was standard form in England and Europe during the Middle Ages. In most of the American colonies, business was conducted in central markets. However, in the major trading centers, such as Charleston, dual-use buildings were popular. Survivors can be found on King, Broad, Elliott and East Bay in the famous Rainbow Row. The balcony is considered one of the best examples of 18th century ironwork in the city. A valuable Georgian building, note the hipped roof, quoins, dentil cornice and belt courses between the floors.

35 **43-47 BROAD STREET:** (SE corner at Church.) Saddlers and harness makers built their shop here c. 1855. This handsome Neo-Grec commercial building has the grid-like facade, stylized triangular pediment and cornice details and support piers that were typical in the 1870's.

46-40 Broad Street

38 and 40 Broad Street

36 **46 BROAD STREET:** (The Greek temple bank building.) Shepheard's Tavern once was on this site. Charleston's colonial taverns were community centers where important events often occurred. At Shepheard's, for instance, one of the first Masonic Lodges in the United States was organized, and later the first Scottish Rite Lodge was begun here. Theater was performed in Charleston as early as 1703, but the first record of a theatrical season in the city dates to 1735 with a newspaper announcement of a tragedy, "The Orphan," to be performed at Shepheard's. The tavern also served as a courthouse and a post office. Balls and banquets were held here, and the first Chamber of Commerce in America was organized here in 1773. The tavern burned in 1796 but was immediately rebuilt. It was demolished in 1928, for the bank.

18th Century residential scale of Broad Street at 29, 31, and 33

37 **40 BROAD STREET:** Built for a merchant in 1806 and updated in 1891 with a Neo-Grec cornice and lintels. This part of Broad Street has an unusual concentration of Neo-Grec alterations on the 18th and 19th century buildings, reflecting the economic recovery after the Civil War and repairs made to buildings damaged in the 1886 earthquake. Other late 18th and early 19th century buildings with Neo-Grec ornament include 41, 37 and 36 Broad Street.

38 **35 BROAD STREET:** The building dates to 1792, built for merchants, with a Palladian window in the dormer on the front slope of the hipped roof.

39 **33 BROAD STREET:** Built as a home and a shop for John Smith in 1786, having a handsome wooden shopfront with fluted pilasters that probably dates to 1821.

40 **34 BROAD STREET:** A marble bank building of 1962 and remarkably well-mannered architecture for that era. The portico features columns with the Tower-of-the-Winds capitals so popular on 19th century Charleston buildings. The building lacks the symmetry of more literate classical buildings, but is far more in harmony with Charleston's streetscape than most late 20th century buildings.

41 **30 BROAD STREET:** (Next to the bank.) This 3-story Federal house of 1800 was nearly demolished in 1974 by First Federal Savings and Loan. Preservationists protested and the old facade of Charleston "grey" brick was preserved.

42 **26 BROAD STREET:** A shoemaker built his establishment here in 1791. The later shopfront has a Neo-Grec stylized cornice and an arcade of fluted engaged columns.

43 **31 BROAD STREET:** Built by a watchmaker in 1792 and updated with fashionable Neo-Grec details about a hundred years later.

44 **29 BROAD STREET:** Like so many commercial buildings along Broad Street, the facade is much later than the original. The Civil War, the earthquake, as well as the urge to be fashionable, resulted in a number of facade alterations. This 1790 building now wears a Second Empire mansard from the late 19th century.

45 **25-27 BROAD STREET:** The Neo-Grec facade is believed to have been applied after the 1886 earthquake. This double building was built in 1839 by William Wragg Smith, attorney.

46 **23 BROAD STREET:** Dates to 1786, having been built by a tailor. The facade was altered in 1838.

47 **21 BROAD STREET:** The original structure dates to c. 1802. The present Neo-Grec facade is believed to have been added after the 1886 earthquake.

48 **18 BROAD STREET:** Where other city centers may have an old structure or two huddling between mammoth glass boxes, Charleston's anomaly is an 8-story commercial palazzo on a street of one to three story 18th and 19th century buildings. Charleston's first skyscraper was built in 1910, causing considerable controversy. The mayor at the time, R. Goodwyn Rhett, was also the president of the People's National bank who built it.

21 Broad Street

Designed in the tripartite mode, the base is rusticated granite, the middle detailed with balconies and the top ornamented with cartouches and Romanesque arches. The architect was Victor Frohling of Thompson and Frohling of New York. During the late19th century, creative American architects who had studied at the Ecole des Beaux Arts in Paris, creatively adapted the language of Renaissance palaces to American business buildings. The Italian marble leopards were carved in the 18th century. People came to visit the building just to ride the elevator, a novelty for the city. The building has a bleak poorly-maintained look today as the ornate American Renaissance cornice was destroyed by a tornado in 1938 and has not been replaced.

Coffee Break: *Jake's, 19 Broad. Note the grandeur of the façade, c. 1838, above the aluminum storefront. It was inspired by The Choragic Monument of Thrasylus in Greece and is attributed to Charles Reichardt, who designed one of the grandest Greek Revival buildings ever built in America—the Charleston Hotel on Meeting Street, which was torn down in the architectural dark ages of the 1960's. Brent's at 40 Broad, open M-F 7:30am-3pm. Blind Tiger, 38 Broad, opens at 11am.*

| *16 Broad Street* | *9 and 11 Broad Street* |

49 **15 BROAD STREET:** An example of the antebellum taste for ornate terra cotta window pediments, fancy cornices and elaborate ironwork. Built for both commercial and residential use, the Italianate alteration was made in the 1850's. At various times, it has contained a hardware store, banks, real estate and insurance offices, the British consul, lawyers, brokers, a snack shop and barbers.

50 **16 BROAD STREET:** Wachovia Bank is located in several buildings. At the northeast corner of State Street, the 2-story, 3-bay building of 1817 has a wooden Eagle on the gable, a symbol of the original occupant, the Bank of the United States.

51 **11 BROAD STREET:** E. B. White designed this handsome Italianate commercial building in 1856 for S. G. Courtenay, booksellers. The Courtenay Bookstore Building was the city's most modern, complete bookstore and also a publisher. William Gilmore Simms, South Carolina poet, novelist and editor, is said to have written some of his novels on the counters of Courtenay. In the 1940's Robertson's Cafeteria was located here, serving like a London coffee house as a meeting place for businessmen and politicians to gossip and exchange views. The brownstone facade was done by stonecutter W. G. Chave of New York. In the 1970's the storefront was restored by owner Joseph P. Riley, Jr., who later became Mayor of Charleston.

52 **9 BROAD STREET:** This brownstone commercial building was a brokerage exchange built in 1856 for William Pinckney Shingler and T. J. Shingler, designed by E. B. White, with stonework by Chave. The Italianate style was exceedingly fashionable at the time. White was also the architect of the City Market Hall, the steeple of St. Philip's church and Grace Church.

53 **3 BROAD STREET:** Built in 1853 for Edward Sebring, president of the S. C. State Bank. On the first floor was the bookstore of Samuel G. Courtenay, with Walker Evans and Cogswell, publishers, upstairs. The architect was Edward C. Jones, who introduced the Italianate style to commercial architecture in Charleston with the design for Sebring's brownstone bank building which is next door.

54 **ONE BROAD STREET:** The first Italianate Renaissance Revival commercial building in Charleston, of Connecticut brownstone, with a welcom-

One Broad Street

ing corner entrance, noble lion head keystones at the first floor. It was designed in 1853 by Jones, the architect who introduced the Italianate style to houses with his design for the Ashe villa at 26 South Battery. Gene Waddell has observed that the bank shows indebtedness to the work of the English Architect Charles Barry and closely resembles a London Building. The bank moved out in 1863 when Federal troops were bombarding the city. It was later owned by George A. Trenholm, cotton broker and blockade runner, said to have been the model for Rhett Butler of *Gone with the Wind*. Trenholm lived in Radcliffeborough in a mansion not unlike Tara.

A NEW ARCHITECTURAL LANGUAGE

Edward C. Jones became recognized as one of Charleston's most talented architects of the mid-19th century with his design for Trinity Methodist Church on Meeting Street (Ansonborough) in 1850—an imposing church with a pedimented Roman portico of Corinthian columns. Three years later Jones shifted stylistically to a picturesque mode that abandoned the symmetry of the classical language. Jones introduced the Italianate with arches, asymmetry, bracketed cornices and lintels to commercial architecture here on Broad Street and in the Browning & Leman Store building (demolished) on King Street. The store had rustication and arched windows similar to 1 Broad and a bracketed cornice. A Baltimore newspaper praised the interior as surpassing "anything in New York or London." Jones brought the Italianate to domestic architecture in 1853, too, with his design for the J.A. S. Ashe villa at 26 South Battery (The Waterfront). Other important Italianate buildings attributed to Jones are the Isaac Jenkins Mikell house at 94 Rutledge and 30 and 32 Montagu Street (all in Harleston Village).

55 **OLD EXCHANGE BUILDING:** The wonderful vista of Broad Street is the high style colonial Exchange Building of 1773 with a rusticated ground story, Gibbs door surrounds, Palladian windows and cupola. The steps, hand rail and balusters are of imported Portland stone. (For history, and details of George Washington's visit, see the Waterfront tour.)

Old Exchange Building

35 Meeting Street

Charlestowne

Charlestowne is in the oldest area of the city. It was part of the old walled city, and the street pattern dates from the 17th century with the addition of some charming alleys. (They weren't so charming then.)

Despite fires, earthquakes, hurricanes and wars, many pre-Revolutionary structures survive. The neighborhood was particularly devastated by the Great Fire of 1740 in which some 300 houses were destroyed south of Broad Street and east of Church Street.

"Whatever else Charleston may be, she is different from any other city in America," wrote Elizabeth O'Neill Verner. Those who move to Charleston "must love the city as we love it to become one of us."

This intense civic pride is evident in the beautiful gardens, window boxes and urns, the collective personal efforts to beautify a beloved city. The incredible assemblage of classical Palladian colonnades, sub-tropical gardens and lacy iron gates can be almost overwhelming. Heed the advice of Samuel Gaillard Stoney: "Lose your way as often as possible... try to feel as well as see the town, because, like all other considerable human entities, Charleston is largely a matter of feeling." And that of Verner: "Catch the tempo of the town...slow your hurrying feet; move to the rhythm of the Moonlight Sonata."

→ Begin the walk at Broad and Church Streets.

Coffee Break: Brent's on Broad, 40 Broad Street

CHURCH STREET was named for St. Philip's Church, sited gracefully just south of Cumberland Street. When the first St. Philip's was built, this was the end of the street, and the city walls ran across what is now Cumberland Street. As you stand here on Broad and Church, you can see what Prof. Robert Russell describes as "one of the two most memorable urban views in all America." (The other view is that of the Old Exchange Building, seen from the middle of Broad Street.) The termination of a vista with a beautiful building was an art practiced with skill in Charleston. This vista of St. Philip's Church extending into Church Street was almost lost in 1835 when the church burned. The city asked that the new Church be moved back in order to make the street straight. Fortunately, the Vestry disagreed, believing that a view of a fine steeple was more valuable than traffic concerns. They moved the church only part way back.

→ Walk south on Church Street.

▮ **107 CHURCH STREET:** Built soon after the Great Fire of 1740 which burned from Broad and Church to Granville's Bastion at Water Street. The whole west side of this block was destroyed.

→ Go left on Elliott Street.

Elliott Street

ELLIOTT STREET was laid out in 1683, known as Callaibeuf's Alley or Poinsett's Alley, after Huguenot families who owned property there and later named for the Elliott family whose wharf was nearby. In the 18th century, this was "the great dry goods mart of Charleston," recalled Charles Fraser in *Reminiscences*. When the fashionable shopping promenade moved to King Street, the street declined, and "by Confederate days it was celebrated and shunned for endemic crime and yellow fever," noted Stoney. Restoration efforts did not spread here until the 1940's when Mrs. Henry Chisholm rescued #16, #18 and #20 and created a picturesque parking lot within the remains of an old warehouse building.

28 Elliott Street *22 Elliott Street*

2 **28 ELLIOTT STREET:** Built c. 1815 on an old foundation which, according to tradition, was Poinsett's Tavern, built c. 1732 by Elisha Poinsett, an ancestor of Joel Poinsett, the diplomat who brought the poinsettia plant from Mexico. A serene walled garden with a lion statue can be glimpsed from the street.

3 **22 ELLIOTT STREET:** George Gibbs built his shop/home here in 1793, moving in 1812, as the ambiance of the street was declining. When Commodore and Mrs. Stanley Jupp bought the house in the 1950's, seven families, some 40 people, lived here.

→ Go right on Bedon's Alley.

BEDON'S ALLEY has existed since 1704, named for George Bedon, a merchant who owned property here. In 1742, a great hurricane struck Charles Town and the sea came into the town. According to historian Walter J. Fraser, Jr., "the Bedons were fleeing their home and Mrs. Bedon, her three children, two white servants and five black slaves almost immediately were sucked under the rushing, swirling torrent and drowned." The Great Fire of 1778 destroyed the alley as well as Elliott Street.

4 **5 BEDON'S ALLEY:** Built by William Cunningham, merchant, in 1779 as his home and counting house. In 1794, the south wing was added. Restored in 1937 by Miss Susan Pringle Frost, one of the most important preservation visionaries in Charleston. By 1941, Miss Frost had rescued ten homes on Tradd Street, two on Bedon's Alley, nearly a block on East Bay and many others.

→ Go right on Tradd Street.

TRADD STREET was named for Robert Tradd, said to be the first child of English descent born here, or for his father, who by 1679, was living at what is now Tradd and East Bay. There are 22 pre-Revolutionary buildings on Tradd Street between East Bay and Meeting Streets.

5 **25 TRADD STREET**: Dates to c. 1749, the home of Major William Boone. In the 1920's, the Jennings family lived here. Edward I. R. Jennings was one of the city's jazz age artists whose works are in the Gibbes Art Museum.

Tradd Street

→ Walk slightly left on Church Street to:

6 **78 AND 76 CHURCH STREET**: (Attached houses) It is said that George Washington spoke from an earlier balcony here. According to reporter Jack Leland of the *Evening Post*, the legend is that a great number of Charlestonians gathered in front of 87 Church where Washington was staying and that he came across the street and used the balcony as his podium. DuBose Heyward wrote *Porgy* in the 1920's while living in the southern house.

7 **73 CHURCH STREET**: Dates to the early 18th century. In 1733, it was given by Miles Brewton, one of Charleston's wealthiest citizens, to his daughter with "love and affection." It originally had a third story. Mary Brewton's husband Thomas Dale was a doctor and a writer.

8 **71 CHURCH STREET**: Col. Robert Brewton, a son of Col. Miles Brewton, was a wharf owner, militia officer and member of the Commons House of Assembly. The Brewton house, c. 1721, is considered the oldest single house in Charleston. It is a classic Georgian house pointed the wrong way. It shows, according to Prof. Russell, how crucial the piazza and the piazza door are to the single house form. The Brewton house has unfortunately lost its narrow one-story piazza

71 Church Street

with a formal street entrance, which can be seen in a 1906 photograph. Loutrel Briggs designed a rear garden in the formal 18th century style which may be glimpsed from the street.

→ Return to Tradd Street.

9 **77 CHURCH STREET:** (SW corner at Tradd Street) Built c. 1819 by Louis Danjou, a grocer, who lived over his store, as did many tradesmen. In the 20th century, it became the home of the famous garden designer Loutrel Briggs.

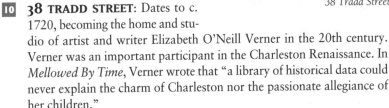

38 Tradd Street

→ Go left on Tradd Street.

10 **38 TRADD STREET:** Dates to c. 1720, becoming the home and studio of artist and writer Elizabeth O'Neill Verner in the 20th century. Verner was an important participant in the Charleston Renaissance. In *Mellowed By Time*, Verner wrote that "a library of historical data could never explain the charm of Charleston nor the passionate allegiance of her children."

→ Continue west on Tradd Street.

11 **46 TRADD STREET:** "Come quickly. I have found heaven," wired artist Alfred Hutty to his wife in 1919, after a brief walking tour of Charleston. Hutty just happened to stop here en route to Florida and wrote that he had "no preconceived ideas of Charleston", that it was with "open vision that I first beheld its quaintness and beauty and tasted the full charm of its old world flavor." The Huttys restored this 1770 home and were important participants in the city's cultural renaissance in art, literature, music and drama. Bessie Hutty was an artist in the garden, which was described as "vibrating with loveliness." Alfred was a founding member of the Charleston Etchers Club and the Society for the Preservation of Old Dwellings. His prints are credited with helping to foster the preservation sensibility by showing the beauty of dilapidated buildings. The Huttys participated fully in the city's social life and are remembered for such eccentricities as a party where guests were asked to bring a dog with a ribbon. The party was pronounced a "howling success."

→ Turn around, return to Church Street and go left.

12 **85 CHURCH STREET:** Built by a planter, c. 1749.

13 **87 CHURCH STREET:** The Heyward-Washington House was built by Daniel Heyward, a rice planter, and was the home of his son Thomas until 1794. Thomas was a planter, patriot, judge, signer of the Declaration of Independence and a delegate to the Continental Congress. During the Revolutionary War, he was captured by Lord Cornwallis and imprisoned in St. Augustine, Florida. Back home his wife bravely defied a British order to light candles in the windows as a gesture of gratitude to the British. A mob assembled and threw things at the house, threatening to tear it down. The house was built in 1772, has notable Georgian interior features, a drawing room mantel attributed to the important cabinetmaker Thomas Elfe, and a 1770 bookcase considered one of the most important pieces of Colonial furniture. When George Washington stayed here in 1791 he kept a journal: "Went to a concert where there were 400 ladies, the number and appearance of which exceeded anything I had ever seen... Breakfast with Mrs. Rutledge." The Heyward-Washington house drawing room narrowly escaped being carried off as a trophy of Americana in 1929.

→   Next door:

14 **89-91 CHURCH STREET**: Built after the Revolution and known as Cabbage Row because African-American tenants put cabbages for sale on the window sills. It was partly the inspiration for the Catfish Row in DuBose Heyward's novel, *Porgy*.

15 **90 CHURCH STREET**: Built c. 1760 by Huguenot Thomas Legare in the Georgian style. The Regency piazzas, with acanthus leaves over the columns, were added c. 1816. DuBose Heyward lived for a time in a small building in the rear. In Charleston, porches are called piazzas. The term began to be used in England after Inigo Jones designed Covent Garden in 1631, surrounding an Italian piazza with an arcade. The British thought piazza referred to the covered walk, and by 1700, Charlestonians were using the word to refer to their porches.

16 **94 CHURCH STREET**: Built c.1760 by John Cooper, merchant. Thomas Bee, planter and delegate to the Continental Congress, bought it in 1771. In 1805, it was the home of Gov. Joseph Alston. His wife Theodosia Burr disappeared at sea in 1812. Like so many important homes in Charleston, it has a plaque installed by the Preservation Society. A handsome example of the Charleston single house.

NORTHSIDE COURTESY

You may have noticed the scarcity of windows on the north side of Charleston houses as well as the doorway which looks like the main entrance but actually leads only to the piazza. Both architectural features are as unique to the city as the tradition of northside manners. They reflect the Charlestonians' intense love of privacy. That extra front door, which screens the piazza from the street is important to "a town that lives so much on its piazzas and so highly values its privacy," wrote Stoney. Charles Anderson, another local observer of Charlestonian character, noted that "a capacity for leisure goes quite naturally with a sense of privacy and a love of peace." Charles Kuralt was introduced to northside manners when he was living temporarily in Charleston researching a book. He longed to look northward at a mockingbird clever enough to whistle back the first four notes of Beethoven's Fifth, but a friend explained to him that in Charleston, "you don't look out your windows overlooking your next-door neighbor's piazza and courtyard. That's their space, and what they do out there is none of your business." Over time, more windows have been punched into the north facades of Charleston homes, and not everyone is rigorous about keeping their blinds closed. It is a custom, however, which many urbanites from the northeast, who share the native Charlestonians' love of privacy, find quite appealing.

→ Go left on St. Michael's Alley.

ST. MICHAEL'S ALLEY is one of those picturesque narrow lanes that was added to the Grand Modell for Charleston. One of America's great inventors and artists took this same route some 180 years ago. Samuel F. B. Morse came to Charleston during the social season and painted close to 100 portraits between 1817 and 1821. He stayed in a boarding house at 36 Church Street (now a garden) and painted in a studio here. According to biographer Carleton Mabee, "When Finley (Morse) left Lucretia of a morning, he had but to walk from Church Street through a short length of St. Michael's Alley to his painting room. His

St. Michael's Alley

formal address was Broad Street, but his windows and private entrance were on the alley, in the shadow of St. Michael's steeple."

17 **8 ST. MICHAEL'S ALLEY**: Designed by E. B. White, who also designed the Huguenot Church, Grace Church and the Market Hall. The balcony was added in the 1920's by Susan Pringle Frost who salvaged it from a demolished building.

→ Turn left on Meeting Street.

18 **72 MEETING STREET**: South Carolina Society Hall, designed in 1804 by Gabriel Manigault, is one of the nation's most valuable Adamesque buildings. The portico, reminiscent of a Palladian villa, was added in 1825, designed by Frederick Wesner. This sort of street colonnade as portico is a unique architectural feature of Charleston, not found in other American cities, although popular in Europe. The South Carolina Society was organized in 1737, mostly by Huguenots.

72 Meeting Street

19 **60 MEETING STREET**: Originally built in 1771, with a rather plain facade somewhat similar to that of 64 Tradd Street which shares a common wall. Bertram Kramer, a bridge and wharf builder, and general contractor, transformed the former tenement into a High Victorian fantasy, complete with mansard, a heavy bracketed cornice, a conical peak and a Moorish arched doorway.

57 and 59 Meeting Street

20 **59 MEETING STREET**: (NW corner at Tradd) The Branford Horry House is a nationally important classic Charleston double house built in the Georgian style c. 1751 by William Branford, a planter and member of the Colonial Assembly. His grandson, Elias Horry, added the Palladian portico in 1830. Horry, a planter and president of the South Carolina Canal and Rail Road Company, when the railroad was the longest in the world, had a sense of good urban design.

21 **57 MEETING STREET**: First Scots Presbyterian Church of 1814 looks as though its design was inspired by Benjamin Latrobe's 1805 design for the Baltimore Cathedral. As you stand in front of the church, look northward toward another lovely vista of the street's porticos extending over the sidewalk. Note, too, the plaque on the fence with map of the walled city, marking the SW corner.

→ Across the street is:

54 Meeting Street   *51 Meeting Street*

22 **54 MEETING STREET**: The Timothy Ford house, a single house with a hip roof, dates to the early 19th century and probably has the most spectacular wisteria in the city. Ford, a patriot in the American Revolution, came to Charleston from New Jersey to practice law. He entertained the Marquis de Lafayette in his home in 1825. Peek through the iron fence at the garden, which is a series of rooms, formally symmetrical.

23 **51 MEETING STREET**: The Nathaniel Russell House is one of the finest Adamesque mansions in America. Russell moved here from Rhode Island and became, according to historian Robert Leath, "the richest merchant of the Post-Revolutionary period." He was known as "King of the Yankees", founded and was the first president of Charleston's New England Society. His wife and daughters were enthusiastic gardeners. An English visitor of about 1818 wrote of the "splendid residence surrounded by a wilderness of flowers and bowers." A Russell descendant recorded that the garden contained "every imaginable plant and flower." In the 1850's the mansion became the town house of R.F.W. Allston when he was governor of the state. Allston, said to be the richest planter in South Carolina, was a patron of the arts. Adamesque was no longer fashionable in the 1850's, but Allston apparently shared the sensibility of Charlestonians who have traditionally cherished their historic houses. Documentation is lacking. Historians speculate that the house might have been designed by Gabriel Manigault or Thomas Pinckney, either of whom might have designed the Middleton-Pinckney house in Ansonborough as well. The garden is open to the public, as is the house.

FLYING STAIRCASES

Charleston has a collection of some of the finest house museums in America, all of which are well worth a visit. Inside the Nathaniel Russell House, for instance, there are incredible moldings, notable Adamesque details, oval rooms, gracious furnishings of the period and a swirling "flying" staircase with no visible support. If you are then inspired to do a bit of redecorating, there is the tempting antiques district on King Street, just north of Broad Street. Reproductions from the museum houses and from private collections are on sale at the shops of Historic Charleston Foundation (105 Broad Street). There you will find such treasures as Regency chairs, copies of those Governor Allston once owned, an 1810 Charleston-made mahogany card table like the one in the Nathaniel Russell music room and the popular blue and white "Canton" china which was found in fashionable dining rooms. Other important Charleston house museums include: Edmonston-Alston House, 21 East Battery (The Waterfront tour), Joseph Manigault House, 350 Meeting Street, the Aiken-Rhett House, 48 Elizabeth Street (Mazyck Wraggborough Garden District), and the Heyward-Washington House, 87 Church Street (Charlestowne).

→ Across the street:

24 **48 MEETING STREET**: Dates to the 1840's, built by Otis Mills, builder of the Mills House Hotel. In the 1850's, this was the home of James Adger, merchant and steamship line developer, reputed to have been the richest man in antebellum South Carolina. The Doric piazzas have been enclosed, and the mansion is used as a school by the First Baptist Church.

→ Walk left onto Water Street and left again onto Church Street.

WATER STREET follows the course of Vanderhorst Creek, the waterway down which William Lord Campbell, the last Royal Governor of South Carolina, escaped in his flight from the rebellious city. It ran just outside the southern boundary of the walled city.

25 **45 CHURCH STREET**: (NW corner at Water Street.) Dates to 1769.

26 **55 CHURCH STREET**:
Charleston gardeners delight in planting the tiniest patch of soil, and here is a spectacular result. In the spring, the Confederate Jasmine perfumes the street-scape, and roses continue throughout the summer.

55 Church Street

GLORIOUS GARDENS

Gardening has been a Charleston tradition for over 300 years. According to Elise Pinckney, "when the first settlement was made on the west bank of the Ashley River in 1670, the plans for the home of the Proprietary Governor called for an extensive formal patterned garden along the river." Historian William O. Stevens has observed that it was different in northern colonies, "when orthodox Quakerism flourished it was considered ungodly to cultivate mere flowers for their beauty. The Puritan had much the same idea." Not Charlestonians. The tradition of the gorgeous flower garden is alive and well. Church Street contains two of the city's most spectacular 20th century gardens, each with a distinct personality. At 55 Church Street, Hugh and Mary Dargan designed an 18th century style formal pattern garden with miniature box hedges, a central sundial, surrounded by antique roses along high walls and growing over the house. Across the street, at 58 Church is the garden of the late Emily Sinkler Whaley with a Loutrel Briggs scheme personalized by Mrs. Whaley's profusion of flowers and now by her daughter. The owners of these gardens graciously open them for the annual spring and fall garden tours. For information, write The Preservation Society, Box 521, Charleston, SC, 29402 and Historic Charleston Foundation, Box 1120, Charleston, SC 29402.

27 **59 CHURCH STREET**: A valuable example of early Georgian architecture, the Thomas Rose House was built c. 1735 and survived the Great Fire of 1740. The garden was designed by Loutrel Briggs in 1954. Note the delicate acanthus leaf ornament on the piazza columns.

Charleston ghosts are said to be mostly handsome and gallant men and pretty and charming women, according to Robert Stockton. One of the city's most famous ghost stories is associated with 59 Church Street. It seems that Dr. Joseph Ladd Brown, poet, physician and gentleman, lived here in 1786 as a boarder with the granddaughters of Thomas Rose. It was his custom to bound up the stairs each evening whistling a quaint English ballad. Brown, from Rhode Island, was professionally and socially well connected, except for one friend, Ralph Isaacs, who was jealous of Brown's social popularity. His jealously erupted one night after a theatrical performance at the Exchange Building. "Seating in theaters then was arranged according to one's social standing," reported the newspaper, so Brown and Isaacs did not sit together. Afterwards a disagreement over the quality of the actress, whom Isaacs had been unable to hear because of his distant seat, led to a duel in which Brown was mortally wounded. In 1962, the News & Courier published a photograph of Brown's ghost and reported that servants in the home claimed to hear him whistling that old ballad.

---

28 **61 CHURCH STREET**: First Baptist Church is called the "Mother Church of Southern Baptists." It was designed by Robert Mills in 1819, the first native-born American who actually studied to be an architect. He was born in Charleston in 1781 and is well known to Americans as the designer of the Washington Monument and important buildings in Richmond, Baltimore and Philadelphia. Talbot Hamlin noted that Mills was the first American designer who realized that a new country needed an American architectural style and who introduced Greek Revival to the southeast.

29 **69 CHURCH STREET**: Built in 1745, one of the largest homes built before the Revolution and one of the great house forms traditional in Charleston— a Georgian double house, usually square with a room in each corner, with a central hall and an entrance on the street.

→ Turn around and walk south on Church Street, crossing Water Street.

30 **41 CHURCH STREET**: The 1909 dream house of architect A. W. Todd, who grew up nearby and as a child imagined what might be built upon a lot so uniquely shaped, only 26 feet wide and 161

61 and 69 Church Street

39 Church Street

feet deep. Todd also built a Harleston Village mansion (40 Rutledge Avenue).

31 **39 CHURCH STREET**: When George Eveleigh built his home, a handsome Georgian double house, c. 1743, it was sited on the south side of Vanderhorst Creek. Eveleigh became wealthy trading in deerskins.

32 **38 CHURCH STREET**: Built c. 1812 by Dr. Vincent Le Seigneur, a native of Normandy who came to Charleston from Santo Domingo in 1793, during the slave uprising in the French colony. Le Seigneur founded the House of Health, one of Charleston's earliest hospitals for slaves. When the house sold in 1974 for $124,740, it was said to be the highest price ever paid for an historic Charleston home. In 1818, Samuel Morse lived at Mrs. Munro's Boarding House, then at 36 Church, now the garden of the Le Seigneur mansion.

33 **35 CHURCH STREET**: Built c. 1770, it was the 19th century home of Dr. Joseph Johnson, Intendant (mayor) of Charleston, 1825-27. Johnson was the author of *Traditions and Reminiscences of the American Revolution*.

→ Go right on Atlantic Street.

ATLANTIC STREET used to be a narrow lane called Lightwood Alley and Lynch's Lane. It was renamed Atlantic in 1837 when it was widened.

→ Turn left on Meeting Street.

34 **18 MEETING STREET**: Built between 1803-06 by Thomas Heyward, a signer of the Declaration of Independence. The entablature of the piazza is particularly intricate with a dentil and modillion cornice and a Greek

15-17 Meeting Street

wave design. Over each column is an acanthus leaf, a motif which can be found on two large homes in Radcliffeborough and on the Governor Thomas Bennett mansion in Harleston Village.

35 **16 MEETING STREET**: "Probably the handsomest and most complete residence in the South and one of the handsomest in the country," exuded the *News & Courier* in 1876, when the Calhoun Mansion was built. Owner George Williams, banker, wholesale grocer, cotton factor and commission merchant, founded the Carolina Savings Bank. His daughter married Patrick Calhoun, a grandson of the statesman, giving the mansion its name. The design by W. P. Russell relates well to Charleston's architectural traditions. It has classical quoins and the entrance portico is similar to that of the 1770 John Edwards House across the street, but larger and with Corinthian columns instead of the Ionic. However, the black and red brick design is an unusual Victorian feature. The interior is decorated with opulent walnut paneling, elaborate patterned ceilings, original lighting fixtures and English aesthetic movement tilework.

36 **15 MEETING STREET**: John Edwards House, 1770, a double house, features a pedimented central pavilion, hipped roof, a double flight of entrance stairs. Edwards was a Patriot, imprisoned in St.

15 Meeting Street

Augustine during the Revolutionary War. During the British occupation, Admiral Marriot Arbuthnot used the house for his headquarters. The graceful curving piazzas were added later by banker George Williams, Jr., a son of the builder of the Calhoun Mansion.

→ Turn around and walk back up Meeting Street to:

GARDENERS' DETOUR: During the summer, go left onto Lamboll Street to see a lavish display of blue plumbago.

31 Meeting Street

37 **24 MEETING STREET**: Designed in 1822 by the talented English Regency architect William Jay, who maintained offices in Charleston and Savannah. Jay's Charleston works are not well documented, but historians speculate about his possible involvement in two other works, a mansion in Radcliffeborough and the Fireproof Building. Note the piazzas with the correct sequence of orders and the recessed arched windows, a recurring theme in Jay's work.

38 **31 MEETING STREET**: Built c. 1792 by James Ladson, an officer of the Continental Line, state legislator, Lt. Governor, and delegate to ratify the U. S. Constitution. In 1840, the house was altered and the main entrance was moved from Ladson to Meeting. Christopher P. Poppenheim, a planter and King Street hardware merchant, bought the mansion in 1877. Mrs. Poppenheim created a formal garden. The fountain was copied from a large park in Bad Nauheim, Germany.

39 **35 MEETING STREET**: The William Bull House, c. 1720, is one of the oldest houses in Charleston, a Georgian double house with quoins and a hipped roof. The piazza and wings are later additions. Bull was a Lt. Governor of South Carolina.

40 **37 MEETING STREET**: The Otis Mills House, built before 1775, with the large bays added later. It became the home of Mills in 1846. He loaned the mansion to

35 Meeting Street

Gen. Pierre G. T. Beauregard, the Confederate commander, during the Civil War.

→   Turn around and return to Ladson Street. Go right on Ladson Street.

LADSON STREET was named for Lt. Gov. James Ladson, who built the wooden house at 31 Meeting Street. The street existed as a driveway and was extended to King Street in the early 20th century.

41 **2 LADSON STREET**: Lt. Gov. William Bull gave this site to his son-in-law John Drayton in 1746. Drayton is believed to have built the house, as the drawing room on the second floor has a mantel similar to the mantels in Drayton Hall. A subsequent owner added a semi-circular Adamesque bay. About 1900, the facade was given its present Colonial Revival treatment.

2 Ladson Street

→   At the vista of Ladson Street is:

42 **27 KING STREET**: This Georgian mansion, reminiscent of the Villa Cornaro by Andrea Palladio, has been called the finest townhouse ever built in Colonial America. Miles Brewton, a slave merchant, built his home between 1765 and 1769, but he lived here only a short time before he and his family were lost at sea in 1775. Brewton's sister, Mrs. Rebecca Brewton Motte, lived here during the Revolution when it became the headquarters for Sir Henry Clinton and Lords Rawdon and Cornwallis. Notable features include the elliptical fanlight of the main doorway and the two-tiered portico with Tuscan and Ionic columns of Portland stone. The property, which includes outbuildings such as the "Gothick" stable, has remained in the family of Brewton's relatives. The garden originally extended all the way to Legare Street.

→   Continue left on King Street.

43 **23 KING STREET**: Built by Thomas Lamboll before 1755, this is one of the oldest wooden houses in the city, possibly as early as 1721.

44 **21 KING STREET**: The Patrick O'Donnell House was built in 1856 by a building contractor. It may have been designed by Edward C. Jones, who introduced the Italianate style to Charleston three years earlier. This elaborate Venetian palazzo became the home of Thomas Pinckney in 1907. Josephine Pinckney organized the S. C. Poetry Society here in 1920.

45 **19 KING STREET**: Thomas Lamboll built this house for his third wife Elizabeth, whom he married in 1743. In 1750, Mrs. Lamboll "excited great interest in the science of horticulture and gardening by planting a large and handsome flower and kitchen garden upon the European plan," wrote a local botanist. The Lambolls corresponded

21 King Street

with John Bartram and sent him asters, double columbine, honeysuckle, jessamine, larkspur, stock and lunaria. The Lamboll's garden, said to be the first of its kind in the city, was located on the block to the south of their home, extending to the water, which is now South Battery where Lamboll had his wharf. Lamboll was a merchant and trader.

15 Lamboll

28 Lamboll Street

→ Go right on Lamboll Street.

46 **15 LAMBOLL STREET**: Benjamin Howard, a wholesale druggist from Tennessee, built this Colonial Revival house, c. 1908. The pedimented portico with giant Ionic columns continues the Palladian tradition. However, the house lacks classical symmetry.

47 **14 LAMBOLL STREET**: Built in 1850 as an investment by contractor Patrick O'Donnell, who obviously had a taste for unusual ornamentation. A quirky, delightful presence in the streetscape.

48 **28 LAMBOLL STREET**: Built c. 1777 on former marsh land, this was Kincaid's Eastern Tenement (apartment building).

5 Legare Street

8 Legare Street

→ At the vista of Lamboll Street is:

49 **5 LEGARE STREET**: Quoins and Doric colonnades on what looks to be a stone house (brick with scored stucco) as you approach Legare Street. John Nash had used this technique for his Regent Street terraces to give them the grandeur of palaces. Charlestonians did follow London fashion.

→ Go right on Legare Street.

50 **8 LEGARE STREET**: Built c. 1857, this Italianate mansion was the 20th century home of Burnet Rhett Maybank, mayor, governor and U. S. Senator. The iron gate is attributed to Christopher Werner.

51 **15 LEGARE STREET**: A wooden single house, dating to 1772, by John Fullerton, a builder, for himself. During the 1780-81 occupation of Charleston, British officers were quartered here.

15 Legare Street

52 **14 LEGARE STREET**: The Francis Simmons House is one of the finest Adamesque mansions in America. The lightness and delicacy of the detail typical of the style can be seen in the slender columns, delicate ornament and the segmental arches.

The pineapple gates were added by George Edwards, merchant and planter, who bought the house in 1816. Something of a mystery surrounds Francis Simmons. Immediately after his marriage, he left his wife on their wedding day and built this house for himself. His wife lived at 131 Tradd Street, and apparently husband and wife maintained a friendly but distant relationship. According to a newspaper account, he presided at her dinner parties and

14 Legare Street

hosted her receptions, and "when they met on the afternoon drive around the Battery, as she rode in her carriage, he rose in his and bowed." There is a beautiful pattern garden, recreated to an 1820's design.

53 **29 LEGARE STREET:** A typical single house, built c. 1835 by Rev. Paul Trapier Gervais, who published sermons and a political pamphlet. In 1895, the novelist Josephine Pinckney was born here.

54 **32 LEGARE STREET:** Built before 1740 by Solomon Legare, a Huguenot silversmith. It is famous for its Sword Gates of 1848, which are identical to those designed for the Guard House, once at Meeting and Broad. The gates were crafted by Christopher Werner and may have been designed by Charles F. Reichardt, architect of the Guard House and the Charleston Hotel, two significant lost landmarks. A number of legends are associated with the property. Philippe Noisette, the Charleston horticulturalist for whom the Noisette rose is named, may have designed the grounds in the 19th century.

32 Legare Street

55 **37 LEGARE STREET:** Dating to 1820, this became the home of John Bennett, the celebrated writer and illustrator, in 1903. Bennett was a major figure in the Charleston Renaissance, one of the founders of the Poetry Society. Over drinks in this house, he introduced DuBose Heyward to a publisher for *Porgy*.

→ Go Right on Tradd Street.

106 Tradd Street

56 **106 TRADD STREET**: Built before 1772 by Col. John Stuart, this is one of the finest Georgian mansions in America. The drawing room's elegant Georgian paneling was sold to the Minneapolis Museum of Art. In 1934, it became the home of skyscraper architect John Mead Howells, who had the lost decorative friezes and carvings duplicated and painstakingly replicated for the drawing room, a model of which may be seen in the Charleston Museum. He built the wall, and a garden was laid out in the style of Le Notre, the landscape architect who planned the garden at Versailles. Howells is famous as the architect of the Chicago Tribune tower, 1922, and the Daily News building in New York, 1930.

Tradition says that during the Revolution, Gen. Francis Marion attended a party here, during which the host locked the door and insisted his guests continue drinking. Not being a big drinker, Marion escaped by jumping from the second story, breaking his leg.

THE CLASSICAL LANGUAGE OF CHARLESTON

Strolling Charleston's colonnaded streets, it's easy to feel transported to London, Bath or almost anywhere in Italy. The pervasive classical language of the city is largely derived from the Renaissance architect Andrea Palladio, whose influence upon English architects was extensive. Charleston bookshops carried British publications with detailed drawings of Palladio and notable English architects. Charleston's builders were prolific and inventive in adapting their designs. The open porches and loggias, so practical for the Mediterranean climate were welcome in Charleston and can be found on the most modest to the most ambitious of her buildings. The recurring use of raised basements, projecting pedimented porticos, colonnades, Palladian windows and a wide variety of pilasters, columns and capitals bring a Palladian grandeur to the city's streetscapes all the way up to Line Street. And beyond the Old and Historic District, you may want to visit Drayton Hall on the Ashley River.

Built between 1738 and 1742, Drayton Hall has been called the first truly Palladian house in America, reminiscent of Palladio's Villa Pisani. It is open to the public and can be reached by car or tour bus. For information, call 843-766-0188. www.draytonhall.org

→ Go left onto Orange Street.

ORANGE STREET was once part of a public pleasure garden for concerts and the site of an orange grove. In 1767, the garden was divided into building lots by Alexander Petrie.

57 **3 ORANGE STREET**: Built c. 1770 for the widow of Alexander Petrie, a silversmith.

58 **4 ORANGE STREET**: A Charleston single house, built before 1774.

3 Orange Street

4 Orange Street

59 **7 ORANGE STREET**: Built by Col. Charles Pinckney, c. 1769.

60 **II ORANGE STREET**: Built c. 1770, this was the home of Samuel and Caroline Gilman who were at the center of a literary circle. Gilman, a graduate of Harvard, was an essayist, poet and pastor of the Unitarian Church. His wife was a well-known writer and editor of *The Southern Rose*.

Coffee Break: *Fast & French, 98 Broad Street.*

"The handsomest shopping street in America"

King Street

K ing Street was one of the most urbane shopping promenades of 19th century America, lined with a "dazzling display of goods emulating a Turkish Bazaar", as Charles Fraser wrote in 1854. Today that dazzle is returning to the many blocks of 18th and 19th century buildings. Shoppers are once again discovering the pleasure of strolling and shopping leisurely along a street of wooden shopfronts with small-scale moldings and ornamentation to delight the eye. A parade of one-of-a-kind boutiques and antique shops occupies restored buildings of great beauty, charm and civility. In the last few years, national companies like Saks Fifth Avenue, Abercrombie and Fitch, and Ann Taylor have moved in with more to come.

King Street has survived many ordeals. After the disastrous fire of 1838, there was a flurry of rebuilding, and by 1853, a Baltimore newspaper reported that the Browning and Leman department store, which stood then at King and Market, (where the Riviera Theater is now), was "probably the most beautiful as well as the most extensive establishment in the world." King Street had revived as a regional shopping mecca.

Then came the Civil War.

King Street is a prominent example of the city's preservation ethic and its tenacity to repeatedly restore itself after numerous catastrophes—hurricanes, fires, earthquakes and wars. The Great Fire of 1861 ravaged much of King Street even before the bombardment by Union Forces in 1863. At war's end, King Street was a shambles. It was rebuilt with optimism and an awareness of architectural fashion. And by 1875, Arthur Mazyck wrote in his GUIDE TO CHARLESTON, ILLUSTRATED, *that the city was "Beautiful as a dream, tinged with romance, consecrated by tradition, glorified by history, rising from the very bosom of the waves like a fairy city, created by the enchanter's wand."*

In 1874, *Scribner's Monthly* wrote of the street: "There the ladies promenade, evening morning and afternoon, shopping; there is located the principal theater, the tasty little Academy of Music and there, also, are some elegant houses."

Two months after the great earthquake of 1886, the *News and Courier* reported, "King Street, the pride of the city, (where) the handsome stores are nearly all repaired and present their usual holiday appearance."

King Street, however, almost did not survive the 1960's and 1970's. Like the commercial centers of so many American cities, its vitality was sapped by suburban shopping malls. It declined to a shabby street of aluminum store fronts, gaudy signs and boarded-up buildings. Mayor Joseph P. Riley Jr., recalled walking along King Street at Christmas in 1975 — "There was no one at all on the street."

"O modernization, what crimes are committed in thy name," wrote Ada Louise Huxtable in 1976 in the New York Times, bemoaning the widespread use of plastic and aluminum to replace ornate facades on Victorian shopping streets. Beauty was replaced by bleakness, and, predictably, the shoppers disappeared.

King Street today is a success story in the making, the result of historic preservation and a visionary mayor, elected in 1975, promising to revitalize downtown. During the "dark ages" of the 1960's and '70's, preservationists protected as best they could this extraordinary assemblage of small scale historic buildings

The revitalization of King Street has been so successful that now the street is in danger of having its small shop-keepers pushed out by the rush of large national retailers opening around Charleston Place. Traffic, while still not horrendous by world standards, has increased in the last few years, far beyond the liking of most Charlestonians. Many fear that the pleasure of the promenade may be ruined for visitors as well as residents if traffic is not controlled.

Much of the appeal of King Street is the 18th century scale. Though the facades are mostly 19th century, the streetscape still has the feel of a Colonial city. It has been called the "handsomest shopping street in America."

→ Begin the walk at Broad and King. Walk north on one of the most mistreated blocks of King Street, mutilated by 20th century "development" — the brutalistic parking garage and a bleak office building — before its inclusion into the Old and Historic District. On your right, just beyond Berlin's, is the new Judicial Center, designed by Jaquelin Robertson of Cooper Robertson Architects, sensitively designed to fit into the context.

I   **125 KING STREET**: (Tellis Pharmacy) Built in 1888, its neon sign is the oldest in the city (and one of the few), installed by the grandfather of the present owner. In 1986, Evans and Schmidt Architects restored the Victorian shopfront, using an old photograph.

125 King Street

A UNIQUE COMMERCIAL ARCHITECTURAL MODE

Note the narrow piazza on 125 King Street with stairs leading up to what was once the residential part of the building. The traditional Charleston single house with south-facing piazza, a combination shop/residence, was the prevailing mode on the street. Piazzas which have been enclosed for use as shops are known as piazza vestiges. The presence of these and the surviving piazzas is a unique architectural feature bringing a residential flavor to a commercial street and adds considerable charm, texture and rhythm.

2 **147 AND 149 KING STREET**: (The Preservation Society) Dates to 1878, built by a prosperous German grocer to be two stores and two apartments above. The Preservation Society has information for visitors, gifts and a bookstore. It is well worth a visit. At 149 is the headquarters for the Ben Silver Corporation (specializing in handmade English silk ties and blazer buttons) which has another store in the Piccadilly Arcade in London.

THE PRESERVATION SOCIETY OF CHARLESTON

Organized in April 1920, as the Society for the Preservation of Old Dwellings, the Society is the oldest community-based membership organization in the nation. The name was shortened in 1956 and the focus of the Society's concerns broadened. Best known for its fall candlelight tours of houses and gardens, the Society also has an important Heritage Education Program in cooperation with public elementary schools and a Home Maintenance Assistance program to assist low-income home owners. The Society publishes books, gives annual awards, installs historic markers and produces position statements on projects which affect the historic character of the city. The Society is a crucial voice in preserving the charm and the ambiance of Charleston.

3 **150, 152 AND 154 KING STREET**: (At the NE corner at Queen) More examples of the commercial/residential mode that was so popular along King Street, built by Patrick J. Coogan, the city treasurer, who lived at 154. All three facades are believed to have been similar to 150, with pilasters, classical capitals and a wide bracketed cornice.

4 **160 KING STREET**: (The building with the large bay windows) The southern annex of the Library Society, added in 1996, incorporating a facade saved from the earlier building of 1889 built by the Carolina Rifles for their armory. The club was among a number of groups formed after the Civil War, when Confederate veterans did not trust the Union troops to maintain order. Carolina Rifles was organized in 1869 as a social club, as armed military units were banned

160 King Street

by the Union troops who occupied Charleston. The Charleston Library Society was organized in 1748 by a group that included planters, merchants, lawyers, a doctor and a school master "to save their descendants from sinking into savagery." It is the third oldest private library of its kind in the United States. The Society is credited with helping to establish both the Charleston Museum and the College of Charleston. The main building, just north of the annex, dates to 1914.

5 **159 KING STREET**: A shop/residence of 1866 built for George Flach, watch maker and jeweler, with Greek Revival grills and a crenelated Gothic parapet. Subsequent businesses here included a furniture and crockery shop, Chinese laundry, fruit shop, barber shop, shoe shine parlor and candy store. This part of King Street is known as the "antiques district" of Charleston.

6 **165 KING STREET**: A Renaissance Revival style house, replacing an earlier building destroyed in the 1861 fire. It was built for a grocer and originally had two tiers of piazzas overlooking a garden to the south. A restoration in 1972 unfortunately did not replace the Modern/Georgian store front, which is at odds with the Italianate cornice and lintels.

7 **169 KING STREET**: (Helen Martin Antiques) At the turn of the century this was the shop of John Rugheimer, a well-known merchant tailor, famous as the arbiter of fashion in gentlemen's clothing in the south. Rugheimer's work received awards at the South Carolina State Fair and at the Chicago World's Fair.

8 **175 KING STREET**: Note the narrow piazza with blue awning. You will see a few of these survivors as you walk up the street.

9 **178 AND 180 KING STREET**: Mixed-use shop/residences were traditional. Homes were reached by stairs to 2nd floor piazzas. Many people still live over shops on King Street.

10 **183 KING STREET**: A fanciful two-story classical building of about 1840 with an 1880's facade of white columns and pediment. Note the piazza vestige with Eastlakian spindle work on the window at the second level.

11 **186 KING STREET**: (RTW) Considered one of the most valuable historic buildings on King Street because of its unusual ornate wooden facade. Built in 1800 to be a combination dry goods shop and residence, it has long southern piazzas. In the

183 King Street

1970's, the building was condemned as uninhabitable. The street level had been defaced with a modernistic brick front. In 1979, an enlightened owner restored the building, replicating the historic shop front which has fluted engaged columns, from an old photograph.

→ At Clifford Street:

186 King Street

12 **191 KING STREET**: (George C. Birlant) William Enston, the furniture dealer and philanthropist, built his shop in the Tudor Gothic Revival style in 1850. Note the trefoil colonnade at the street level.

13 **193A KING STREET**: A piazza vestige with Gothic ornament.

14 **192-198 KING STREET**: Col. Blum's Range was designed by Charleston architect Francis D. Lee in 1853 to be an inn with shops on

193A King Street

the ground floor. (Lee was also the architect of a Gothic Revival church at Charlotte and Elizabeth streets.) In 1982, the building was restored to its original use and became the King's Courtyard Inn.

192 - 198 King Street

→ At Fulton Lane:

204 King Street

15 **200 KING STREET**: The great fire of 1838 apparently burned to within inches of this building, evidenced by its jutting out beyond buildings to the north. The street was widened in the burned area. Dating to 1806, this is one of the over 200 18th and 19th century buildings that line King Street between Broad and Spring Streets. The 18th century scale and the replacement of bleak 20th century aluminum shopfronts with traditional wooden ones has attracted shoppers back to the street.

16 **202 KING STREET**: The Rugheimer Building of 1912 was designed by Walker & Burden for John Rugheimer, whose firm, one of the oldest custom tailoring establishments in Charleston, was founded during the Civil War, when Rugheimer was a seaman and a blockade runner. The business continued until 1972.

17 **204 KING STREET**: Very sophisticated new construction, designed after hurricane Hugo destroyed an earlier building in 1989. Architects Evans and Schmidt responded creatively to the context in both scale and detail: the fenestration, handsome shop fronts with rusticated piers, and the arches relate well to the streetscape. Above the shops is the Fulton Lane Inn.

ARCHITECTURAL GOOD MANNERS

When etiquette expert Marjabelle Young Stewart released her annual list of the most polite cities, Charleston was ranked Number One (although it isn't polite to brag.) The same courtesy can be seen in some new buildings. Modern architects like to design "look-at-me" buildings, but certain of Charleston's architects have deferred graciously to their new building's context, using historical forms creatively. In addition to 204 King, other courteous buildings are 211 King (Saks), 55-59 Vanderhorst (Radcliffeborough houses), 46 Rutledge (Harleston Village house) and 7 Savage Street (Charlestowne house). Avoid Calhoun Street, which has some of the city's most mediocre ill-mannered architecture. Locals debate which is the ugliest: Nations Bank "toadstool" building at Gadsden Street, the Medical University and Eckerd buildings at Ashley Avenue or the new College of Charleston library at Coming Street.

18 **208 KING STREET:** This Richardsonian Romanesque building originally was a YMCA, designed by S. W. Foulk in 1889. It once had a tower with a peaked roof. Red brick ornamented with rough stone and broad rounded arches are a hallmark of the style, named for Henry Hobson Richardson, best known for Trinity Church, Boston, 1873.

19 **211 KING STREET:** Saks Fifth Avenue has not been opening downtown stores in recent times, but Charleston's downtown is different. King Street is a model for historic preservation leading to economic development. Sandy Logan of LS3P Architects, creatively detailed the facade so that it does not read as one long horizontal building and thus fits gracefully into a street of narrow vertical buildings.

Saks, Riviera Theater

20 **214 KING STREET:** Built after the great fire of 1838, with the popular ornamental iron grills near the parapet and later Neo-Grec window surrounds.

Coffee Break: The Sweetwater Cafe. 137 Market Street.

21 **216 KING STREET:** (The Body Shop) A shop/residence built in 1839 for a dry goods merchant, remodeled in 1908 as a cafe by the colorful Vincent Chicco, who emigrated from Italy in 1868 and also ran Chicco's Cafe on Market Street. He was known as the "King of the Blind Tigers." A blind tiger was a bar that circumvented the state wide prohibition law of 1892 by charging the patron to see a mythical "blind tiger" and then giving him a drink for free.

22 **225 KING STREET:** The Riviera Theater, considered the city's best example of Art Deco, was built in 1939 by Albert Sottile, the theater magnate. It stands on the site of a magnificent department store that was remodeled into the Academy of Music where Sarah Bernhardt and Lillian Russell appeared. The "Aztec Temple" design of the Riviera was a familiar theme also widely used for furniture, belt buckles, radios and clocks. Note the inlaid sidewalk.

23 **226 KING STREET**: Charleston Place caused a great controversy in the 1980s. As first proposed, it would have been much taller and would have overwhelmed the historic district and the skyline of the whole city. It took nine years, but the preservation community finally was able to have the project scaled down and redesigned by John Carl Warnecke. It has been a major factor in the stabilizing and revitalization of the downtown area. Not everyone loves it, but it is almost universally credited with anchoring downtown from further deterioration.

24 **229-233 KING STREET**: (Beginning with Old Towne Restaurant) Three identical Greek Revival tenements built after the great fire of 1838. Note the ornate iron grills between the buildings at the second floor and the Greek anthemion grills near the roof.

Coffee Break: Starbucks, 239 King Street.

25 **237 KING STREET**: A High-style Tuscan Revival shop/residence built in 1870 and designed by Abrahams & Seyle for a grocer. Men's social clubs held meetings in the upstairs drawing rooms. Note the iron store front with Corinthian columns, ornamental lintels, the cornice, arched windows and the Italianate piazza vestige.

26 **243 KING STREET**: (SW corner at Beaufain) The Siegling Building was built as a home and a shop for John Siegling, whose business in 1973 was the oldest music house in America, having been founded in 1819. The Greek Revival building—note the grills at the parapet—was later altered at the street level. The interior of Siegling's store was highly praised for its grand stairway and lace and velvet curtains.

→   At Beaufain Street:

229 - 239 King Street

243 King Street

27 **245 KING STREET**: Built after the fire of 1838 and remodeled in the late 19th century. Note the Neo-Grec incised lintels and the fanciful cornice.

28 **249 KING STREET**: Designed by the prolific Charleston architect John Henry Devereux, who also designed the post office on Broad Street. It was highly praised in the press. Note the baroque pediment and the bracketed cornice. The storefront is a later alteration. In 1876, the J. R. Read dry goods company was located here. Their stock was said to compare most favorably with that of any similar concern in the country and included dry goods of every description: gloves, hosiery, fabrics and "fancy goods."

245 - 253 King Street

29 **251 KING STREET**: In the late 1850s, this was the bookstore of John Russell, where the city's intellectual elite met.

BOOKSTORE SOCIAL SALONS

During the 19th century, a salon society developed in Charleston, according to historian David Moltke-Hansen. "Ideas and books entered the drawing room, and lectures became suitable entertainment for both sexes." John Russell's bookshop, which was located at various addresses on King Street, was one popular meeting place. According to Lacy Ford, "members of the so-called Russell's Bookstore Group, a literary set, held informal gatherings in the back of Russell's Bookstore." The Group, which included William Gilmore Simms, Paul Hamilton Hayne, James Louis Petigru, Basil Gildersleeve, Henry Timrod, William John Grayson, Charles Fraser and other prominent Charlestonians discussed the latest books and ideas and started RUSSELL'S MAGAZINE in 1857. When the actor Louis Fitzgerald Tasistro visited Charleston, he observed that "the most fashionable lounging-place where the ladies of Charleston are accustomed to assemble is Hart's Circulating Library in King Street... Reading constitutes, in fact, the principal recreation with all classes in Charleston." In 1855, of the nine retail bookshops in Charleston, eight were located on King Street, with that of Samuel Hart located at 300.

30 **253 KING STREET**: (Demetre Jewelers) Built before 1861. Albert Sottile opened a motion picture theater here in 1907.

31 **254 KING STREET**: (Victoria's Secrets, NE corner at Hasell Street) The famous firm of Hayden, Gregg & Co., jewelers and silversmiths were here in the 19th century. Built in the Greek Revival style—with the popular grills—in 1839. The lion head earthquake bolts on the Hasell Street facade were added after the earthquake of 1886.

32 **267 KING STREET**: C. 1875 and restored using old photographs in 1993. In the 19th century, it was an art gallery.

33 **270 KING STREET**: The Masonic Temple Building (SE corner at Wentworth) was designed in the Tudor Gothic style by John Henry Devereaux in 1871.

34 **273 KING STREET**: (SW corner at Wentworth) This handsome Italianate building has been partly restored to its 1880's appearance, although it is still missing its beautiful dome.

270 King Street

285-287 King Street

Coffee Break: Sermet's Corner, 276 King Street.

35 **281 KING STREET**: The S. H. Kress & Co. building of 1931. The reeded pilasters, chevron and zigzag designs and foliation are characteristics of Art Deco and are familiar all over America, built at a time when "corporate style" did not necessarily mean second rate architecture.

36 **285 KING STREET**: An especially beautiful shopfront on a building with a classical balustrade and lavish ornamentation. In 1867, the famous bookstore of John Russell was located here.

37 **287 KING STREET**: This was once the popular shop of R. W. Hamblin, who sold millinery, dry goods and notions. In 1993, the Neo-Grec facade was restored, using a photograph from the 1890's. The stylized Neo-Grec mode used geometric shapes, segmental arches, narrowed piers and broad linear relief on pilasters and was popular in New York in the 1870's and 1880's. It has been cited as a "distinctive American School" by historian Sarah Bradford Landau.

→ Cross Society Street.

38 **300 KING STREET**: Believed to have been built between 1790 and 1809. In the mid 19th century, it was the bookstore of Samuel Hart.

39 **304 KING STREET**: Built in 1911 by Albert Sottile as the Princess Theater and rehabbed into a bar and grill.

40 **306 KING STREET**: One of the most successful businesses on King Street was located here in the 1880's—The Tea Pot, run by the entrepreneur Samuel Wilson, who lived in Harleston Village at 11 College Street. Wilson sold fancy groceries, teas, coffees, spices, fine wine and liquors. The building dates to 1810. It's historical integrity has been diminished by an inappropriate 20th century shopfront.

41 **313 KING STREET**: A fine example of the Federal style, built for a saddler and harness maker as a store and residence in 1812 and restored in 1964 by the clothier Jack Krawcheck. Mr. Krawcheck also built a southern annex, which was sensitively designed by Simons and Lapham to complement the older building and is ornamented with balconies. The new annex was built of old materials that Mr. Krawcheck began to collect before World War II. "He was proud," reported the *News and Courier*, "that he did not smash up old houses to obtain the materials... he felt that nothing was too good for his Charleston building, because... Charleston has been good to him." The owner and the architect exemplify the love and respect Charlestonians have for the fabric of the city and its heritage.

42 **318 KING STREET**: Another example of the piazza vestige, this one enclosed in 1860. It's neighbor at #316 is in dire need of restoration.

43 **319 KING STREET**: The American Hotel was built in 1839 when the vitality of King Street was moving uptown, just as it is today. The building was restored in 1975. One of several fashionable hotels on King Street and an architecturally valuable commercial building, the hotel was created by combining several older buildings behind the Greek Revival facade, featuring six fluted pilasters.

318, 316 King Street   *324 - 314 King Street*

44 **324 AND 322 KING STREET**: "Millinery creations of the choicest description" were once sold here. The shop specialized in hats from Paris, London and New York. And there was once a storefront to match the sophistication of the hats, made of cast iron fluted pilasters. The News and Courier reported in 1889, "The Nagel Building is assuming handsome proportions. The metallic front, which was manufactured in Charleston by R. M. Masters, gives it a pretty appearance." This once-grand building is badly in need of restoration. Three cast iron pilasters survive, but between them are two slanted "modern" shop fronts of aluminum and brick.

45 **327-329 KING STREET**: (NW corner at George) Originally built as a double tenement c. 1855 for a prosperous German grocer. In 1923, John Newcomer remodeled it as the Gloria Theater for Albert Sottile.

46 **336-338 KING STREET**: Dates to the late 18th century, built by John Cunningham, shopkeeper, who was also a founder of the Second Presbyterian Church.

Coffee Break: Modica, 41A George Street, has very special Italian coffee made in a hand-crafted espresso machine, paninis, gelatos.

336-338 King Street

47 **341 KING STREET**: Built in 1817 as a shop/residence for James White in the Federal style with quoins and an elaborate gable. There used to be a piazza on the south side. Now there is a passage used as a short cut to and from the College of Charleston.

48 **345 KING STREET**: The hardware merchant Christopher P. Poppenheim, who lived in a mansion on Meeting Street, built his shop here in 1883. He later moved to a larger building at 363 King.

49 **363 KING STREET**: When completed in 1891, this commercial building was described in the press as "a dream in granite, pressed brick and terra cotta." It was built for Poppenheim, designed by Charleston architect W. B. W. Howe, who also designed the mansion of Charles Drayton at 25 East Battery and the William Enston homes on upper King Street. A close look in the upper windows on the right side of this facade will reveal that its Victorian exuberance is only facade deep, and the modern building behind is not related to the front.

363 King Street

50 **369 KING STREET**: The building has a Neo-Grec cornice and a piazza vestige on the south side.

51 **371 KING STREET**: The Garden Theater Building of 1917, built for theater magnate Albert Sottile, exhibits the influence of the Ecole des Beaux-Arts, as designed by C. K. Howell and David B. Hyer. The two-story Roman triumphal arch is flanked by giant Corinthian pilasters. Classical motifs in terra cotta ornament the facade.

→   At the SW corner at Calhoun:

52 **381 KING STREET**: This ante bellum shop was built by William Enston, an Englishman who was a Charleston merchant and philanthropist. It reflects the popular Italianate style of the 1850's. Note the piazza vestige.

53 **387 KING STREET**: (Francis Marion Hotel) When it opened in 1924, the Francis Marion was the largest hotel in the Carolinas. W. Lee Stoddard of New York designed it in the Georgian Revival style with a limestone base with terra cotta and limestone trim.

54 **399 KING STREET**: This parking garage disrupts the pedestrian experience. A citizen group — the Rally Round the Square Committee — recently coordinated a vision for restoring the neglected blocks around Marion Square. The plan, which you can see at www.savethecity.org in the December 2003 *Guardian*, recommends refacading the garage with a design that is in harmony with historic buildings.

MARION SQUARE

First conceived after the failed slave insurrection of 1822 as a parade ground and a State arsenal, Marion Square came into its own in 1843 as the site of the new South Carolina Military College, better known as the Citadel. The arsenal building on the north side of the square was built in 1825 and enlarged several times. The Citadel moved north in the 1920s. The former Citadel building was converted into a hotel in the 1990s. Today Marion Square is at a crossroads. Much of its former graciousness was lost to urban decay during the mid-20th century. Several of these eyesores are slated to be replaced. Residents are urging that new buildings be in harmony with local classical architecture—see The Vision for Marion Square in the December 2003 issue of the Guardian at www.savethecity.org. The much-despised County library building, built at the northwest corner of Marion Square in 1958, is slated to be replaced with a hotel designed by Fairfax and Sammons Architects, the cutting-edge New Classicist firm that coordinated the Vision. They are also designing a mixed-used building to replace the much-despised building on the southwest corner. On Saturdays, from April to December, there is a lively Farmers' Market in the Square.

55 **403 KING STREET**: Built c. 1808 as a private home, sensitively restored by Bill Huey in 2000 for St. Matthew's Lutheran Church with a new copper roof, new stucco and a rebuilt dormer with a graceful Palladian window.

56 **405 KING STREET**: St. Matthew's Lutheran Church of 1867 was designed in the Gothic Revival style by John Henry Devereux. The *Charleston Daily Courier* wrote, in 1872, that "the powerful buttresses, towering pinnacles and carved crockets of the lofty steeple give it an air of fairy beauty." The 297 foot steeple made it the tallest building in South Carolina at the time.

405 King Street

57 **409 KING STREET**: (NW corner King and Vanderhorst) The old Aimar Drug Store Building was built in 1808 as an investment by Lucretia Radcliffe. The Aimar Drug Store was located here from 1852 until 1978. It was valued not only for the medicines it sold, but also as a source of spices, aphrodisiac, "dragon's blood", brimstone, frankincense and "Aimar's Premium Cologne Water."

ARCHITECTS' DETOUR: Go right on Hutson Street. At mid-block on the north side is one of the city's celebrated parking garages, rating high marks for its respect for the city's urban fabric. The segmental-arched windows of the attic story echo those of its neighbor. The rusticated base is an attractive presence in the streetscape. It was designed by Stubbs Muldrow Herin. The white tower in the distance is that of Second Presbyterian Church on Meeting Street.

409 King Street

438 King Street

Coffee Break: Kudu Coffee, 4 Vanderhorst Street, serves breakfast and snacks all day. King Street Grocery, 435 King Street. 39 Rue de Jean, 39 John Street, serving French bistro food, is open from 11:30am on.

58 **415 AND 417 KING STREET**: Dates to 1856 as a store and residence. Note the intact Renaissance Revival cornice and lintels.

59 **426 KING STREET**: A former home with hipped roof, built in 1815, and later converted to commercial use.

→ Cross John/Warren Streets. The block on the western side, between Warren and Radcliffe Streets is undergoing revitalization. Once shabby buildings at 439, 441 and 455 have been restored with handsome wooden shopfronts.

60 **438 KING STREET**: Built in the 1870's by the entrepreneur Harris Livingstain to be his home and place of business. Large and Italianate, the Livingstain building was designed for lavish entertaining and a large household. The house was equipped with a speaking tube that connected to the store. The ornate interior with tall ceilings included gas chandeliers and a dining room that seated thirty people. Note the ornate paneled piazza entrance with heavy brackets.

61 **445 KING STREET**: (Across from 438) The building with green tile dates to 1910, but may be the remodeling of an earlier building. One of the few commercial buildings in the city with extensive use of decorative terra cotta. The building was unfortunately trashed at the street level with an aluminum storefront.

62 **442 KING STREET**: Not long ago, this Greek Revival single house was in ruins and flanked by empty lots. It was once the home of planter James Ferguson, who built it in the late 1830's and is one of the earliest surviving residential buildings in the area. In 1840, it became a bakery and is still known as the Amme Bakery Building for the firm that baked here for 75 years. Twice in the 1970s, the BAR refused to permit demolition. Architect Glenn Keyes restored it in 2000 and designed the creative well-mannered buildings on both sides based on old photographs. The three buildings demonstrate the important role preservation and contextual architecture play in the economic development of a downtown.

63 **446 KING STREET**: The Art Deco American Theater dates to the 1930's. The owners are pioneers in the revitalization of King Street, also restoring 442, and reconstructing 440 and 444. Their current project is the rescue and restoration of the William Aiken House.

64 **456 KING STREET**: One of the city's finest Adamesque buildings, the William Aiken house, was built in 1811, this was the home of the father of Governor William Aiken. Aiken senior was president of the South Carolina Canal and Railroad Company which ran the first railroad to use steam locomotives to pull a train in regular service in 1830. Around the corner on Ann Street you may see a replica of the steam engine, The Best

William Aiken house, 456 King Street

Friend of Charleston, the first regularly scheduled train in America. As we go to press, the fate of the museum is uncertain.

→ Turn right onto Ann Street. If you have young children with you, there is a Children's Museum on the south side of the street.

65 **29 ANN STREET**: (Mid block, on the right) Camden Depot Gate, designed by Edward C. Jones in 1849 with crenelated Gothic towers.

→ Turn around and return to King Street and go right (north)

Coffee Break: Paolo's, 41 John Street, serves authentic espressos and gelatos from noon on, daily.

66 **479 KING STREET**: Built in 1881 of red brick with a dog-tooth brick cornice, marble window sills and lintels.

67 **474-476 KING STREET**: These two buildings with the ornate Neo-Grec cornices and lintels have recently been restored. Neo-Grec became fashionable in New York in the 1870s and 1880s.

474 and 476 King Street

494 King Street

68 **494 KING STREET**: The Bluestein Building, with a unique facade featuring blue-glazed brick and Neo-Grec ornamentation. Built in the 19th century and remodeled in 1913. The City bought the facade in order to maintain the architectural character of the street and to signal a commitment to the revitalization of upper King Street. After the building was damaged in a fire in 1987, the City hired Evans and Schmidt Architects to restore the facade and the storefront. Mayor Riley noted that the building was "one of the most beautiful and architecturally significant buildings in this area."

This neighborhood is in transition. It still contains boarded-up buildings (some incredibly beautiful ones), remnants of the economic decline which began in the 1960s, when many residents moved to the suburbs. Historically, King Street was an important regional shopping district. In the 1890s the blocks above Marion Square were called the "New Jerusalem" of Charleston. A number of prominent Jewish families still have ties to the area. The Francis Marion Hotel closed in 1989 after damage from hurricane Hugo. The transformation of Upper King in the last decade has been dramatic. The restoration of the Bluestein Building at 494 King was an important step in the renaissance of the area. The Francis Marion Hotel was restored. Many local unique businesses have moved into the area. There is such a large cluster of home furnishing shops that have moved into the area, it has become known as a design district. New restaurants are also opening here. The city is putting in slate sidewalks and appropriate lighting fixtures similar to those below Calhoun Street.

69 **515 KING STREET**: (SW corner at Morris Street) The building has lost its cast iron shopfront, but retains pilasters and a piazza vestige buried behind brick. This building, along with 507 and 509 (c.1895 for a grocer and tobacconist) are examples of buildings that could be restored to good effect.

515 King Street

ARCHITECTS' DETOUR: Serious students of architecture will enjoy continuing up King Street to Spring Street to view the Victorian commercial architecture awaiting restoration. This area was recently zoned as part of the Old and Historic District. Retail vitality began to pick up in late 1994, when the city calmed traffic by making King a two-way street above Calhoun Street. Wide one-way streets tend to become speedways, not conducive to strolling and shopping.

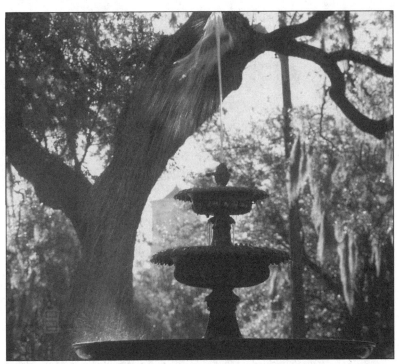

Fountain in Wragg Square

Mazyck Wraggborough Garden District

The planter aristocracy began to move into the Mazyck Wraggborough area at the beginning of the 19th century, building enormous town homes designed for lavish entertaining. Initially, the planters and their families came to escape the malaria so prevalent on the plantations during the summer— "Charleston became a planters' summer resort," noted historian Samuel Gaillard Stoney. Soon they began to spend a good part of the year in town, returning in January for the social season. The planters, noted for their hospitality and ceremony, set the pace. They built their mansions on gracious wide streets, creating an idyllic suburb of classical grandeur that many visitors to Charleston never see.

Charleston enjoyed a golden era of development in the 18th century similar to that of Bath, England. Professor Robert Russell has noted that both cities catered to the same kind of country aristocrat with a taste for parties and elegant living. The expression of that lavish taste continued well into the 19th century in Charleston and may be seen here in the opulent antebellum homes of Mazyck Wraggborough.

"NEVER HAVE I BEEN TO A DULL PARTY"

The social agenda included plays, balls and concerts in the winter, with horse races and outdoor musical programs in the summer. All year there were social clubs, dinners, lectures, musical and literary groups and private parties. Charlestonians have traditionally led a full social life. Historian Walter Fraser, Jr. noted that Charleston's taste for dancing and music was "unrivaled in America" and that even politics was upstaged by parties. Henry Laurens observed in 1763 that sessions of the Legislature were shortened "in favor of the ball." Even after the heyday of the antebellum planter, the art of party-giving survived. "Never have I been to a dull party," wrote Elizabeth O'Neill Verner in the 20th century. "It is the thing Charleston does best of all—give a party. Nowhere else do gaiety and dignity blend with such perfect harmony." The city continues to exude an air of festivity and elegance reminiscent of the novels of Jane Austin.

During these antebellum years, according to historian George Rogers, there was a division in the city "between the planters of this part of town and the merchants who lived more generally in what was the old walled town near the docks." Today, the neighborhood is being restored to its former splendor.

Walking about Mazyck Wraggborough is rather like meeting the Wragg family—Mary, Ann, Judith, Henrietta, Elizabeth, Charlotte and John. These were the children of Joseph Wragg, who was granted the area by the Lords Proprietors in 1715. Wragg's company was the largest slave trading house in Charleston. Like other prosperous merchants, such as the Manigaults, Hugers and Mazycks, the Wraggs also became planters in the 18th century.

Joseph Wragg was said to have had one of the finest libraries with books on law, history, literature and gardening—a library "suited to the needs of a businessman who was also a cultivated gentleman," according to historian Frederick Bowes. A "good companion" was expected to have an acquaintance with Greek and Latin and to exercise good judgment, wit, courtesy and cheerfulness.

Wraggborough was laid out by the Wragg family in 1801, who, with great civic generosity and a sense of good urban design, reserved two acres as public land—Wragg Square and Wragg Mall. Just to the southeast, the area known as Alexander Mazyck's pasture, is bounded by Chapel, Elizabeth and Calhoun streets and the Cooper River, and was surveyed in 1786. Mazyck Wraggborough Garden District has a very active neighborhood association.

→ Begin the walk at Meeting and John Street, right by the Visitor Center.

1 **WRAGG SQUARE** was once lined on the northern side with a handsome row of homes known as Aiken's Row, built after 1832 by Governor William Aiken. The architectural historian Talbot Hamlin, noting the importance of colonnades on Charleston homes in the 1830's, wrote that on Aiken's Row "the alternation of the colonnaded porches and rich foliage creates a street picture of great beauty." Sadly, that streetscape

Aiken's Row on Wragg Square

was interrupted by the demolition of five of the homes on the Row. Mazyck Wraggborough was not zoned as part of the Old and Historic District until 1975.

→ Walk through Wragg Square to:

2 **48 ELIZABETH STREET**: The Aiken-Rhett House was built c. 1818 by John Robinson, a merchant and land speculator, who bought a number of lots nearby on Judith Street. In 1827 the house was bought by William Aiken and inherited by his son in 1833. William Aiken, Jr. was a member of the planter aristocracy, active in politics and Governor of South Carolina in 1844. He is reputed to have been the largest slaveholder in South Carolina at the beginning of the Civil War. Aiken and his wife

48 Elizabeth Street

spent lavishly, transforming their home into a showplace for entertaining, replacing Federal details with more fashionable Greek Revival, acquiring art. In 1839, a ball there was described by Francis Kinloch Middleton as "the handsomest I have ever seen...the orchestra from the theatre played for the dancers...the supper table was covered with a rich service of silver. The lights in profusion (with)...a crowded and handsomely dressed assembly." In 1863 a reception for Confederate President Jefferson Davis was given here, and for several months during the Civil War it was the headquarters of Confederate Commander Gen. Pierre G. T. Beauregard. It was recently a site for the filming of the mini-series *North and South*. Descendants of the family of Gov. Aiken lived here until 1975. The mansion is now a remarkable museum, open to the public.

→ Walk left on Judith Street.

3 **10 JUDITH STREET:** A double house of the early 19th century, built in the Regency style by John Robinson, designed with a high basement as it then overlooked a marshy creek to the south. Such piazzas and high ceilings offered some relief from the summer heat. When Duc de la Rochefoucault-Liancourt visited Charleston, he observed that "In Charleston, persons vie with one another, not who shall have the finest, but who shall have the coolest, house." The

10 Judith Street

small house on the left stands in what was originally the garden of #10. Robinson also built the homes at number 17, 15, 8 and 6 Judith. In 1902, this was the home of Rt. Reverend Peter Fayssoux Stevens, the first bishop of the Reformed Episcopal Church.

4 **9 JUDITH STREET:** Built by John Tidemann, a German merchant, between 1835-52. Note plaque.

→ Return to Elizabeth Street and go left to Chapel Street.

ELIZABETH STREET: The homes on this block were built at a later date than the planters' mansions, when the area was becoming more densely populated. Preservationists in Charleston have a high regard for the more modest houses of a neighborhood. These so called "background" buildings preserve the sense of place and authenticity which is vital to the appreciation of the architectural gems.

→ Go left on Chapel Street.

CHAPEL STREET: In the early decades of the 19th Century, this was an elegant country district, undeveloped except for a few grand planter mansions, gardens and orchards. By 1968, the area had deteriorated to a run down low-rent neighborhood with unsympathetic alterations to the old mansions. Because the area was somewhat isolated, demolitions that took so many fine homes along Meeting Street and those of Aiken's Row, spared Chapel Street.

→ Immediately on your right are five similar houses.

36 Chapel Street

5 **51-59 CHAPEL STREET**: Capt. Benjamin McCabe, a prosperous business man, built this row in 1890 in a very un-Charleston manner, abandoning the traditional "single house" plan with a side piazza. Instead, McCabe's Row houses are typical American Victorian with front porches. Three of the porches have ornamentation that appears to have been influenced by British designer Charles Eastlake. McCabe lived at 59 Chapel.

6 **36 CHAPEL STREET**: The sidewalk garden in front of this plantation style home clearly signals that a passionate gardener once lived here. You can peek over the fence and see the formal hedges that once enclosed a cottage garden profusion of blooms. The mansion, built c. 1809, by Dr. Anthony Vanderhorst Toomer, a planter, is considered one of the finest homes of the Adamesque period, having fine interior woodwork. The house was recently restored.

GARDENS AND NEW CLASSICISM

During the 20th century Modernist architecture seriously damaged Charleston's historic integrity. Today, neo-classicism is making a comeback — good examples at 40 and 42 Chapel Street. Another recent embellishment is the Chapel Street Fountain Park. The community convinced the city to create it by raising over $12,000 as a challenge grant. Because of the significant amount of green space in the area, which includes Marion Square, the neighborhood is now called Mazyck Wraggborough Garden District. Forty-five Noisette roses (a variety which was developed by Philippe Noisette in Charleston in the early 1880s) surround the park.

7 **34 CHAPEL STREET**: Built c. 1840 by Toomer or his son. The present owner believes Robert Mills may have been the architect. The mansion displays a very early architectural fusion of Greek and Gothic Revival.

34 Chapel Street

8 **35 CHAPEL STREET**: When the city boundaries were extended in 1849 to incorporate this area, a number of modest homes were built, including this one, c. 1852 by Sylvia Miles, a free black woman. At the time, there were a number of free blacks who were tradesmen, entrepreneurs and slave owners. By 1860, about 18% of the black population was free.

9 **28 CHAPEL STREET**: The Elias Vanderhorst House was built after 1832, and like other handsome homes of the era, it combines the Greek Revival (note the piazza) with the Federal (the gracious circular stairs leading to an entrance with an elliptical fanlight.) Vanderhorst was a member of the prominent rice planting family and his home was one of the most spacious in the city. A visitor wrote of the exquisitely furnished drawing room where "memorable entertainments were given and the gods of hospitality held sway." The home remained in the Vanderhorst family until 1915.

28 Chapel Street

→ Continue walking to Alexander Street, and go right.

ALEXANDER STREET: This block was developed between 1880 and 1910, a period of economic ups and downs. After some years of prosperity in the early 1880's, a major cyclone struck the city in 1885, followed by the earthquake of 1886. Low cotton prices caused an economic depression by the 1890's. The architecture here responds well to the context of the neighborhood. Some of the houses were clearly influenced by the earlier plantation style homes and the ones along Aiken's Row. Number 110 has Eastlake style trim on the piazzas similar to that on McCabe's Row. Others are in the traditional Charleston single house style with side piazzas, a style that has continued to be popular because it is well suited to the climate and to the desire for privacy on small urban lots. The street is named for Alexander Mazyck whose pasture used to be here.

→ Turn left and walk east on Charlotte Street.

CHARLOTTE STREET was one of the best addresses in Charleston during the antebellum years. Today these grand houses have been, or are being, restored.

Alexander Street

16 Charlotte Street

10 **16 CHARLOTTE STREET**: Robert Martin, of Scotch-Irish descent, owned a large wagon yard and was in the business of transporting cotton. He bought his lot from Daniel Mazyck of the important Huguenot merchant family and built between 1834 and 1840 one of the grandest mansions of the city. The house is detailed with large quoins at the corners, Doric columns on the basement level, fluted Greek Doric for the piazza above, an egg and-dart on the entrance. The Martin House is famous for having the first stationary bathtub in the city. It is seven feet long, carved from granite and survives in the basement.

11 **20 CHARLOTTE STREET**: Robert Martin built this mansion in 1848 as a wedding gift for his daughter who married Joseph Aiken. Martin, an amateur architect, may have designed the house himself, but the design has also been attributed to Edward Jones, Russell Warren or James Curtis. Whoever designed it produced a daring and sophisticated plan and a bold addition to the streetscape with arched Italianate piazzas on the west facade and two-story Greek Revival columns, cast ironwork with anthemions and Greek frets on the south side.

20 Charlotte Street

12 **29 CHARLOTTE STREET**: Built by a planter c. 1828, it is one of the earliest homes in the area. Later the home of another planter, William St. Julien Mazyck, a descendant of the Huguenot family that developed the suburb.

13 **32 CHARLOTTE STREET**: Believed to be the earliest surviving home

Detail, 20 Charlotte St.

on the street, built c. 1820, in the delicate Adam style.

14 **33 CHARLOTTE STREET**: This handsome double house, built in 1854 by a planter, was a hospital during the Civil War and residence of the notorious Union general in charge of reconstruction after the war.

"I WAS A SORT OF POOBAH"

Major General Daniel Edgar (Dan) Sickles was the military commander of the two Carolinas during Reconstruction until he was removed in 1867 by President Johnson for exercising his authority "too strenuously." Sickles said of himself, that he was "a sort of Sultan, a sort of Roman Consul. I was not only the military commander, I was the governor of those two states; I was the Court of Chancery of those two states. I was the Supreme Court of those two states. I was a sort of Poobah." The Governor of South Carolina, a Confederate veteran, said Sickles' "almost unlimited power" had been used "with moderation and forbearance." However, the Charleston Mercury expressed "relief at his departure," apparently agreeing with the President. Before the war, Sickles had been a Congressman from New York credited with singlehandedly forging the coalition that created Central Park. More notoriously, he killed the son of Francis Scott Key in Lafayette Square in Washington in front of twelve witnesses, for having an affair with his wife. He was acquitted by a sympathetic jury who heard for the first time the plea of temporary insanity. He later forgave his wife. He lost a leg in the Battle of Gettysburg, and went on to become the American minister to Spain. He died at age 94 in New York City. Nat Brandt has written a fascinating account of Sickles in THE CONGRESSMAN WHO GOT AWAY WITH MURDER.

---

15   **36 CHARLOTTE STREET**: Built c. 1830, this was the home of the Cordes family. Many members of this Huguenot family lived on Charlotte Street during the 19th Century. The house is in a traditional style, its piazza columns tend to the Greek Revival, having none of the slender delicacy of those of #32.

16   **40 CHARLOTTE STREET**: Built in 1831, this is one of the earliest homes that can be considered Greek Revival. Hamlin notes that the Greek Revival did not become common in Charleston until the 1840's and attributes this to the excellence of such Adamesque architects as Gabriel Manigault "whose works set a standard so high that Charleston builders who followed found little temptation to seek new forms."

17   **43 CHARLOTTE STREET**: Built c. 1849, with a rusticated and elevated entrance, large quoins ornamenting the corners. According to the *News & Courier*, the house has a ghost—a small girl dressed in mid-19th century costume who has appeared at night and spoken briefly with the inhabitants.

18   **44 CHARLOTTE STREET**: Built c. 1843, showing some influence of Greek Revival with the front piazza which was popular in this neighborhood. The house was threatened with destruction in 1966 but was rescued by an anonymous buyer who made funds available to the Historic Charleston Foundation to buy it.

44 Charlotte Street

22 Elizabeth Street

342 Meeting Street

19 **22 ELIZABETH STREET**: (NE corner of Elizabeth and Charlotte Streets.) The New Tabernacle Fourth Baptist Church was built as St. Lukes Episcopal Church in the Gothic Revival style in 1859-1862, designed by local architect Francis D. Lee. It is considered one of his best works. The congregation donated their lime to the Civil War effort and the building was never stuccoed as intended. In the late 19th century, Rev. D. J. Jenkins, who established the famous Jenkins Orphanage and band, was the minister here.

20 **342 MEETING STREET**: (but set back on Elizabeth Street): The Second Presbyterian Church was designed and built by James and John Gordon in 1809-1911. As you stand on Meeting Street, look back at Charlotte Street and notice how much lower it is. The street was excavated in 1865 and the earth bagged to fortify Fort Sumter.

→ Look left when you reach Meeting Street.

21 **341-345 MEETING STREET**: (SW corner of Meeting and Charlotte Streets.) Originally the factory of the Charleston Bagging Manufacturing Company, one of the city's largest manufacturers in the late 19th Century. In 1942, it became the Chicco Apartments, named for Vincent Chicco who had owned a speakeasy on Market Street. Chicco opposed prohibition and was repeatedly elected to the city council. The building has since been converted into the Hampton Inn.

→ Walk to the right on Meeting Street.

THE SOCIETY FOR THE PRESERVATION OF OLD DWELLINGS

On April 12, 1920, 32 concerned citizens met at the home of Mr. and Mrs. Ernest Pringle, 20 South Battery, to discuss the fate of the Joseph Manigault House on Meeting Street that was to be torn down for a gas station. There was a growing awareness that the heritage of the city was at risk. Alice Ravenel Huger Smith and D. E. Huger Smith had published THE DWELLING HOUSES OF CHARLESTON *two years earlier. That night in April, Alfred Hutty, the artist, spoke about the value of old houses historically and artistically. The group decided to call themselves the Society for the Preservation of Old Dwellings, and Miss Susan Pringle Frost was elected president. Money was pledged to save the Manigault House, In 1933, the property was bought by Princess Pignatelli, a wealthy plantation owner and given to the Charleston Museum, which is across the street. Despite the jail-like building, the Museum contains a fine collection and is well worth a visit. .*

22 **350 MEETING STREET** was designed by gentleman-architect Gabriel Manigault as a home for his brother Joseph. Built c. 1803, it is one of the most important Adamesque houses in America. The mother of the brothers was Elizabeth Wragg who had married Peter Manigault. The Manigaults came to Charleston after the revocation of the Edict of Nantes (1685), and accumulated a fortune as merchants and later became planters. According to historian Robert Rosen, the colonial merchant Gabriel Manigault, their ancestor, was the city's wealthiest merchant and "probably the

350 Meeting Street

wealthiest man in America." Behind the semicircular projection on the north side is a beautiful curving staircase. The house is furnished with an outstanding collection of furniture from the period. The Garden Club of Charleston recreated the garden based on an old photograph. The Joseph Manigault house and garden are open to the public.

Coffee Break: 39 Rue de Jean, 39 John Street, serves French bistro, sushi, hamburgers. Opens 11:30 am daily. Basil, 460 King Street for Thai cuisine. Lunch 11:30-2:30. Paolo's, 41 John Street, serves authentic espresso, lattes, cappuccino, gelatos and Italian cannoli. Open daily at noon.

55 Society Street

Ansonborough

Lord George Anson's winnings after a card game in the 18th century—
Ansonborough—became in the 20th century, a nationally significant
example of historic preservation as economic development. A house
here valued at $2,000 in 1960 might easily sell for 2 million today.

A CINDERELLA STORY

*To walk through Ansonborough now, you would never imagine the shambles
it had become in the 1950's. "A fine candidate for mass demolition," recalled
Time Magazine in 1967, reporting on the "Cinderella" story accomplished
by the Historic Charleston Foundation. In 1959, The Foundation sponsored
the restoration of some 35 acres of antebellum housing in Ansonborough.
After the Irish and German families who had lived here for many years fled
to the suburbs, this area had become a slum. By 1972, over 100 properties
had been restored. This was the first neighborhood rehabilitation program
in the country. Some $8.5 million in private investment had poured into*

the area. The vision of the Foundation and of many private citizens paid off for the entire city. The Foundation was established in 1947 and today conducts many programs dedicated to preserving the architectural heritage of Charleston and the Low Country. The Foundation owns and operates the Aiken Rhett and Nathaniel Russell house museums. In the spring, they organize popular tours of private homes and gardens.

The area is named for a dashing British naval officer, George Anson, who came to Charleston in 1724, and who had a taste for gambling. At age 27, Anson was captain of the HMS Scarborough which patrolled the shores of Carolina to protect the town from pirates.

Anson is said to have won Ansonborough in 1727 in a card game with his friend, Thomas Gadsden. Dr. Joseph Johnson, a 19th century resident of Ansonborough, records that "His lordship was so fond of gambling that he has been censured for even winning money from his humble midshipmen. It was said that Mr. Gadsden played with his lordship, lost a large sum of money, and paid the debt of honor by giving him titles for all these lands." In the mid 1740's, Anson captured a Spanish cargo valued at a million and a quarter pounds sterling, circled the globe and returned to England loaded with Spanish gold. Anson's loot filled 32 wagons and was paraded through the streets of London. The South Carolina Gazette reported that, "the Prince and Princess of Wales and Admiral Anson were at the House in Pallmall to see the Procession." Anson became a baron and later, First Lord of the Admiralty.

Ansonborough was Charleston's first suburb, laid out in 1746. The neighborhood was devastated by a great fire in 1838. The conflagration raged from Society to Market Street, between East Bay and St. Philip and Archdale streets. It destroyed much of the upper King Street retail area and the Ansonborough residential district. After the fire, the State Bank made "fire loans" stipulating that new houses were to be of brick, three stories tall. There is more surviving Greek Revival architecture in Charleston than anywhere in America and most of that is in Ansonborough. It was the *au courant* style at the time of the fire. The Charleston Hotel had just been built on Meeting Street with a Greek Corinthian colonnade which historian Talbot Hamlin called "one of the most superb street facades the movement produced." Undoubtedly this building inspired the widespread use of Greek Revival in the rebuilding of Ansonborough. The hotel was demolished in 1960, but Ansonborough has been transformed from a slum to one of most desirable neighborhoods in the city. Avid gardeners will particularly enjoy the neighborhood as it contains many gardens and colorful window boxes.

→ Begin the walk on Meeting Street, between Society and George Streets.

1 **286 MEETING STREET**: A survivor of the time when this was a fashionable residential street lined with grand mansions all the way to Mary Street. The Wildhagen House, built c. 1807, is considered one of the finest Adamesque houses in the city. This part of Meeting Street has been brutalized by demolition and undistinguished new construction.

→ Across the street, on the SW corner of Meeting and George, is another 19th century survivor:

2 **287 MEETING STREET**. Originally the Deutsche Freundshaftsbund Hall, designed in 1870 in the Gothic Revival style by Abrahams & Seyle who also designed a mansion in Radcliffeborough and a high style Tuscan Revival commercial building on King Street. The iron gates were designed by Albert Simons in 1955. The wrought iron fence was salvaged from one of Charleston's finest Adamesque mansions, that of Thomas Radcliffe, which stood across the street. The Freundshaftsbund was a social and charitable organization of Germans, which had entertainments "frequently of a highly intellectual character" and also balls and concerts.

287Meeting Street

309 Meeting Street

→ Walk north toward the red brick Romanesque building just south of Calhoun Street.

3 **309 MEETING STREET**: Built in 1894 as a funeral home, this is one of Charleston's finest examples of Richardsonian Romanesque, detailed with pale rough-faced masonry, contrasting with smooth red brick. The style is named for Henry Hobson Richardson, who designed Trinity Church in Boston, 1877, the Allegheny Court House in Pittsburgh, 1884 and the Marshall Field Warehouse in Chicago in 1885. His work influenced other architects such as Burnham & Root and Louis Sullivan in Chicago and R. H. Robertson and Stanford White in New York. Richardsonian Romanesque is rare in Charleston.

→ Turn around, return to George Street. Walk to the left.

14 George Street

4 **14 GEORGE STREET**: Alice R. Huger Smith noted that a new architectural taste became evident after the Revolution, exemplified in four grand mansions, which included curving staircases, bays and oval rooms. One of them was the Middleton-Pinckney home at 14 George Street. Other mansions in the Adamesque mode include the Nathaniel Russell House on Meeting Street (Charlestowne) and the Manigault House on Meeting Street (Mazyck Wraggborough), both open to the public. The fourth grand Adamesque mansion, that of Thomas Radcliffe on Meeting Street, was demolished. Historians speculate that Gabriel Manigault, architect of the Joseph Manigault house, may have designed all of these. The Middleton Pinckney mansion was built in 1797 by Mrs. Motte Middleton who, according to local lore, was hidden by her mother in the attic of the Miles Brewton house on King Street, when British soldiers were garrisoned there. After the death of her first husband, she married Thomas Pinckney, son of Chief Justice Charles Pinckney and Eliza Lucas, who pioneered commercial indigo production.

5 **9 AND 11 GEORGE STREET**: Built c. 1813. Two of the houses rescued by the Historic Charleston Foundation in the 1960s.

6 **8 GEORGE STREET**: Late Georgian style double house built 1790 for a planter. Note the Palladian window in the east end. This block escaped the 1838 fire, but it was not spared by 20th century development. The context of the fine house was destroyed in 1972 when the adjacent townhouse complex was built.

7 **4 GEORGE STREET**: Built c. 1854 for a merchant.

→ Walk left onto Anson Street.

8 **93 ANSON STREET**: St. John's Reformed Episcopal Church was built in 1850 as a mission chapel for black Presbyterians. Later used by Irish Catholics, it became a Reformed Episcopal Church in 1971. Walk behind the church to see a charming formal garden featuring the iron work of Philip Simmons.

Every since the 18th century, Charleston's gardeners have been working to make their city the most beautiful in America. The tradition continues with the Noisette Rose Trail, developed as a feature for the International Heritage Rose Conference in Charleston in 2001. Volunteers have planted and are tending Noisette rose gardens all over the city, including the one here on the lawn of the Gaillard Auditorium. Other sites include St. Luke and St. Paul (Radcliffeborough), the Joseph Manigault House (Mazyck Wraggborough), Grace Church (Harleston Village) and the William Aiken House (King Street). In the early 1800's, John Champney, a rice planter, cross-fertilized the China rose with the Musk rose to produce the first rose to be hybridized in America and the first repeat-flowering climbing rose— Champney's Pink Cluster. According to rosarian David Austin, "Philippe Noisette, a nurseryman, also of Charleston, sowed seed from 'Champney's Pink Cluster' to produce a variety known as 'Blush Noisette', which, although not so tall in growth as its parents, was repeat flowering. Thus it was that the Noisettes were born." Philippe sent cuttings of the new rose to a Parisian brother with a nursery, who saw the potential and developed more Noisettes. Residents of Wagener Terrace, where Noisette once had his rose farm, have created a Noisette Garden there, just north of Grove Street and Fifth Avenue.

9 **GAILLARD MUNICIPAL AUDITORIUM:** (NE corner Anson and George Streets) This has been called the "second most devastating thing to happen to Ansonborough", the first being the fire of 1838. The Gaillard site was filled with houses that survived the fire, but failed to survive the wishful thinking of 1960's urban renewalists who believed that a single huge building—a convention center or a Symphony hall—might undo decades of damage to the community's economy. The scale and unfortunate design of the Gaillard are much at odds with Ansonborough. Trees and roses have been planted around the building in an attempt, along with the architecturally superior, award-winning parking garage, to hide it. Within this monster, however, resides one of the finest symphony orchestras in America.

→ The large yellow house at the end of George Street at East Bay is:

10 **332 EAST BAY:** Built by Robert Primerose, a merchant, c. 1817, in the Regency style.

→ On your left is:

11 **321 EAST BAY:** The William Blake House, c. 1789. Blake was one of the wealthiest slave owners in South Carolina. The house deteriorated in the 20th century and was slated to be demolished for a parking lot when it was rescued by Historic Charleston Foundation.

→ Walk north on East Bay to:

12 **329 EAST BAY:** One of Charleston's finest Adamesque style mansions, built c. 1800 by Philip Gadsden, who was a merchant and wharf owner. The building was once in danger of demolition because of high property taxes. Mrs. Dorothy Legge, a founder of Charleston's preservation movement, rescued the mansion by blocking the demolition crane. She convinced the city to lower the taxes if the owner would agree not to demolish. The gates to the garden were designed by Samuel Gaillard Stoney, an architect and historian and

329 East Bay Street

were made by Philip Simmons, a well known Charleston blacksmith and craftsman. Note the gracious entrance with a Gibbs surround.

PROPERTY TAXES VS. PRESERVATION

The Charleston Evening Post reported in 1933 that "During the past year or two there has been an exceedingly regrettable and a very harmful movement among owners of unremunerative properties to destroy the old buildings in order to reduce their tax liability, and there are great gaps left which break the harmony of neighborhood scenery." Charleston continues to be threatened by high property taxes. Historic homes are expensive to maintain, especially in Charleston's heat and humidity. Thus many residents are being forced out of homes their families have occupied for generations. These dislocations are tragic not only for the families but also for the neighborhood, which loses the collective memories, traditions, mores and unique speech of the native Charlestonian. Outside of the United States, historic cities routinely provide subsidies and tax credits for maintenance of homes in historic districts.

317 East Bay

Coffee Break: *Saffron, 333 East Bay. Doe's Pita Plus, 334 East Bay.*

→ Turn around and walk south on East Bay Street to:

13 **317 EAST BAY**: (SW corner of George and East Bay Streets) Built c. 1804 in the Federal style by Benjamin DuPré. Note the Palladian window.

→ Cross George Street and continue on East Bay.

14 **301 EAST BAY**: Built c. 1806 with exceptional Adamesque woodwork, such as that surrounding the entrance. Owner Moses C. Levy was a King Street merchant and during a four year period when there was no regular rabbi at the Synagogue Beth Elohim on Hasell Street, he and two other members of the congregation took turns officiating. While the great fire of 1838 was raging, Levy rushed to the Synagogue and rescued the sacred scrolls.

Across the street is the Harris Teeter supermarket in what was built as a freight depot in 1914 for the Seaboard Air Line Railway. If you walk down to Society Street you can see that behind the market is the west facade of Bennett's Rice Mill which was built c. 1844 by Gov. Thomas Bennett in the Renaissance Revival Style. It was destroyed by a tornado in the 1960's.

→ Return to Laurens Street.

LAURENS STREET: was named for Henry Laurens, a Revolutionary patriot, said to be the wealthiest merchant/planter of the era. He became president of the Continental Congress in 1777. During the war, he was captured at sea and imprisoned in the Tower of London. As evidence of the high regard for Laurens by both Americans and British, he was exchanged for Lord Cornwallis in 1781. In 1782, Laurens, Benjamin Franklin, John Adams and John Jay signed the preliminary treaty of peace. The Laurens home once stood across the street on the southeast corner of Laurens and East Bay, overlooking marshes and the Cooper River.

GRAPEVINES AND CAPERS

In 1775, Henry Laurens wrote to a friend, "I now live in the middle of a garden of four acres pleasantly situated upon the River...Mrs. Laurens takes great delight in gardening." Their botanical paradise was created in the area now bounded by East Bay, Society, Anson and Laurens Streets. Son-in-law Dr. David Ramsay wrote in his HISTORY OF SOUTH CAROLINA that among the other "curious productions" introduced by the Laurenses were "olives, capers, limes, ginger, guinea grass, the alpine strawberry (bearing nine months in the year), red raspberries, blue grapes; and also directly from the South of France, apples, pears, and plums of fine kinds, and vines which bore abundantly of the choice white eating grape called Chasselats Blancs. The whole was superintended with maternal care by Mrs. Elinor Laurens, with the assistance of John Watson, a complete English gardener." Watson shipped shrubs from Charleston to be planted in public gardens in England and later established the first nursery in South Carolina.

15 **40 LAURENS STREET** (NW corner Laurens and East Bay) Built 1809 by Stephen Shrewsbury, carpenter and patriot. The Shrewsbury House has an Adamesque double piazza, hipped roof and an elaborate Adamesque entrance with a fan window and side lights.

→ Continue walking left on Laurens Street.

16 **39 LAURENS STREET**: This house was moved twice by the Historic Charleston Foundation, first from the Gaillard Auditorium site to 42 Laurens, where it was stored on blocks for several years, and then to its present location. It was built c. 1788 and restored in 1975.

17 **5 ALEXANDER STREET**: (on the short street at right) Built c. 1811 by Simon Chancognie, a French consul, altered in the 1880's.

18   **6 ALEXANDER STREET**: Built c. 1803 by a ships' carpenter.

19   **48 LAURENS STREET**: (NW corner of Alexander Street) Built c. 1816, it is a fine example of the small-scale Charleston single house.

20   **55 LAURENS STREET**: (The "grey" brick mansion at the vista of Wall Street.) An Adamesque style house, c. 1818, which escaped the great fire of 1838. The James Jervey House was restored in the late 1940's by John D. Muller. It was a brave reminder of the architectural civility of the neighborhood, at a time when the neighborhood was in decline.

→   The beautiful vista at the end of Laurens Street is:

75 Anson Street

71 Anson Street

21   **75 ANSON STREET**: Built c. 1800 by Joseph Legare. A gracious Georgian single house on a high basement with three tiers of collonades.

22   **79 ANSON STREET**: Built c. 1760 by Daniel Legare, a planter, this is one of the oldest houses in the area.

→   On your left on the SE corner of Laurens and Anson street is:

23   **61 LAURENS STREET**: This handsome house, c. 1800, was moved from the site of Gaillard Auditorium.

→   Go left, walking south on Anson Street.

24   **74 ANSON STREET**: Built c. 1812 and moved to this site by Historic Charleston Foundation from the auditorium site.

25   **71 ANSON STREET**: Built c. 1806 by Thomas Doughty in the Adamesque style. A central room projects into the garden facade as on the Nathaniel Russell House

26 **67 ANSON STREET**: St. Stephens Episcopal Church was built c. 1835, and Henry Horlbeck, a member of the family of builders and architects, is considered the architect. An all-black congregation worshipped here for some 65 years, when in 1987, the congregation became integrated. It is reputed to be the first Episcopal Church (certainly the first in Charleston) that did not charge rent for the pews.

27 **72 ANSON STREET**: One of the most beautiful gardens in Charleston can be glimpsed through the fence.

BEYOND AZALEAS

There are more flowers blooming in Charleston than ever before. The loss of trees to Hurricane Hugo in 1989 brought more sunshine into many gardens, making it possible to expand the palette well beyond azaleas and camellias. A long growing season, sub-tropical climate, intense summer heat and walls create a climate not friendly to many English perennials, but other flowering species flourish. One of Charleston's most accomplished gardeners (at 72 Anson) is meshing her love of abundant blooms and a collector's passion with a traditional Loutrel Briggs design that once featured more shade-tolerant plantings. This inclination is very much in the spirit of such historical horticultural adventurers as Eliza Lucas, Henry Laurens, Thomas and Elizabeth Lamboll, Joel Poinsett and Alexander Garden. These gardeners exchanged seeds and plants with other avid gardeners in this country and abroad. Charleston was the horticultural center of the south. In keeping with that tradition, each October, the Preservation Society of Charleston has special candlelight tours of houses and gardens. The gardens feature an increasing variety of plants that thrive in the South's special climate and long growing season.

→ Go left on Society Street.

28 **44 SOCIETY STREET**: Isaac Reeves House, 1840, was part of the Historic Charleston Foundation rehabilitation project.

29 **36 SOCIETY STREET**: Built in 1840 for a merchant, this Greek Revival home had been divided into apartments. In 1970 a major restoration returned the mansion to a single family home. A traditional double-house entrance replaced the four apartment entrances. The double doors and transom were rescued from a house at 16 Logan Street, which was being demolished. The entrance architrave was designed with Doric pilasters to go with the ancient piazza columns.

→ Turn around and walk west. The lush garden of Henry Laurens once extended to Society Street. Ansonborough is home to many passionate gardeners.

30 **43 SOCIETY STREET**: Built c. 1840 by a member of the Venning family of planters and factors from Christ Church Parish. It is said that he built this home as a wedding present for his son and #46 for himself. He also built #58 and #60 Anson.

→ Continue straight ahead, crossing Anson Street.

31 **49 SOCIETY STREET**: Built after 1839, used as a convent until 1970.

32 **55 SOCIETY STREET**: Ansonborough contains magnificent classical temples. This grand old High School Building of 1841 was designed by Edward Brickell White, architect of a number of Charleston's finest buildings (Market Hall, Centenary Methodist Church at 60 Wentworth Street and the portico of the College of Charleston.) Historian Talbot Hamlin considers White's work more Roman than Greek. Indeed, the Maison Carree at Nimes, France, is believed to have been White's inspiration for the High School. Built AD 14, it is the best preserved Roman temple in existence, so beautiful that Thomas Jefferson told a friend that he would gaze at it for hours at a time "like a lover at his mistress." Jefferson imitated the Maison Carree in his design for the State Capitol in Richmond. Charleston's Roman temple now contains apartments.

55 Society Street

33 **56 SOCIETY STREET**: Built c. 1840 by Dr. Joseph Johnson, medical scientist, astronomer, historian, Intendant (mayor) of Charleston. A grand single house with generous porportions, it was recently the home of novelist Josephine Humphreys.

34 **58 SOCIETY STREET**: Built after the great fire of 1838 for a commission merchant.

35 **62 SOCIETY STREET**: Saved from demolition in 1970 after protests by the Historic Charleston Foundation and the Historic Ansonborough Association. It has been restored as a single family dwelling.

36 **64 SOCIETY STREET**: C. 1839, Federal Style.

63 Society Street   *275 Meeting Street*

37 **63 SOCIETY STREET**: Built after 1839 as a Presbyterian lecture room, it became a concert hall and in 1861 was remodeled as a German Church in the Romanesque style by Louis J. Barbot. In 1946, it was altered again by the American Legion. It is now being restored back to the Romanesque facade. Although Henry Hobson Richardson popularized the Romanesque mode in the 1880's, Charleston architect Barbot, was using it earlier.

38 **66 SOCIETY STREET**: Built c. 1840 with a "fire loan." Note the unusual ornamental ironwork on the third floor.

39 **272 MEETING STREET**: (NE corner Meeting and Society.) Built c. 1872. Stokes Business College occupied the building in 1898 until the 1930's, offering secretarial education "for women entering the previously all-male careers in offices." It was restored in 1984 for commercial and residential use.

→   Across the street is:

40 **275 MEETING STREET**: This Ansonborough temple—Trinity United Methodist Church—was built in 1850, designed by Edward C. Jones in the Roman Revival style with Corinthian columns. It is said to have been inspired by the Madeleine, which was built in Paris, 1806-1842. The interior is ornate and features a Tiffany window.

→   Go left (south) on Meeting Street to:

41 **262 MEETING STREET**: Built 1887 for the City Fire Department. Designed by Daniel G. Wayne, who also designed the Second Empire Rogers Mansion in Harleston Village. The beautiful iron pavilion over the artesian well dates from 1885.

→   Go right on Wentworth Street.

42   **60 WENTWORTH STREET:** Centenary Methodist Church, designed c. 1842 by Edward Brickell White. During construction of the church, White's design was criticized by a letter writer to the newspaper, who pointed out the architectural solecism of having lateral doors behind the columns. White thoroughly agreed and revealed his losing battle with the church's building committee over the doors. Nonetheless, the church is considered an important example of the Greek Doric temple in America, along with Bethel Methodist church on Pitt Street (Harleston Village) and the Beth Elohim Synagogue on Hasell Street. The repetition of colonnades on private homes and public buildings is crucial

60 Wentworth Street

to Charleston's unique sense of place. Preservationists would like to see this detail used in new comstruction

→   Turn around and walk east on Wentworth street, crossing Meeting Street.

43   **43 WENTWORTH STREET:** This Greek Doric temple was built as a Methodist church in 1838. Now St. Andrew's Lutheran Church, the interior is also Greek Revival.

44   **38 WENTWORTH STREET:** Built c. 1847, the William McElheran House is considered a "major success story of historic preservation." It had become a ruin by 1974, but protests saved it from demolition. In 1860, it was bought by carriage makers, and during the Civil War cannon carriages for the Confederacy were made here.

45   **33 WENTWORTH STREET:** Built in the 1840's, it has been owned by the wife of an apprentice iron worker, a brewer, a steamship company clerk, and a poet from New York.

46 **31 WENTWORTH STREET**: Note the charming courtyard garden.

47 **24 WENTWORTH STREET**: Francis Quinlan McHugh, an attorney, built half a dozen brick houses in the area with fire loans. He built this double house in c. 1840.

48 **19 WENTWORTH STREET**: Built c. 1847 by an engineer and machinist, it has Greek Revival details. This lot was originally part of a plantation belonging to Col. William Rhett and was divided into lots by his great granddaughter in 1799. The front fence is a notable example of mid-19th century ironwork.

→ Turn around and return to Anson Street. Walk south on Anson Street. Go left at Hasell Street. (Pronounced Hazel in Charleston.)

49 **44 HASELL STREET**: Built by 1849 by James Stocker, a commission merchant. Note the Greek Revival anthemion grills in the parapet.

44 Hasell Street

36 Hasell Street

50 **42 HASELL STREET**: Built before 1848 by George Cannon, Jr. Note the fluted Doric columns on the piazza. Many great houses on Hasell Street show the influence of Greek Revival, which was a fashionable style when the street was rebuilt in the 1840's, following the 1838 fire.

51 **36 HASELL STREET**: Built before 1851 by a planter who is said to have used it as his townhouse. Note doorway.

52 **37 HASELL STREET**: Built c. 1840 in the Greek Revival mode with a later doorway.

53 **33 HASELL STREET**: Built immediately after the fire, this was the first of seven single houses built at the eastern end of Hasell Street. It was a model for the others and has special finishing details such as the elaborate side lights of the entrance door on the piazza, which are ornamented with leaded glass. In 1870, this was the home of a colorful wholesale grocer who moved many times as his fortune increased. He first lived at lower East Bay, then here, later to Wraggborough and finally to Cannonborough. The street doorway here has been Victorianized as have others, but much of the the Greek Revival detailing survives. Many homes in the neighborhood are constructed of Charleston "grey" brick. The context of the street is very harmonious.

→ Turn around and return to Anson Street.

54 **45 HASELL STREET**: (Seignious Store Building, c. 1852. SE corner of Hasell and Anson Streets) The building had become ramshackle by 1950 and was saved by the Historic Charleston Foundation.

→ Cross Anson Street and continue walking west.

55 **48 HASELL STREET**: A Lutheran Church temple of the Tuscan order, designed by Edward Brickell White in 1842. White was also the architect of the Doric temple church at 60 Wentworth, Market Hall and Gothic churches in Harleston Village and the French Quarter. A versatile architect, he also designed the steeple of St. Philip's church in the tradition of English Renaissance architect Sir Christopher Wren.

48 Hasell Street

56 **50 HASELL STREET**: A number of large homes were constructed on Hasell Street with great attention to detail and to fashion. In c. 1846 a planter built his home here of "grey" brick which has been stuccoed and painted.

57 **51 HASELL STREET**: This is believed to have been the home of Col. George Washington Glover and "his young bride Mary Baker Glover (the future Mary Baker Eddy)." Col. Glover died in 1844. Subsequently Mrs. Glover married Dr. Asa Gilbert Eddy, and in 1866 she originated the doctrine of Christian Science.

58 **54 HASELL STREET**: Built c. 1712 for Col. William Rhett, one of the oldest houses in Charleston. The piazzas were added later. In 1706 Col. Rhett commanded a small fleet which drove off a combined French and Spanish invasion and in 1718 he captured the notorious pirate Stede Bonnet and his crew.

60 Hasell Street

59 **60 HASELL STREET**: Beyond a spacious formal garden, this Italianate home looks as if it were a grand mansion. Actually it is only one room deep. Built c. 1847, it was for many years the home of Admiral Paul Pihl who was the model for Pug Henry in Herman Wouk's *The Winds of War*.

ARCHITECTS' NOTE: Look carefully at the entrance of 64 Hasell, which is embelished with an unusual amount of very sophisticated classical detail. Historian Gene Wadell identifies the Ionic capitals as being identical to those used inside the Beth Elohim Synagogue, which was built at the same time—1840. The capitals are copies of those used on the Erectheum in Athens. The Greek theme continues with anthemion designs on the doors and pilasters and in the ornate ironwork.

Coffee Break: Jestine's Kitchen, 251 Meeting Street.

→   Cross Meeting Street.

60 **86 HASELL STREET**: Built c. 1797.

61 **95 HASELL STREET**: St. Mary's Roman Catholic Church was built in 1840, replacing an earlier church, which burned. The parish was established in 1789 and was the first Roman Catholic church in the Carolinas. The interior is the most elaborately painted church in Charleston. The church has recently been restored. Evidence suggests it may have been designed by Patrick Keeley. He was a prolific architect for the Catholic church in the northeast and also the architect of the Cathedral of St. John the Baptist on Broad Street and St Patrick's Roman Catholic Church at 134 St. Phillip Street.

THE LARGEST JEWISH COMMUNITY IN AMERICA.

A community of Sephardic Jews existed in Charleston as early as 1700. They were joined in the 1740's by immigrants from London and Amsterdam who were familiar with the indigo trade. By 1800, Charleston was the center of the largest Jewish community in the country.

62 **90 HASELL STREET**: Considered one of the finest Greek Doric temples in America, Kahal Kadosh Beth Elohim is the oldest synagogue of Reformed Judaism in the United States and the oldest synagogue in continuous use. First organized in 1749, it became Reformed in 1824. The design of the temple has been attributed to Cyrus Lazelle Warner of New York and recently to Tappan and Noble (by historian Gene Wadell). Prof. Russell notes that Warner was paid as much for his modifications as Tappan and Noble received for their original plans, suggesting substantial modifications by Warner.

Coffee Break: Palmetto Café (inside Charleston Place). Starbucks, 239 King Street. Vickery's, 15 Beaufain.

90 Hasell Street

7

LAURENS ST.

SOCIETY ST.

WENTWORTH ST.

ANSON ST.

HASELL ST.

6

MARKET ST.

5 HAYNE

PINCKNEY ST.

7

N. MARKET ST.

8

Walk Ends Here

S. MARKET ST.

4

EAST BAY

MEETING ST.

CUMBERLAND ST.

CHURCH ST.

3
2
1

STATE ST.

Walk Starts Here

QUEEN ST.

VENDUE RANGE

CHALMERS ST.

BROAD ST.

Market Hall

Market Hall

The Market Hall area lies just south of the old residential suburb of Ansonborough and just north of what was the old walled city. The wall ran along Cumberland Street, and there are plaques at both Meeting Street and on East Bay, marking the northern corners of the wall. What is now Market Street was originally Ellery's Creek, which was filled in. Market Street was laid out in the 1730s, but was not developed until later in the century.

Charles Fraser, the painter and writer, who was born in 1782, remembered when the city's market was in a small wooden building on Tradd Street, and the old beef market stood where City Hall is now. "This I saw burn down in the great fire of June, 1796," he wrote. "...That terrible conflagration commenced in the afternoon in Lodge Alley near the Bay." After the fire, the beef market moved up here, where there was a thriving wholesale business. Wholesalers who began to locate in the area after the Revolution, rebuilt the area, after the great fire of 1838, in the various current architectural styles of the mid-19th century. One of the nation's grandest hotels, The Charleston Hotel, was built here, attracting such guests as Daniel Webster, Jenny Lind, Thackery and Queen Victoria's daughter Louise.

Today many fine old mercantile buildings surrounding Market Hall have been refurbished, and the area hotels once again are attracting visitors from all over the world.

→ Begin the walk at Market and East Bay. The large classical building facing you is:

1 **200 EAST BAY:** One of Charleston's grandest landmarks, the Renaissance Revival U. S. Custom House, was designed by Boston architect Ammi Burnham Young, who designed a similar custom house in Boston, which has been praised for its "striking originality." Young was the architect for many custom houses and post offices for the federal government. His numerous works helped to establish the classical tradition

200 East Bay

of federal buildings. This impressive temple, with Roman Corinthian porticos, stands on the site of Craven's Bastion, a part of the wall that surrounded Charles Town in 1704. Charleston architect E. B. White supervised the construction, which took over twenty five years, 1853-1879, as it was interrupted by the Civil War.

→ Walk to the right (south) along East Bay to the NW corner of Cumberland Street and East Bay.

2 **205 EAST BAY:** Only the elegant cast-iron store front on this commercial building survived the earthquake of 1886. However, like Charlestonians all over the city, the William M. Bird Co., which sold paint then and now, picked up the pieces and rebuilt, embellishing their building with more ornate lintels and a Victorian cornice, which has been removed.

→ Turn around and walk toward Market Street. On your left will be:

3 **207, 209 & 211 EAST BAY:** In 1894, George W. Steffans bought this building for his wholesale grocery business, which was a successful one, with accounts all over the south. A hundred years later, the building was restored.

→ At N. Market Street, go left.

205 East Bay

4 **34 N MARKET STREET:** This is the old Church of the Redeemer which dates to 1916, when it was built for seaman by the Charleston Port Society on land donated by a member of the Pinckney family. It has been converted into a restaurant.

THE OLD CITY MARKET

The one-story sheds from East Bay to Meeting Street once contained meats and county produce. They are on a filled-in creek, on land donated in 1788 by the Pinckney family with the stipulation that it always be used for a market. The sheds are of uncertain age, having been rebuilt several times after fires and most recently after a destructive tornado in 1938. Today the market sheds are occupied by a wide variety of vendors.

→ Continue to Meeting Street. As you cross Anson and just before Church Street, notice the ornate doorway of the Doubletree hotel at 181 Church. It once embellished a mid-19th century warehouse building which burned. The classical entrance reflected the prosperity of the firm of George W. Williams & Co., which began as a grocery business and later became one of the city's most successful banking houses.

→ At the NE corner of Meeting & N. Market Streets is:

5 **112 N. MARKET STREET:** (The Planter's Inn) Built about 1840, it was known as the Hornik Dry Goods Building before this handsome commercial building was rehabilitated into an inn.

→ Walk to the right (north) on Meeting Street.

6 **209-235 MEETING STREET:** A remarkable block of commercial buildings, many with ornate cast iron storefronts—a block which has been nationally admired by historic preservation officials as an important ensemble of the various architectural styles that were prevalent between 1840 and 1915.

235 Meeting Street

209-215 Meeting Street

This array with Greek Revival grills, Italianate arches, stylized Neo-Grec features and elaborate, flamboyant midcentury eclectic facades was rehabilitated in 1985 as part of the Charleston Center project. Wholesalers here once sold boots and shoes, "fancy goods," cabinets, crockery and glassware, dry goods, buggies and harnesses. There is an increasing appreciation for the value of such fine historic commercial buildings. The texture, rhythm and ornamental detail is a pleasing relief from the flat hard edges of the brown aluminum storefronts that line so many American shopping streets. The architecture is similar to that of the Soho Cast Iron Historic District in New York City.

Coffee Break: *Gita's Gourmet in the Market opens at 9:30am daily, serves coffee to go. Café Café, 177 Meeting Street, opens at 7am and serves food at day. Mistral, 99 South Market, serves French food from 11am on.*

→   Turn around and walk south on Meeting Street.

7 **188 MEETING STREET:** The Roman Revival temple that is Market Hall was designed in 1841 by Edward Brickell White, one of Charleston's most sophisticated architects of the antebellum years. It is said to be modeled after the Temple of Fortuna Virilis in Rome, but historian Gene Waddell believes it may have been inspired by Thomas Jefferson's Virginia State Capitol in Richmond or by Robert Mills's courthouses in South Carolina.

It has a rusticated base and a pedimented Roman Doric portico. The Doric frieze is ornamented with sheep and bull skulls and triglyphs. Lavish ironwork adorns the double flight of stairs. More examples of the Palladian grandeur created by White include a number of temple-front buildings in Ansonborough, the Roman Ionic portico for the main building of the College of Charleston (Harleston Village) and a commercial building for the Charleston Gas Light Company (Gateway Walk). Stylistically versatile, White introduced Gothic Revival into Charleston with his designs for the Huguenot Church (French Quarter) and Grace Episcopal Church (Harleston Village). He also designed the steeple for St. Philip's Church and two Italianate commercial buildings on Broad Street. Meat and produce were sold in the market stalls. It was never a slave market. The Confederate Museum is on the second floor.

THE NEW YORK OF THE SOUTH

White's monumental Market Hall expresses the civic aspirations of Charleston during the antebellum decades, when the city was often described as the "New York of the South." City Hall had moved into the handsome neoclassical bank building at Broad and Meeting Streets. The Fireproof Building had been built in 1826, a Greek Revival temple theater building in 1837, the Charleston Hotel (one of America's finest Greek Revival structures) in 1839 and the Hibernian Hall in 1840. Market Hall was one of many in this parade of high-style urbane structures on Meeting Street. Today, Meeting Street around Market Hall is an embarrassment to Charleston, a hodge podge, with a few historic survivors surrounded by parking lots, motels and mediocre new construction that speaks not of grandeur, but rather of mediocrity and loss of vision. One of the worst is Liberty Center, 151 Meeting, which intrudes upon public space, not with a graceful colonnade, but with sheer bulk, its parking garage built on the sidewalk.

→ Continue south on Meeting Street.

8 **171-173 MEETING STREET**: (Meeting Street Inn) Built in 1874 as a restaurant/saloon and home by Adolph Tiefenthal, a native of the German Rhine Country. It replaced an earlier building—the New Charleston Theater of 1837. That theater, designed by Charles Reichardt as a Greek Revival temple, was one of the great losses in the fire of 1861.

Coffee Break: Cafe Cafe, 177 Meeting Street.

8

PINCKNEY ST.

HAYNE ST.

N. MARKET ST.

S. MARKET ST.

ANSON ST.

CUMBERLAND ST.

MEETING ST.

Walk Ends Here

35   36

Walk Starts
Here

QUEEN ST.   27   28

1   LODGE 4
ALLEY 3

EAST BAY

26   33   34
25   24   23   2
29   5   6
30   9 7
31
32

STATE ST.

CHALMERS ST.   21   20   VENDUE RANGE

22   18 12 8
17 13   10
14   GENDRON
11
BROAD ST.   19   15   CORDES

16

CHURCH ST.

EAST BAY

TRADD ST.

Chalmers Street

French Quarter

The French Quarter played a major role in Charleston's distinguished history as a great mercantile and shipping center. It was part of the Grand Modell for Charles Town, platted by the Lords Proprietors in the 17th century. The name was coined in 1973, when preservationists applied to the National Register of Historic Places for recognition of the Lodge Alley block where there was historically a high concentration of French merchants.

On August 20, 1973, Robert Stockton reported in the *News & Courier* the ominous news that "Baier and Company received permission to demolish 14 structures to make way for a $6 million high-rise condominium project...Most of Lodge Alley, with its ties to Colonial and Revolutionary history, will become part of the condominium parking area."

Some 4.5 acres of American history were to be leveled. The skyline of the entire historic city would be ruined. The Save Charleston Foundation was organized, which raised funds from across the United States in order to buy the property from the developer. A national treasure was saved. The restoration of the historic structures for mixed uses—a hotel, offices, condominiums, restaurants, shops—was a model of historic preservation as sound economic development.

Warehouse buildings across America have been restored and rehabilitated into inviting and successful commercial/residential areas—from Soho and Ladies' Mile in New York to Ghiradelli Square in San Francisco. The French Quarter includes buildings that are older than any of these. It would have been a great loss to the history of American commercial architecture and to the economic vibrancy of Charleston had the fourteen warehouse buildings of the Lodge Alley complex been razed.

Today the neighborhood is one of the most picturesque residential neighborhoods and has become the center of Charleston's growing artistic community, containing many art galleries and craft shops. And this part of Charleston continues to exude a continental flavor that so impressed an 18th century French traveller, who noted that Charleston was "more European than the rest of America...most of the inhabitants having been reared in Europe, had more taste and experience, were more like the French than Northerners, which must generally give them an advantage over the latter." The French visitor noted that in no other city had he found "more benevolence and hospitality, more agreeable manners."

→ Begin the walk on State Street, just south of Cumberland Street.

LODGE ALLEY COMPLEX: This block, on the south side of Cumberland Street, between East Bay, State Street and Lodge Alley is the block that was threatened with demolition in 1973. Today the complex is a time-share resort surrounded by restaurants, offices, shops and homes.

→ Go right (west) to State Street, and walk left on State to:

Lodge Alley Inn

■ **37 STATE STREET:** The classical builders and architects of Charleston created a countless variety of doorways that contribute beauty and texture to the streetscape, unlike "modern" designers today whose doors are often difficult to find, tend to all look alike as bleak gozintas, (Philip Johnson coined the term gozinta—goes into the building)

37 State Street

42 State Street

devoid of such ornament as the swag and fluted columns which welcome you here. The ornamental lanterns are another gracious note.

2 **42 STATE STREET**: This dignified pink house with quoins, built c. 1816, might have been standing in the shadow of the high rise condominium. The context and beauty of the whole streetscape here would have been overwhelmed by the change in scale.

Walk through **LODGE ALLEY**, the picturesque, cobbled walkway, located between 42 and 44 State. If you look over your shoulder, you can see the steeple of St. Philip's Church. Charleston is a city of beautiful vistas, many of them punctuated by church spires. Lodge Alley is one of Charleston's oldest thoroughfares, appearing on a map of 1739. It was named for the Marine Lodge here, where in 1774 the Huguenot Dr. John Ernest Poyas directed the building of a float for the Charleston Tea Party parade. Buildings along the alley were built by the Bonneau family and by Etienne Poincignon who was a successful tin smith and real estate investor.

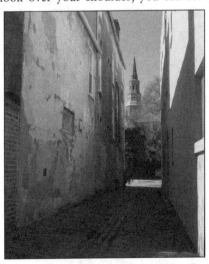
Lodge Alley

→ At East Bay:

3 **191 EAST BAY**: The windows overlooking Lodge Alley are those of what was the Cordes home. Etienne Poincignon remodeled it and the Porcher family home, c. 1845, into a commercial building with an ele-

191 East Bay

East Bay Streetscape

gant Italianate store front. The building that faces East Bay was built c. 1800 as the home of Theodore Gaillard.

→ Walk left to:

4 **195 EAST BAY**: Built for merchant Isaac Barrett in the 1850's. It is now connected to #199 and contains the popular High Cotton Restaurant. Just inside the courtyard entrance to the Lodge Alley resort, note the plaque commemorating the Save Charleston Foundation.

→ Turn around, walk south on East Bay Street.

5 **185 EAST BAY**: Built for grocers in the 1890s, now a popular restaurant.

6 **180 EAST BAY**: The French merchant Stephen Lefevre built soon after 1794 what Stockton called "Charleston's most French building." It formerly had a high hipped roof of pantiles. The French influence can still be seen in the window grill design.

195 East Bay

180 East Bay

7 **167 EAST BAY**: dates to c. 1835, recently an art gallery, now a restaurant. Restaurants compete with galleries for space in the area. Three times a year the French Quarter Gallery Association organizes an art walk. Galleries remain open in the evening and refreshments are served.

8 **161 EAST BAY**: Formerly the grocery and liquor store of Frederick W. Wagener, designed by Richard Southard in an ornate Queen Anne style. That same year, 1880, Southard designed a smaller Queen Anne building for Mayor William A. Courtenay on East Bay, which was highly praised for its beauty and style. It was demolished for a parking lot.

161 East Bay

→ Walk west along Queen Street. Just behind Wagener's store building is:

8 **3 QUEEN STREET**: Queen's Gate Apartments is the former warehouse of Wagener, who made a fortune in wholesale groceries and liquors. His store, at 161-165 East Bay, and warehouse were built in 1880. Commercial buildings of the late 19th century quite often had imposing facades facing main thoroughfares and more modest ones on side streets.

Warehouse (3 Queen Street to the left)

→ Across the street is:

9 **2-4 QUEEN STREET**: Buildings in the French Quarter which once housed cotton, rice and groceries have been inventively adapted for uses as dwellings and offices. In the 1970's, this antebellum warehouse became the studio of Carolina sculptor Willard N. Hirsch.

→ Return to East Bay and go right.

Vendue Range

VENDUE RANGE is on land-fill created in the 18th century. This area was a center of shipping and trade. In the early 1700's, the tonnage shipped through Charleston exceeded that of New York. Today Charleston is the second largest port for container shipping on the east coast. Vendue Range is lined with old commercial buildings built by Samuel Prioleau, Thomas Napier and other merchants of French descent. In 1774, Prioleau had a wharf here with ten stores on the north and nine stores on the south side of the Range, plus several blocks of stores on East Bay. Prioleau was a patriot during the Revolution and was imprisoned at St. Augustine by the British in 1781, along with Arthur Middleton, Thomas Heyward and Hugh and Edward Rutledge.

→ At the SE corner of Vendue and East Bay is:

[10] **162 EAST BAY**: (Vendue Inn) The building was built by Samuel Prioleau soon after 1783 and was for many years the offices of the Clyde Steamship Line. The ships carried goods and travelers, "the saloons and state rooms being all on deck, securing very thorough ventilation and the tables are luxuriously supplied," noted a quidebook.

→ On the east side of East Bay, between Gendron and Cordes Streets is a warehouse block:

Colonnade,157 East Bay

11 **160 EAST BAY**: Prioleau's Range, built by Samuel Prioleau, Jr. before 1813 and altered into Greek Revival by his son, who added the fifteen decorative iron grills with a Greek Anthemion design. Prioleau served in the state legislature, was Intendant (mayor) in 1824, and was a merchant and lawyer with 80 slaves.

153-155 East Bay

12 **157 EAST BAY**: One of the most beautiful commercial buildings in Charleston, with a Corinthian cast iron fluted colonnade and arched windows. Its Palladian grandeur creates a street wall that is pedestrian-friendly, unlike the bleak modern aluminum store fronts. The tinted glass, however, mars its beauty, makes a shop look abandoned, closed.

COLONNADES

Colonnades can be found throughout Charleston on a variety of different building types—homes with piazzas, churches, schools, municipal and commercial buildings. This recurring architectural theme gives cohererance to the streetscape and is a crucial architectural feature that knits together the urban fabric into a tout ensemble unique for an American city.

13 **155 EAST BAY**: This handsome antebellum commercial building was built by Etienne Poincignon.

14 **153 EAST BAY**: Built c. 1779, once the tavern of Edward McCrady.

15 **141 EAST BAY**: One of Charleston's most talented 19th century architects, Francis Lee, designed this astonishing building in 1853 for a bank. Lee's approach to architecture is known as mid-century eclecticism. According to Prof. Russell, Lee and his partner, Edward C. Jones, and Edward Brickell White were the leading practitioners of this approach in

141 East Bay

Charleston, designing buildings to be memorably picturesque rather than stylistically correct. Although many of the details are Moorish, such as the horseshoe arches and the use of contrasting stone to create stripes, the building is also classically balanced, roofed with a cornice instead of a minaret and with Greek Revival piers at the corners. Lee also designed a Gothic Revival Church on Charlotte and Elizabeth Streets and the interior of the Unitarian Church.

In 1970, Lee's Moorish fantasy was a ruin in danger of being demolished for yet another parking lot. Senator Ernest F. Hollings rescued it and restored it to be his office.

→ Across the street, between N. Atlantic Wharf and MidAtlantic Wharf is:

16 **140 EAST BAY STREET:** (Between N. Atlantic Wharf and Mid-Atlantic Wharf.) In 1988, under Mayor Riley, the city has built parking garages that are superior architecturally to most office buildings. This one, with shuttered openings and office spaces on the ground floor successfully conceals its utilitarian purpose and fits in admirably with the ancient warehouses of the area. It has won 3 awards, including the Presidential Design Award from the National Endowment for the Arts.

→ Turn around, return to Unity Alley and walk left to:

17 **2 UNITY ALLEY:** This building was originally entered from 153 East Bay and contained McCrady's tavern, for which the present restaurant is named. On the second floor was the Long Room of that tavern. In 1972, the wrecking ball threatened this irreplaceable landmark of Charleston and American history. W.H.J. Thomas reported in the *News and Courier* the findings of local historians. The tavern is one of only a few documented 18th century taverns that survive. Entertainments were given in the Long Room of the tavern, which is considered to be the earliest extant playhouse in America. When Richard Hutson was elected Intendant (mayor) of Charleston in 1783, he and his friends went to "Mr. McCrady's, where an elegant entertainment was provided, and where the Citizens, on the novel and pleasing occasion, had the happiness to congratulate the Intendant on his election." In 1791, George Washington was entertained and served a "very sumptuous" dinner in the Long Room. The building was sold in 1801. It became a French coffee house, and as late as 1865, was being used for "a coffee house and restaurant."

Coffee Break: East Bay Coffee House, 157 East Bay.

→ Go right on State Street

18 **22-24 STATE STREET**: Built c. 1841 by Joel Robert Poinsett as a multi-family dwelling with shops at the street level.

→ Turn around and walk back to:

19 **7 STATE STREET**: This classically designed building, c. 1819, is a former insurance headquarters of the Union Insurance Company. On June 5, 1830, a dinner was given here to honor Joel R. Poinsett, who had just returned to Charleston, having served as Minister to Mexico.

FAMOUS CHARLESTON GARDENERS

Charleston is famous horticulturally for three flowers named after early Charlestonians. Joel Poinsett, of Huguenot descent, was a noted statesman, diplomat and U. S. Secretary of War. Poinsett maintained two gardens in Charleston, and because of his keen interest in plants, he supplied American nurseries with plants he discovered on his travels. An exotic red flower he brought home from Mexico is named for him—the poinsettia. The Noisette rose commemorates Philippe Noisette, whose early 19th century nursery developed it. The gardenia was named in honor of Dr. Alexander Garden by his friend and mentor Linnaeus, the Swedish botanist who established the modern system of plant classifications.

→ Turn around and return to Chalmers, a cobbled street, and go left.

CHALMERS STREET was named for Dr. Lionel Chalmers, whose home here was destroyed by the great fire of 1778. Chalmers was a scientist who studied the weather and diseases. He corresponded with leading scientists in Europe and was published abroad.

Corner of Chalmers and State Street

20 **6 CHALMERS STREET**: The Old Slave Mart Museum was built in 1859 as a slave market and later used as a dwelling. In 1938, it became a museum of African and African-American arts, crafts and history.

6 and 8 Chalmers Street

15 Chalmers Street

21 **8 CHALMERS STREET**: The German Fire Company Engine House, designed with a hybridized Castellated/Italianate facade by E. B. White, who also designed the 1850's crenellated Citadel expansion.

22 **15 CHALMERS STREET**: The Pink House, which is believed to have been a tavern during Colonial days, was built c. 1712, and is one of the oldest buildings in Charleston. The gambrel roof is one of the few surviving. The house is built partly of Bermuda stone, which was imported here until about 1770. This was once the studio of artist Alice R. Huger Smith, a prominent member of the creative community which flourished in Charleston during the 1920's and 1930's, (the Charleston Renaissance.) The Piping and Marching Society of Lower Chalmers Street, a literary and social club, was started here in 1949.

DID THE CIVIL WAR BEGIN ON CHALMERS STREET?

The rather plain building at 23 Chalmers is the rear of the Confederate Home building at 62 Broad Street, and is particularly important in Civil War history. The right part of the building housed the courthouse for the United States District Court in 1860. When news of Abraham Lincoln's election victory was announced, the jurors rebelled and refused to continue with the proceedings. Judge A. G. Magrath rose and said, "So far as I am concerned, the Temple of Justice, raised under the Constitution of the United States, is now closed." This was the first official rebellious act against the Union, according to historian E. Warren Moise. Six months later the building was used as the Confederate States Court for the District of South Carolina. Judge McGrath was appointed to preside by Confederate President Jefferson Davis. Moise wrote an account of this in Preservation Progress.

23 **36 CHALMERS STREET**: (The grey stuccoed house with Greek anthemion grills below the cornice) A free black woman, Jane Wightman, built

38 and 36 Chalmers Street

this house c. 1835. In 1930, it became the home of Josephine Pinckney, prominent author during the Charleston Renaissance. She added the Federal style piazza entrance.

24 **38 CHALMERS STREET**: Jane Wightman also built this house c. 1844. It was the birthplace of Elizabeth O'Neill Verner in 1883. Verner spent much of her adult life in the neighborhood as an artist. In her 1941 book, *Mellowed by Time*, she wrote of the "infinite variations" of Charleston—a "blend long mellowed by time. Music—suave manners—wit and humor—a love of beauty—epicurian tastes—soft voices— a fearless lack of hypocrisy and an easy tolerance, are contributions.. to that elusive flavor—charm." Verner's childhood home later became the home of Laura Bragg, director of the Charleston Museum. Bragg restored the house in 1927, adding Georgian and Federal details, which were designed by local architect Albert Simons.

At the vista of Chalmers Street, the large Greek Revival temple building is Hibernian Hall (see the Broad Street tour).

→ Go right onto Meeting Street. At the corner is:

25 **108 MEETING STREET**: The Historic Charleston Foundation gift shop, which is well worth a visit.

→ When you exit the shop, go right along Meeting Street.

26 **116 MEETING STREET**: Dates to 1887, designed by Daniel G. Wayne, who also designed the Francis Silas Rodgers mansion on Wentworth Street. Note the decorative brickwork.

→ Go right on Queen Street.

QUEEN STREET was one of the original streets on the Grand Modell and was called Dock Street for a boat dock in the marsh then at the corner of Queen and East Bay. A great fire destroyed much of the area in 1796. Many buildings date from the late 1790s.

Corner of Queen and Church Streets

7 **54 QUEEN STREET:** (Thomas Elfe House.) Built in 1760, this was the home of furniture-maker Elfe, who was born in London and was a contemporary of Thomas Chippendale. Elfe emigrated to Charleston in the mid 18th century and was considered the best master craftsman of his time.

28 **46 QUEEN STREET:** Abraham Sasportas built this multifamily dwelling in 1796-1802. A French-born Jewish merchant, Sasportas was an agent for French privateers who sold their goods in Charleston.

→ At the SW corner of Queen and Church Streets:

29 **135 CHURCH STREET:** What is now the Dock Street Theater was once the Planters Hotel. Planters Punch is said to have been created here. In 1918, according to Stockton, the hotel had become a "ruin inhabited by tramps." It was slated for demolition when Elizabeth O'Neill Verner and others were instrumental in getting the building boarded up until funds for its restoration could be found. Secretary of State James F. Byrnes, (a South Carolinian), obtained federal money to remodel it into a theater in 1937. Plays and musical events of a high quality are presented here.

30 **136 CHURCH STREET:** Local architect E. B. White was one of the first American architects to design in the Gothic Revival Style. The first such church in America was Trinity Church in New York, designed in 1839. White's design for the French Huguenot Church dates from 1844, and he later designed Trinity in Columbia and Grace Episcopal in Charleston in 1847. In 1680, 45 Huguenots arrived here subsidized by King Charles, who believed their skills as farmers, grape growers, wine makers, weavers, brick makers and in other trades would contribute to the settlement. Among these immigrants was a pastor. He organized the French Huguenot Church in 1681, and it is the only remaining independent Huguenot congregation in America.

French Huguenots began arriving in Charleston in large numbers after the revocation in 1685 by Louis XIV of the Edict of Nantes, which guaranteed religious freedom to the Huguenots. A wave of French Catholics, exiles from Acadia, arrived in 1755. And in the 1790's, after the slave revolt in Santo Domingo, more French Catholics fled to Charleston.

Given the history of wars between England and France, French immigrants were not initially welcomed with enthusiasm, but the General Assembly did pass a law enabling them to become citizens. These new Charlestonians contributed their skills as teachers of French, music, dance and pastry making. They established French coffee houses, built many buildings and were successful businessmen. Some of the greatest fortunes in the city were amassed by the Manigault and Mazyck families, contributing greatly to the success of the city as a commercial center.

Charleston architects Albert Simons and Samuel Lapham have noted that the city's French strain manifests itself in "an appreciation of and a desire for the monumental and judiciously proportioned in architecture, and it is the presence of this character in so many buildings of comparatively small dimensions that gives the city much of its individuality and charm."

Charleston's loyalty to the French was particularly evident in 1793 when Citizen Genet visited the city and was greeted jubilantly here but rather cooly when he visited Washington in Philadelphia.

→ Go right on Church Street.

31 **134 CHURCH STREET**: The French Huguenot Church Rectory, in the 18th century Georgian style, is believed to be pre-Revolutionary.

32 **132 CHURCH STREET**: The Douxsaint House probably dates from the mid 1700's and was built by Huguenot Paul Douxsaint, a merchant and planter.

132 Church Street

→ Turn around, return to Queen Street and go right.

33 **22-28 QUEEN STREET**: Johnson's Row, a notable row of brick tenements, was built in the 1790's by William Johnson and his son. Johnson made his fortune as a blacksmith and later as a planter. His son was a judge and politician.

34 **20 QUEEN STREET**: The Footlight Players were organized in 1932 during the Charleston Renaissance. Two years later they bought this antebellum warehouse and converted it into their theater. The Footlight Players is one of the oldest community theater groups in South Carolina. Get tickets if you can.

THE CHARLESTON RENAISSANCE

French Quarter residents played an important role in the early 20th century, an era that has come to be known as the Charleston Renaissance. Laura Bragg, director of the Charleston Museum, 1920-1931, ran a salon for artists, writers and musicians at her home, 38 Chalmers Street, which has been compared to Gertrude Stein's salon in Paris. And, in fact, Stein, Carson McCullers and other well known writers were visitors in the Bragg home. Josephine Pinckney, author of THREE O'CLOCK DINNER lived at 36 Chalmers. Alice Ravenel Huger Smith, water colorist and etcher, had a studio at 17 Chalmers. She and her father collaborated on the 1917 book THE DWELLING HOUSES OF CHARLESTON, the first survey of Charleston architecture. Miss Smith was a founder of the Charleston Etchers Club, along with Alfred Hutty, Elizabeth O'Neill Verner (who was born on Chalmers Street) and John Bennett, the novelist. The Etchers Club played a significant role in the history of American printmaking. Other groups which flourished during the Renaissance included the Poetry Society of South Carolina, the Footlight Players (on Queen Street), Gibbes Memorial Gallery (on Meeting Street), the Charleston Museum, Charleston Symphony Orchestra, the Society for the Preservation of Old Dwellings (later The Preservation Society). Charlestonians continue to enjoy a rich cultural life.

→   Return to Church Street and go right.

35 **139 CHURCH STREET**: A favorite architectural detail, found on both dwellings and commercial buildings, is the ornamental iron grill at the parapet.

139 Church Street

36 **146 CHURCH STREET**: St. Philip's Protestant Episcopal Church is the city's oldest Episcopal congregation and the first Anglican church south of Virginia. The first church was built c. 1681. When the

Dock Street Theater, St. Philip's Protestant Episcopal Church and the Huguenot Church

second church was built in 1723, an observer wrote of the "large and beautiful building, exceeding any that are in his Majesty's Dominion in America." After the church burned in 1835, the exterior was rebuilt by Joseph Hyde, closely following the 18th century design. The interior was modified and shows the influence of St.-Martins-in-the-Fields, which was designed in London in 1721 by James Gibbs. Gibbs popularized Palladian architecture, and his *Book of Architecture*, 1728, is known to have been available in Charleston. In 1848, E. B. White designed the steeple in the Wren-Gibbes tradition. George Washington attended services here in 1791. A stroll through this cemetery is a walk back into the history of South Carolina. Here you find the graves of Col. William Rhett, Edward Rutledge, Charles Pinckney, John C. Calhoun, Edward McCrady, and Dubose Heyward. George Washington attended services here in 1791.

Coffee Break: *Jimmy Dengate's, 5 Cumberland Street, serves old-fashioned southern food, 11am-2pm. The fried chicken is reknowned. Joseph's, 129 Meeting Street opens at 8am, has delicious beignets, salads, small meals.*

9

LIBERTY ST.

WENTWORTH ST.

BEAUFAIN ST.

MAGAZINE ST.

MARKET ST.

10

9 ●Walk Ends Here

8

ARCHDALE ST

6 7

CLIFFORD ST.

CUMBERLAND ST.

QUEEN ST.

KING ST.

Walk Starts Here

MEETING ST.

5 4

3

1

2

BROAD ST.

QUEEN ST.

CHALMERS ST.

STATE ST.

ELLIOTT ST.

CHURCH ST.

W N E S

St Philip's Churchyard at Church Street

Gateway Walk

ateway Walk was the inspiration of Garden Club President Mrs. Celia Peronneau McGowan, who, on a visit abroad, had been charmed by the gardens in Paris as oases amid the bustling city. A plan for such a Parisian pleasure in the middle of Charleston was developed by the noted landscape architect Loutrel Briggs. Gateway Walk opened in April 1930 and was recently restored by the Garden Club. This will be a short walk, meandering through graveyards and a sculpture garden. Allow time to read the tombstones and enjoy the peacefulness of this unusual urban setting.

THE GARDENS OF LOUTREL BRIGGS

No one has influenced the style of the Charleston garden more than the landscape architect Loutrel Briggs. Briggs, was born in 1893 in New York City and developed a practice there before first visiting Charleston in 1927. He soon began designing gardens for northerners who knew his work and who were moving to Charleston. One of his first commissions here was in 1929 for Mrs. Washington Roebling (64 S. Battery), widow of the man who supervised the building of the Brooklyn Bridge. Briggs designed more than 100 small gardens here, noted for their formal symmetry and use of such native plantings as camellias, azaleas, loquat trees, tea olives, wisteria, yellow jessamine, oleander and star jasmine. Briggs saw the urban garden as an outdoor room or series of rooms, furnished with ponds, statuary and benches. Many Briggs gardens have been carefully preserved and restored and may be seen on the annual house and garden tours given in the spring and fall by Historic Charleston Foundation and The Preservation Society. The South Carolina Historical Society, which is located in the Fireproof Building, 100 Meeting Street, open to the public, has some 300 Briggs drawings in its collection.

→ Begin the walk on Cumberland and Meeting Streets. Note the plaque on the SE corner with the map of the walled city of 1704. This was the NW corner of the walled city. Walk east on Cumberland.

1 **79 CUMBERLAND STREET:** The Powder Magazine was finished in 1713 and is the only surviving public building from the era of the Lord's Proprietors, which ended in 1719. It was built at a time when the settlers were threatened by the Indians on land and the Spanish by sea. Open to the public.

→ Continue east on Cumberland to Church Street and right to the graveyards of St. Philip's Episcopal Church. If you are lucky, the gates will be open.

2 **146 CHURCH STREET.** The cemetery of St. Philip's church includes the graves of William Rhett, who captured pirates, John C. Calhoun, vice-president of the United States, Edward McCrady, the historian, Edward Rutledge, signer of the Declaration of Independence and

St. Philip's Church and Cemetary   *St. Philip's Cemetery*

Governor of South Carolina, DuBose Heyward, author of *Porgy* and many other important Charlestonians. The gate is open from 9 a.m. until 4:30 p.m.

→ The Gateway walk continues into the graveyard of the Circular Church. If the gate is locked, return to Church Street, going left and left again on Cumberland. The side gate on Cumberland is usually open. If not, walk left on Meeting to the front gate.

Circular Church

Circular Cemetary and Parish House

3 **150 MEETING STREET**. The churchyard of the Circular Church is the city's oldest burying ground. It contains significant funerary art, the largest collection of New England slate gravestones south of Boston, and the graves of Dr. David Ramsay, physician and historian, and Thomas Bennett, mill owner, architect and the father of Gov. Bennett. Stevenson and Greene of New York designed the Circular Congregational Church in the Richardsonian Romanesque style. Robert Stevenson trained with the famous firm of McKim, Mead and White and designed many churches after opening his office in the 1880's. Ernest Greene worked for Frederick Withers, a specialist in church design, before becoming a partner with Stevenson in 1891. The firm designed Trinity Congregational Church in East Orange, N. J. in 1891 and several handsome commercial buildings in the Ladies' Mile Historic District in New York. The Circular Congregational Church was established in 1681 by French Huguenots, Scotch and Irish Presbyterians and

Circular Church Cemetary

Congregationalists. An earlier church, designed in 1806 by Robert Mills was destroyed in the great fire of 1861. Bricks from the earlier building were used for the present building, built in 1891. Within the graveyard is the Parish House, designed in 1867 in the Roman Revival temple style, influenced by Palladio and Mills.

MEETING STREET is named for the White Meeting House which was located here, where early settlers met to worship. Later these settlers formed the Circular Congregationalist Church.

Coffee Break: Joseph's, 129 Meeting Street; Diana's, 155 Meeting Street.

4 **141 MEETING STREET:** The talented local architect E. B. White designed this Palladian commercial building for the Charleston Gas Light Company (now the S. C. Electric and Gas Company) in 1876, an era in which commercial buildings were often more elaborate than dwellings. The iron gates were brought from an earlier building occupied by the Gas Light Company.

5 **135 MEETING STREET:** The Gibbes Museum of Art is the headquarters of the Carolina Art Association, founded 1857. South Carolina architect Frank P. Milburn designed it in the Beaux Arts style, 1904. It reflects the influence of the American Renaissance, the period between 1876 and 1917, when American architects such as McKim, Mead and White, Richard Morris Hunt and Daniel Burnham, the archi-

135 and 141 Meeting Street

tectural stars of the Chicago Worlds Fair of 1893, were popularizing the use of elaborate classicism for urban buildings. The style emanated from training at the Ecole des Beaux-Arts in Paris, which looked to the language of the Italian Renaissance. Thus, the Gibbes has the familiar Palladian themes of the raised entrance, rustication, symmetry and a grand pedimented portico, which had been popular themes in Charleston since Colonial times. Within the Gibbes is a fine collection of American paintings including many portraits of notable Charlestonians, an outstanding collection of over 400 miniature portraits, ten remarkable miniature rooms and Japanese woodblock prints. The gallery collections include works by Benjamin West, Rembrandt Peale, Gilbert Stuart, Samuel F. B. Morse, Thomas Sully, Charles Fraser and Philip Pearlstein.

In 1857, after a popular exhibit of Charles Fraser's writings and paintings, a group of Charleston's cultural elite organized to found the Carolina Art Association. Fraser painted hundreds of miniature portraits, many of which are on exhibit at the Gibbes Museum. He was also an attorney, civic leader, historian and designer of the steeple on St. John's Lutheran Church at 10 Archdale Street. Fraser's work was renowned nationally and internationally. When the Marquis de Lafayette visited Charleston in 1825, he sat for a portrait by Fraser and was given a Fraser miniature as a gift from the City. Lafayette wrote that the portrait was "a very high specimen of the state of the arts in the United States." Locally Fraser was admired as a "faithful citizen, a pillar and an ornament." Reminiscences of Charleston, *which Fraser wrote in 1854, is a valuable history of the city.*

→   The Gateway Walk continues to the right (north) of the Museum, into the Gibbes sculpture courtyard. Walk through the Gov. William Aiken iron gates, passing the Charleston Library Society (King Street Walk) on your right. Cross King Street and walk through the gates and into the churchyard of the Unitarian Church. The hours when the gates are open is irregular.

Dr. Samuel Gilman, former pastor of the church, essayist and poet, is buried here. Dr. Gilman was the author of "Fair Harvard" where he taught mathematics. Mrs. Caroline Gilman edited and published The Rose Bud, the first children's newspaper in the country, and she is said to have laid out a formal garden on the south side of the church.

6   **6 ARCHDALE STREET:** The Unitarian Church was being built when the British occupied it and destroyed the new pews. It was completed in 1787. In the 1850's, it was remodeled by F. D. Lee, whose plans were inspired by the Henry VIII chapel at Westminster Abbey. The lacy fan tracery ceiling is considered to be some of the finest Gothic Revival work in America.

7   **10 ARCHDALE STREET:** St. John's Lutheran Church was built in 1818, designed by Frederick Wesner, a local architect and plantation owner who also designed the portico of the South Carolina Society Hall. A steeple was added

6 and 10 Archdale Street

19 Archdale street

in 1859, to the plans of Charles Fraser. The cemetery contains the graves of Wesner and of John Adam Horlbeck, a builder of the Exchange Building. The church and churchyard are open 9:30 a.m. to 5:00 p.m.

→ Exit the cemetary onto Archdale Street. Directly in front of you is:

8 **19 ARCHDALE STREET**: Philip Porcher, a planter, built this Georgian home with a hipped roof in 1773. The piazza is a later addition. Porcher was a Loyalist, whose real estate was confiscated during the Revolution. However, his property was returned to him after influential citizens testified to his "universal good character."

9 **21 ARCHDALE STREET**: This house and #23 were built by Dr. Samuel Wilson, whose wife was Catherine Mazyck. It dates to about 1804. The Greek Revival piazza is a later addition.

21 Archdale Street

10 **23 ARCHDALE STREET:** Considered one of the best Adamesque style houses in the city, it was built c. 1808 of Carolina grey brick.

23 Archdale

→ For one of the most memorable views in Charleston, walk to the corner of Archdale and Market Streets, and look east, over to Market Hall. This is a view recently recovered by the construction of the Saks Fifth Avenue building, which was built out to the street providing a solid street wall to frame the vista of Market Street, an example of good urban design.

Coffee Break: *Vickery's, 15 Beaufain Street (Caribbean food.) Starbucks, 239 King Street.*

10

RADCLIFFE ST.

WARREN ST.

VANDERHORST ST.

ST. PHILIP ST.

92

93 94 *Walk Ends Here*

91

HALSEY ST.

CALHOUN ST.

RUTLEDGE AVE.

SMITH ST.

PITT ST.

COMING ST.

69-65

GREENWAY

COLLEGE OF CHARLESTON

90

87

BULL ST.

85 83 81

80-78

77 75

73-70

GATE

64 GEORG

88 86

89

84 82

76 74

56 63

57

GLEBE ST.

62

29 30

31 32

33 35

36 37

47 49 50

51 52 54 55

BARRE ST.

MONTAGU ST.

48

53

58 59

34

22

24 23

46 44

WENTWORTH ST.

60 61

28

GADSDEN

26

27

25

21

19

20

18

38 45

39 43

42

41

BEAUFAIN ST.

17

16

15

14

40

FRANKLIN ST.

Walk Starts Here

MAGAZINE ST.

CLIFFORD S

ASHLEY AVE.

COLONIAL LAKE

1

2

QUEEN ST.

13

12

3

LOGAN ST.

ARCHDALE ST.

KING ST.

CHISOLM ST.

COLONIAL ST.

RUTLEDGE AVE.

11

10

4

5

6 7

9 8

SAVAGE ST.

NEW ST.

BROAD ST.

N
W E
S

Houses on Rutledge Avenue, the east side of Colonial Lake.

Harleston Village

Harleston Village is the largest of the fashionable planter suburbs and was laid out in the the 18th century. The streetscape today reflects the history of Charleston's expansion over the many creeks and marshes of the area. Because of the size and isolation of the original building lots, the first mansions were as large as those found downtown but built with the broad part of the house facing the street. Envision these grand homes as they were built—their long piazzas overlooking the marshes, peacefully isolated from the bustle of the commercial city, but close enough to participate fully in its rich social and cultural life.

In addition to the huge planter mansions, Harleston Village contains buildings of national importance: handsome Georgian and Greek Revival homes, three of the most significant Adamesque mansions in the city, important Classical and Gothic Revival works by Charleston's versatile architect Edward Brickell White and the finest collection of Victorian architecture in the city. There is an incredible display of ornamented Queen Anne gables, fancy Second Empire mansards and decorative brackets, incised Eastlake ornament and spindlework, cupolas and graceful S-curved towers. As the neighborhood became more densely populated and the creeks filled in, smaller houses were built in the traditional single house style with side piazzas, the narrow end of the house facing the street. Charleston builders were skillful in fitting their fanciful creations into the historic streetscape and in embellishing single houses and piazzas with Victorian flourishes.

When Sir Nikolaus Pevsner, the noted architectural historian, visited Charleston in 1973, he warned the city not to let its Victorian architecture disappear. Sir Nikolaus expressed concern that many preservation laws did not protect Victorian architecture as rigorously as Georgian. Indeed, protecting buildings in Charleston has always been a concern.

By the 1960's Harleston Village had deteriorated. Many houses had been subdivided into apartments. Even the planter mansions were in danger of demolition. In 1966, preservationists succeeded in having the Old and Historic District enlarged to include most of Harleston Village, but there were still bulldozers to be confronted. When the College of Charleston expanded, many houses were unfortunately lost. The Preservation Society rescued houses from the site of a parking garage and moved them to other sites in the neighborhood.

Civic-minded and farsighted investors rescued houses from demolition by neglect. Architectural reporters W. H. J. Thomas and Robert Stockton increased public awareness by writing house histories in regular columns in the *News and Courier*.

Today, Harleston Village is once again one of the city's most desirable neighborhoods. Its variety of architectural styles, forms and ornamentation combine to create a neighborhood through which you will wish to stroll slowly. The neighborhood is named for Affra Harleston, a young woman who sailed from England on the Carolina, the first ship to reach the Carolina coast in 1670. Her family had lost its money in the rise of Cromwell, and she sailed as an indentured servant. A shipboard romance developed between Affra and first mate John Coming, and they were married in 1672 after she was released from servitude. Coming received a grant of land near White Point (the Battery) which he traded for land in what is now Harleston Village. The Comings had no children, and her nephew John Harleston inherited the land and laid out the streets of the neighborhood a century later, in 1770.

In 1786, English and Scottish merchants established the first golf club in America on Harleston's Green, between Calhoun and Beaufain Streets, from Rutledge Avenue to the Ashley River.

Harleston Village includes an area known as the Mazyck lands, which were granted to James Moore in 1698 and willed to Isaac Mazyck, a French Huguenot, in 1712. Mazyck was a self-made man who became wealthy as a merchant, trading with the West Indies as early as 1688. His property was bounded by Broad, Beaufain, Smith and Archdale. Within this area was a square block reserved for public use where the Work House, Magazine, District Jail and hospital were located.

→ Begin the walk on Magazine and Archdale Streets, which is just north of Broad and slightly west of King Street.

MAGAZINE STREET, where we begin this walk, is named for a series of powder magazines that were built on the western end of the street.

1 **21 MAGAZINE STREET**: The Old Jail, at the corner of Magazine and Franklin streets, was built here in 1802 and remodeled several times. An addition designed by Robert Mills was replaced in 1855 by the octagonal wing at the rear, designed by Barbot & Seyle who expanded the main building in the Romanesque Revival style. (They also designed the large classical temple church building at 68 Spring Street, now the Karpeles Manuscript Museum.)

21 Magazine St.

In 1822, pirates were imprisoned in the Old Jail, and during the Civil War, Federal prisoners were confined here. The building continued to be used as a jail until 1939. It was briefly a museum. At the other end of this block once stood the notorious Work House for runaway slaves.

Across the street is the **Robert Mills Housing Project**, built in 1937. Charleston Mayor Burnet Maybank was the first mayor to make use of Federal Housing Funds. Designed by Simons and Lapham, it was a pioneer of low-rent housing. It was one of the finest early housing projects.

→ Go left onto Franklin Street. On your left, just past the jail, you will see:

2 **20 FRANKLIN STREET**: (City of Charleston Housing Authority) The Old Marine Hospital was designed by Robert Mills, Charleston native and America's first professionally trained architect, in 1833. Mills is most famous for the Washington Monument, the Monumental Church in Richmond, the Treasury Building

20 Franklin St

in Washington and the Fireproof Building on Meeting Street. The Hospital was built for the care of merchant seamen and has been called the city's first Gothic Revival building. Actually it is a classical building with Gothick ornament (an 18th century design approach, which used Gothic details to embellish symmetrical classical structures). When the hospital was built, it overlooked the marshes of the Ashley River. It also served as a military hospital for the Confederacy and as a school for black children. In 1895, it was occupied by the Jenkins Orphanage for black children, founded by Rev. D. J. Jenkins. The famous Jenkins Orphanage Band toured Europe and the United States.

12 Franklin Street

17 Franklin Street

GARDENERS' DETOUR: Before crossing Queen Street, walk left to a formal 18th century style front garden (colorful in the spring) at 140 Queen Street. Return to Franklin Street, crossing Queen Street.

→ On the left, just after crossing Queen Street, is:

3 **12 FRANKLIN STREET:** Note the lintels with incised Neo-Grec details. The Neo-Grec style was developed in France in the early 19th Century. Richard Morris Hunt has been credited with introducing it to America in the 1850's. It is characterized by incised linear ornamentation, stylized geometric and floral forms and broad linear relief on pilasters and columns, according to historian Paul R. Baker.

4 **17 FRANKLIN STREET:** Built c. 1852, in an era when brownstone was fashionable. Brownstone was used for window sills and door trim and the piazzas were painted to match. Full-length windows opening onto the piazza were a popular feature of Charleston Greek Revival houses. During a hurricane in the 1940's a great many wine bottles floated from under the house from what is believed to have been the wine cellar of a French consul who lived here during the 1870s.

5 **15 FRANKLIN STREET**: Etienne Poincignon, a prosperous tinsmith and real estate investor was a French Catholic who fled to Charleston from Santo Domingo after the slave insurrection of 1793. Other French refugees lived nearby on Archdale Street. The house, built in 1850 when Greek Revival was being replaced by mid-century Eclecticism, shows the Greek influence in the parapet honeysuckle-anthemion cast iron pieces. DuBose Heyward, author of *Porgy*, lived here as a child.

6 **13 FRANKLIN STREET**: Charleston's single house adapted well to changing architectural fashions. Here is a c.1849 house with its side piazza and entrance embellished with stick-style columns.

13 Franklin Street   *9 Franklin Street*

7 **9 FRANKLIN STREET**: This early Bracketed style house has a gable ornamented with grills under the eaves, a popular ornamental motif often seen on the parapets of Greek Revival buildings, as on 15 Franklin.

→   Turn right onto Broad Street.

Coffee Break: *There are few restaurants in Harleston Village. For a cool drink and a snack, there is Burbage's, 157 Broad Street, a neighborhood grocery store. By Colonial Lake there are benches (and a trash basket.)*

BROAD STREET: The great fire of 1861 destroyed much of this area. The fire began at Hasell and East Bay and swept across the peninsula to Tradd Street and the Ashley River. Some 575 houses burned. Miss Emma Holmes was among those who lost their homes in that fire, and she wrote in her diary that this neighborhood was "Oh, so changed that I could not realize where I was. All seemed a frightful dream, though I stood among a forest of chimneys." The neighborhood was rebuilt after the Civil War and today contains a fine collection of fanciful Victorian architecture that was fashionable at the end of the 19th Century.

164 Broad Street

170 Broad Street

8 **164-166-168 BROAD STREET**: These houses, all built by Samuel Wragg Simons, reflect his improving financial situation. The smallest house at 168 was built first, in 1886. Five years later, Simons built 166 and 164. The grandest house of Simons row is 164, where he lived. Note the picturesque asymmetry, the tower with the S-curved roof, projecting bays, fish-scale shingles and the fancy gables, all popular Victorian details.

9 **170 BROAD STREET**: Victorians loved pattern upon pattern and style upon style. Here is a notable Charleston stick style example with a Georgian Palladian-windowed balcony, ornamented gables and fancy shingles.

10 **180 BROAD STREET**: Tower-of-the-Winds capitals ornament this Greek Revival house built about 1850, a survivor of the 1861 fire. It was used as a prison for Union officers during the Civil War.

180 Broad Street

CONFEDERATE COURTESY AND A UNION SWORD

During the Civil War, Major Orlando J. Smith of the Sixth Indiana Cavalry was imprisoned in the O'Connor home at 180 Broad Street. "We were treated," said Major Smith, "exactly as well as the Confederates. We were hungry sometimes and so were they." The prisoners were also given a good deal of freedom, allowed to play ball by Colonial Lake, known then as "The Pond." After the war, Smith became a successful writer, editor and publisher in Chicago. As head of the American Press Association, his writings appeared in papers all over the country. Years later a stranger appeared before Smith, carrying the sword Smith had lost in battle in 1864 when he was wounded and captured. The Southerner returning the sword said he had been reading Smith's newspaper articles and was impressed by the fair and friendly tone. Smith's sword is now at DePauw University in Indiana of which he was a founder.

→ As you continue west on Broad and turn right on Rutledge you come upon COLONIAL LAKE, named such in 1882, but traditionally referred to as the Rutledge Street Pond. An act of 1768 of the General Assembly called for the construction of the lake and for the area around it to be held as a common.

RUTLEDGE AVENUE: was named for statesman John Rutledge who was President and Governor of South Carolina, a delegate to the Continental Congress and the Constitutional Convention. He lived at 116 Broad Street, where much of the U. S. Constitution was drafted. Rutledge Avenue, from Beaufain Street northward was laid out when Harleston Village was platted in 1770. It was extended over the city marshes to Broad Street in 1849. The loss of a handsome Victorian house at the southwest corner of Rutledge Avenue and Broad Street in 1973 prompted the Harleston Village Association to ask the city to protect the other Victorian and Classical Revival houses in the Colonial Lake area.

22 RUTLEDGE AVENUE: Bradford Lee Gilbert designed this mansion with a Mediterranean flavor, incorporating Italianate and Gothic details, about 1902 for Dr. Manning Simons. Gilbert was a New York architect who designed the first skyscraper in New York City with a metal skeleton instead of load-bearing walls—the Tower Building of 1888. Gilbert was also the chief engineer for the Erie Railroad and he remodeled the original Grand Central Depot. In Charleston, Gilbert was the architect of the South Carolina Interstate and West Indian Exposition of 1901. The design of Dr. Simons's home is less ornate but similar to the facade of the New York Building in the Exposition.

22 Rutledge Avenue

Bradford Lee Gilbert was the major architect of the South Carolina Interstate and West Indian Exposition of 1901, organized by Charleston businessmen in hopes of reviving the city's stagnating economy. It was inspired by the successful White City built in Chicago in 1893 for the World's Columbian Exposition. Charleston created its make-believe city on a 250-acre site—a fantasy of alabaster/plaster palaces displaying the latest in technology, sunken gardens, rare tropical plants and lush plantings of roses, azaleas, camellias and oleanders. The Liberty Bell was borrowed from Philadelphia. Thirty-one states and several foreign countries participated. Some 500,000 visitors came, including President Theodore Roosevelt and Mark Twain. Several million dollars were pumped into the economy and new businesses moved into Charleston. However, the Exposition Company went into receivership. Photographs of the Ivory City are on exhibit in the Charleston Museum. The only surviving fragment of the Exposition buildings is the domed bandstand at the end of Cleveland Street in Hampton Park. And even this has been relocated and rebuilt. After the demise of the Exposition, the site was redeveloped as a city park.

30 Rutledge Avenue

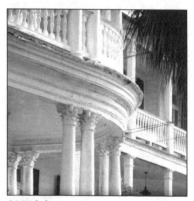

36 Rutledge Avenue

12 **30 RUTLEDGE AVENUE:** Anna Wagner built the house in 1902 at 28 St. Philip Street. In 1975, it was slated to be demolished for a parking garage. Wagner's granddaughter and the Preservation Society rescued it and had it moved to this site. Moving houses is a last resort of Charleston preservationists.

13 **36 RUTLEDGE AVENUE:** Maintaining an old house is an expensive undertaking. The graceful, curving piazzas have been restored. When restoration is done successfully, the result is inevitably higher real estate taxes. Charleston's historic districts need tax reform if they are to survive.

40 Rutledge Avenue

14 **40 RUTLEDGE AVENUE:** This gorgeous Colonial Revival, which dates to about 1900, was built by Albert W. Todd, an architect and state senator.

15 **42 RUTLEDGE AVENUE:** Built c. 1856, this was the oldest of the houses in the Colonial Lake area that was unprotected in 1973 when the Harleston Village Association lobbied for an extension of the Old and Historic District.

16 **46 RUTLEDGE AVENUE:** Charleston has traditionally been noted for its civic courtesy, exemplified by its streetscapes where houses display variety, yet fit gracefully into the overall context. This is such a house, designed in 1983 by Douglas Boyce, Jr. in the traditional single-house mode. It received a Carolopolis Award from the Preservation Society, which annually recognizes excellence in restoration and new construction.

17 **52 RUTLEDGE AVENUE:** This Edwardian pile was built in 1912 for the president of a lumber company. Note the fancy shingles, stained glass, Palladian window and octagonal tower.

→   After crossing Beaufain, you will see on your right:

52 Rutledge Avenue

18 **64 RUTLEDGE AVENUE:** 1908, Colonial Revival. Not an old house in Charleston, but with its neighbor at 66, it contributes to the visual pleasure of the streetscape.

64 Rutledge Avenue

19 **67 RUTLEDGE AVENUE:** Col. James H. Taylor's home, c. 1851, was designed in the Persian Villa style, with Moorish arches ornamenting the piazza. Daniel Webster was entertained here. Descendants of the Taylor family occupied the house for over 100 years. Rev. Dr. James H. Taylor, who was living here in 1956, recalled the "tub races in the pond" (Colonial Lake) and the trolley cars which ran up Rutledge and over a curved wooden bridge spanning the creek at what is now Calhoun Street.

THE GARDENS OF HARLESTON VILLAGE

Architectural restorations here outshine the gardens. Residents continue to cherish lawns with a few green shrubs. However, there are several gems for gardeners. At 74 Rutledge, a glorious patterned garden, laid out in the 1790's, is believed to be the oldest in the city. There are good examples of the Charleston taste for geometric symmetry and formality, which has prevailed since Colonial days—a large garden of roses, statuary and parterres, some of which is believed to date from 1854, is visible through the hedge at 94 Rutledge. Another formal garden may be seen through the gates at 144 Wentworth Street. Charming new gardens, very much in the spirit of the 19th century, may be seen at 36 Montagu Street and at 54 Montagu, where there is a large formal garden.

A must-see is the campus of the College of Charleston, which has been transformed into a lush arboretum featuring landscaping plants, many labeled, which flourish in Charleston—roses, azaleas, yew, aspidistra, holly ferns, holly, red maple, boxwood, magnolia, sago palms, palmettos, pittosporum, fatsia, liriope and Spanish moss. Just to the east of Randolph Hall, the walled Kathleen Lightsey garden, entered through an ornamental iron gate, is a typical small courtyard garden with urns, a fountain and a border of flowers.

→   Notice on your right, just before you come to Wentworth Street the pattern garden of:

20 **74 RUTLEDGE AVENUE:** The pattern garden was laid out in the 1790's and is one of the oldest in the city. There were once many such small pattern gardens in Charleston, inspired by French and English parterres of the 17th, 18th and 19th Centuries.

74 Rutledge Avenue

→ Across the street, on the SW corner of Wentworth and Rutledge Streets, you will see:

21 **73 RUTLEDGE AVENUE:**
Originally built in 1852, the house was remodeled in c. 1893 by Isaac W. Hirsch, a King Street merchant. He added a high fashion Second Empire mansard, stained glass and a large bracketed bay window. Architectural reporter W. H. J. Thomas speculated that the architect may have been T. H. Abrahams of the firm of Abrahams & Seyle known for designing a high style Tuscan Revival commercial building on King Street.

→ Cross Wentworth Street and the second house on your left is:

22 **81 RUTLEDGE AVENUE:** The Glover-Sottile House, c. 1826, was built by noted physician Dr. Joseph Glover in the Regency style. Giovanni Sottile, Italian Consul, bought the house in 1906 and restored it. Note the delicate ironwork and the dignified arched entrance with a Gibbs surround.

→ Turn around, walk back to Wentworth Street, and go right.

23 **164 WENTWORTH STREET:** (On the NW corner of Wentworth and Rutledge Streets) Part of the mansion dates to 1835. The front facade was remodeled in 1889 in the Victorian Italianate style for Carsten Wulbern, a wholesale grocer. Note the bracketed cornice, elegant fluted columns and the handsome entrance with stained glass side lights.

24 **166 WENTWORTH STREET:** Before the era of mass production, it was necessary for a builder to be a skilled craftsman. The historic fabric of Charleston was created by the taste of 18th and 19th Century carpenter/builders such as Job Palmer who built this house for himself.

→ Take a short detour at the corner of Wentworth Street and Ashley Avenue. Go left to see the front of the house at the SE corner of Wentworth and Ashley, which is:

25 **76 ASHLEY AVENUE:** Built c. 1855 for the rice planter John Hume Simons, who married his cousin Mary Hume Lucas. During the Federal bombardment of Charleston, the huge double drawing rooms were used for church services by the Roman Catholic congregation of St. Mary's on Hasell Street.

→ Directly across the street, at the SW corner, is:

77 Ashley Avenue

26 **79 ASHLEY AVENUE:** Daniel Fairchild, a brick and lumber factor, built his home in the Greek Revival style. The then-fashionable brownstone lintels and sills were later painted over. Notice the belt course between the floors and elongated quoins, also important details of the era.

27 **77 ASHLEY AVENUE:** Charleston is noted for its distinctive doorways, such as this one with Ionic pilasters. The city's builders were adept in their use of the classical language to give entrances importance and dignity. While most "Modern" entrances are bleak and utilitarian, those on Charleston's 18th and 19th century homes seek to be beautiful and distinctive, are welcoming, often impressive. Such a variety of ornamented doorways brings texture and rhythm to the city's streets.

→ Return to Wentworth and go left (west) to Gadsden Street past some colorful front gardens. Turn right onto Gadsden Street.

GADSDEN STREET was one of the original streets of Harleston Village, laid out in 1770 and named for Christopher Gadsden, Patriot general and Lt. Governor of South Carolina during the revolution.

28 **19 GADSDEN STREET:** (The white house with red roof and blue shutters) When it was built c. 1828, this house overlooked the Ashley River and its marshes.

→ Turn left onto Montagu Street.

MONTAGU STREET: was named for Sir Charles Greville Montagu, the Royal Governor of South Carolina, 1766-1768.

29 **64 MONTAGU STREET:** Thomas Bennett, the building contractor, architect and mill owner, built this house before 1813. About 1800, the Bennett family bought many lots in the area. The superb craftsmanship of this family of builders contributed much to the city's streetscapes. Bennett owned and operated, in partnership with Daniel Cannon, a number of wind and tidal-powered lumber mills just to the west of his home.

→　　Turn around and go east on Montagu. At the NW corner of Montagu and Gadsden is:

30 **62 MONTAGU STREET**: At this writing, this notable antebellum mansion has been allowed to fall into ruins. Demolition by neglect is a serious problem above Calhoun Street, however it is unusual to find a mansion of this character neglected in Harleston Village.

62 Montagu Street

60 Montagu Street

31 **60 MONTAGU STREET**: The Gaillard-Bennett House, a spectacular Adamesque mansion, c. 1802, has received the restoration that #62 desperately needs. It was built by Theodore Gaillard, a rice planter and factor. Note the gracious entrance, fluted columns with Tower-of-the-Winds capitals, modillion cornice and elliptical window of the portico gable. The rusticated base is a Palladian motif. From 1851, it was the home of Washington Jefferson Bennett, son of Governor Thomas Bennett, operator of the family rice and lumber mills. The Bennetts added the ornate cast iron porches and curving front wall. Robert E. Lee was a guest of the Bennetts in 1870. After a party in his honor, Lee addressed a gathering from the second story balcony.

32 **54 MONTAGU STREET**: Until about 1880, this house and #60 stood alone on the block in a rural area of creeks and marshes. Built c. 1815 in the Adamesque style by Dr. Edward Washington, a popular physician and Intendant (mayor) of Charleston, it has been featured on television in This Old House, has beautiful formal garden.

33 **44 MONTAGU STREET**: (The yellow house mid-block hidden behind palmettos) The main rooms of this Greek Revival villa are on the second floor in order to take advantage of what once was a view of the Ashley River. It was built c. 1847 on landfill by John Harleston Read.

34 **43 AND 45 MONTAGU STREET**: These very similar Victorian houses were built in the late 1890's using what was called German siding, a weather board beveled at the top.

93 Rutledge Avenue

94 Rutledge Avenue

→ At the NW corner of Rutledge and Montagu:

35 **93 RUTLEDGE AVENUE**: This Italianate mansion with Tower-of-the-Winds capitals was built c. 1850 by Edward L. Trenholm, a cotton export merchant, whose company operated blockade runners during the Civil War. He was in business with his brother George Alfred Trenholm, Confederate Secretary of the Treasury and the alleged model for Rhett Butler in *Gone with the Wind*.

Tower-of-the-Winds capital

→ At the NE corner of Rutledge and Montagu:

36 **94 RUTLEDGE AVENUE**: Palladian villa grandeur built by a wealthy Edisto planter, Isaac Jenkins Mikell, c. 1853 for his third wife. It has an elevated and pedimented portico, and it has recently been attributed to Edward C. Jones, one of the city's most important architects, on very solid stylistic grounds. It is believed that part of the present formal garden is from the original design. At one time this was the home of Mayor John Ficken, later becoming the Charleston County library. It was threatened with demolition in 1960 when the value of such opulence was not appreciated.

CAPITALS SOLVE AN ARCHITECTURAL MYSTERY

The variety of capitals adorning the city's colon-naded streetscapes provide not only great visual pleasure, but recently a capital also helped solve an architectural mystery. There are a number of impor-tant buildings in Charleston whose architects are unknown—St. Michael's Church and the building that houses Ashley Hall School, for example. The Isaac Jenkins Mikell mansion at 94 Rutledge was the work of an unknown hand until historian Gene

Ram's Head Capital

Waddell and a College of Charleston student obtained special permission to visit Kensington, a privately owned plantation in Richland County, to research a paper on Edward C. Jones. Jones is known to be the architect of Kensington, built just before the Mikell mansion. The ram's head capi-tals on Kensington turned out to be identical to the capitals on the Mikell mansion. Since these intricate capitals are found nowhere else, Waddell concluded that Jones was the architect of both buildings.

→ Continue east on Montagu. The next house on the left is a pink Victorian:

37 **40 MONTAGU STREET**: One of the most beguiling of Charleston's Victorian fantasies, this house was built in 1891 by Bernard Wohlers, who managed a grocery store. The influence of Charles Eastlake combined with a hint of Queen Anne and the Shingle Style cre-ates a house of great charm. Such Victorian creations are not fully appreciated in Charleston with its

40 Montagu Street

vast collection of colonial and antebellum houses. In a less fortunate community, a structure of this originality would be among the most cherished landmarks. The house was restored in 1963.

→ Turn right on Smith Street. At the corner of Smith Street and Wentworth Street, notice the large building on the SE corner.

38 **149 WENTWORTH STREET**: The Francis Silas Rodgers Mansion has been converted into one of the city's grandest hotels, was designed by Daniel Wayne in 1885. It is Charleston's finest example of the Second Empire style. Rodgers was a cotton factor, phosphate manufacturer, shipper and public servant. The four-story mansion contains 13,883 square feet. Rodgers had 12 children, and the top floor once had a family school room—and billiard parlor. Rodgers was a member of the City Council and organized the city's first professional fire department. He was on the Board of Firemen and vigilantly on the look-out for fires from the cupola on the roof. The family would gather on the tin roof to watch fireworks at Colonial Lake.

→ Continue south on Smith Street.

149 Wentworth Street cupola in background

39 **34 SMITH STREET**: (The NE corner of Beaufain and Smith) George Robertson, a merchant, built this large Italian villa c. 1855. It may well remind you of the Palladian grandeur of the Battery. In fact, Robertson built a house very similar to this at #1 Meeting Street.

→ Turn left onto Beaufain Street.

40 **89 BEAUFAIN STREET**: This handsome Regency home was built c. 1815 for William Steele, a lumber merchant. It was once the home of Duncan Nathaniel Ingraham, a Civil War naval hero who married Harriott Horry Laurens, granddaughter of the statesmen Henry Laurens and John Rutledge. Note the marble piazza door surround, the lunette of the pediment and the segmental arches of the piazza.

→ Turn left onto Pitt Street.

PITT STREET: was named for William Pitt, Earl of Chatham and a champion of colonial rights. The Lanneau family built most of the homes on the block. Bazile Lanneau, a French Arcadian, arrived in Charleston in 1755. He grew up under the protection of Henry Laurens, became a Protestant and prospered as a currier and tanner. In 1778, Lanneau bought the west side of this block from Isaac Harleston.

41 **2 PITT STREET**: Built before 1788 by Bazile Lanneau and moved here in 1974, rescued by the Preservation Society. Charleston has an impressive record of preserving historic structures by, as a last resort, moving them. This site is appropriately opposite Lanneau Row. The two-story kitchen building for this house was moved to 76 Beaufain Street.

42 **4 PITT STREET**: Rachel Lazarus built this house c. 1815. It, too, was moved by the Preservation Society from the parking garage site on St. Philip Street. Other houses moved include those now located at 72, 74 and 76 Beaufain and 30 Rutledge.

43 **I, 3, 5, 7 AND 9 PITT STREET**: Lanneau's Row, built by Bazile Lanneau and his family "stands as a monument to the family's endeavors and the fashion consciousness of the 1830s and 1840s when these five homes were built," wrote architectural reporter W. H. J. Thomas. Note the Greek Revival anthemion grills at the parapets of #5, 7 and 9. A sixth member of the Row was demolished prior to 1966, when the neighborhood was incorporated into the Old and Historic District. In 1973, when the owner of #3 wanted to demolish his house, the Board of Architectural Review denied the request. Charleston protects streetscapes rather than isolated landmarks—history is not just the story of kings and queens.

THE BOARD OF ARCHITECTURAL REVIEW

The BAR was created as part of Charleston's famous preservation ordinance of 1931, which was the first to protect an entire district. The seven-member Board reviews alterations, new construction and demolition requests within the Old and Historic District, which includes most blocks south of Calhoun Street plus the neighborhoods of Radcliffeborough, Mazyck Wraggborough Garden District and the commercial corridor of King Street up to the Crosstown. The BAR's legal mandate to protect the historic character of the District and the rigorousness of their decisions is crucial to the city's economy, as tourism has become the city's biggest industry. The authenticity of Charleston's streetscapes attracts over four million visitors a year, who pump nearly $3 billion annually into the economy.

44 **13 PITT STREET**: Brownstone was popular in 1858 when Henry Gerdts, a wholesale grocer and commission merchant built his home, which has possibly the most elaborate brownstone ornament in the city. Note the carved entrance with a pediment supported by brackets and the correct Ionic and Corinthian columns on the piazzas. The Italianate, with brackets, had been introduced in 1853 by Edward Jones.

13 Pitt Street

138 Wentworth Street

→ Turn left on Wentworth

45 **137 WENTWORTH STREET**: (A small grey house in the middle of the block) Catherine Lopez, a "free woman of color" bought this house in 1838.

46 **138 WENTWORTH STREET**: Edwin L. Kerrison, a founder of Kerrison's Department Store, built his home c. 1839-1842. The design, which is attributed to Russell Warren of Rhode Island, has the popular Tower-of-the-Winds capitals. This feature, plus a heavy row of dentils under the cornice, closely resembles the details of a house in Providence by Warren, according to historian Beatrice St. Julien Ravenel. Other historians have noted a similarity between this mansion and that of Joseph Daniel Aiken at 20 Charlotte Street. Warren was noted for his "vivid and original houses in the Greek Revival style," according to Talbot Hamlin, and he designed homes in Newport, where many Charlestonians vacationed in the summer. Warren spent winters in Charleston, where he owned property.

→ Turn right onto Smith Street then right onto Montagu Street.

47 **34, 32 AND 30 MONTAGU STREET**: These three homes with the arched piazzas, so reminiscent of a memorable house on South Battery (#26), are believed to have been designed by the same architect, Edward C. Jones, in 1854, a year after he designed the Col. Ashe Italianate house on the Battery.

48 **25 MONTAGU STREET**: Built c. 1847 by John Robinson, a factor, and later owned by one of America's pioneer surgeons in gynecology. Dr. Theodore Gaillard Thomas, who bought the house in 1869, originated several operations, including substitutes for the Caesarian section, and invented surgical instruments.

34, 32, and 30 Montagu Street

20 Montagu Street

49 **24 MONTAGU STREET**: (Set back from the street, with the red roof) This small single house was built c.1804 by Daniel Bruckner, a merchant. The one-story piazza is partly enclosed. This house was built when the area was still open country, which is why it is set so far back from the street.

50 **20 MONTAGU STREET**: (At the corner) The James Moultrie House is considered one of the most handsome and delicately proportioned Adamesque houses in the city. It was built c. 1809, at the same time as the Nathaniel Russell House on Meeting Street (another Adamesque treasure and open to the public) was being built. Originally the home of Daniel Cobia, planter and butcher, it was sold to the Moultrie family in 1834. Dr. Moultrie, a kinsman of Gen. William Moultrie, the Revolutionary War hero, was one of the most prominent medical men of the era. He helped lead the campaign to found a medical school for South Carolina and was chairman of the physiology department in the new college. Edward McCrady, the historian, lived here from 1879 to 1891 and probably wrote much of his famous four-volume history here.

51 **18 MONTAGU STREET**: Built by a Goose Creek planter, c. 1788, this is the oldest house on Montagu Street and one of the few 18th century Georgian period homes in Harleston Village. In 1811, it was the home of Chancellor Henry William DeSaussure, who had been appointed first director of the U. S. Mint by George Washington. Like so many of the huge homes in the area, this house was converted into apartments.

16 Montagu Street

12 Montagu Street

52 **16 MONTAGU STREET**: In 1971, this home was praised in the press for being one of the "most conscientious" of the restorations taking place. The owners, Mr. and Mrs. G. A. Z. Johnson, Jr. reduced the number of apartments and restored period details of this handsome early Greek Revival/late Federal dwelling, which was built c. 1830 as the home of a merchant.

53 **13 MONTAGU STREET**: Built in the Georgian period, c. 1789, by Jacob Williman, a prosperous butcher, currier, tanner and plantation owner. It was one of the earliest houses in Harleston Village.

54 **12 MONTAGU STREET**: Built by a mariner in 1812, it is now the home of the Johnsons who recognized the quality of the houses on Montagu Street and restored civility, period details and fresh paint to a number of splendid houses on this block.

55 **6 MONTAGU STREET**: When John Rudolf Switzer, a prosperous saddler built his home, c. 1803, this was still semirural. It became the home of planter Robert Trail Chisolm in 1812. By 1962, the house had fallen into ruin. Unsightly additions destroyed its Adamesque delicacy. The house was rescued by the Johnson family and was one of their pioneer restorations.

→ Turn right onto Coming Street.

56 **36 COMING STREET**: Built in 1842 by a planter on what was called the Glebe lands—some 17 acres given to the Church of England in Charles Town by Mrs. Affra Harleston Coming in 1698. It is now owned by the College of Charleston. The piazza is fashionably Greek Revival; the hipped roof, fenestration respond to the Georgian fabric of Charleston.

57 **34 COMING STREET**: Built by a vintner in 1771-78 also on Glebe lands.

→ Turn left onto Wentworth Street.

58 **114 WENTWORTH STREET**: This early 19th century grocery store building was restored in 1975 by the College of Charleston for offices.

59 **100 WENTWORTH STREET**: Grace Episcopal Church, an early example of Gothic Revival in America, was designed by Edward Brickell White in 1847. White was probably familiar with the work of Richard Upjohn, whose design

100 Wentworth Street

for Trinity Church in New York (dedicated in 1846) was considered the first church building in the United States to be truly Gothic. White was one of the first American architects to join in the revival of Gothic, having designed the Huguenot Church in 1845 and Trinity Church in Columbia in 1847. Prof. Russell considers Grace to be White's Gothic masterpiece.

60 **107 WENTWORTH STREET**: Charleston cherishes eccentricity, and according to *News and Courier* reporter W. H. J. Thomas, this house has a rich history. Built c. 1796 and later remodeled, the house was owned by the Johnson family in the 19th Century. James Johnson (1796-1865) was married here and it is said that when he removed his coat, his bride fainted "as she had never seen a man in shirt-sleeves before." Mr. Johnson originally practiced law but found it "not compatible with my conscience" and became a merchant. According to tradition, during the 1886 earthquake, several Johnson spinsters climbed up on the roof of the house and prayed, not to save themselves, but to save the steeple of Grace Church. Dr. William Henry Johnson (1871-1934), was a colorful orthopedic surgeon and amateur inventor. Dr. Johnson began the department of orthopedics at the Medical College and made his own splints and braces in a backyard blacksmith shop. He brought the first X-ray to Charleston, never sent bills to his patients and exercised by throwing his anvil about the backyard. He also practiced sharpshooting by aiming at, and rarely missing, bees. He invented a pressure cooker which connected to the radiator of his car in order that he might drive in the country and cook dinner simultaneously.

61 **99-106 WENTWORTH STREET**: This charming row of Victorians is built upon what was, in the 18th Century, the expansive rose garden of 107 Wentworth.

→ Turn left onto Glebe Street.

GLEBE STREET is named for the Glebe lands, 17 acres that were, as mentioned earlier, given to the minister of the Church of England in Charles Town by Affra Harleston Coming in 1698. The lands were divided into lots in 1770 and the street was created in 1797. (Glebe lands are lands belonging to, or yielding revenue to, a parish church.)

62 **6 GLEBE STREET**: St. Philip's Glebe House was built in 1770 and is now the home of the President of the College of Charleston. The College's first classes met here. It is one of the city's finest Georgian homes.

63 **7 GLEBE STREET**: The design of the Mount Zion A.M.E. (African Methodist Episcopalian) Church has been attributed to Francis D. Lee. Built in 1847 as the Glebe Street Presbyterian Church, the design is said to be influenced by the work of English architect Sir John Soane. In 1882, the church became the Mount Zion African Methodist Episcopal Church.

6 Glebe Street

66 George Street

→ Turn right onto George Street.

64 **66 GEORGE STREET**: The Roman triumphal arch entrance to the College of Charleston was designed by E. B. White in 1850. As you walk through the arch, Randolph Hall will be directly in front of you. Built in 1828, it was designed by William Strickland. (Strickland was a student of Benjamin Latrobe, an architect of the U. S. Capitol in 1803. Strickland's other notable works include the Second Bank of the United

Randolph Hall

States and the Merchant's Exchange in Philadelphia, the Tennessee State Capitol and churches in Nashville.) In 1850, Charleston architect E. B. White added the portico and the wings. At the left, the Towell Library building, (now Admissions), was designed in 1854 by George E. Walker in the Italianate manner, with handsome quoins and tall arched windows. These buildings are considered nationally important.

THE COLLEGE OF CHARLESTON

The College of Charleston was founded in 1770, making it the 13th oldest college in America, although it did not begin to enroll students until 1785. It is also the oldest municipally-supported college in the country since Charleston began to appropriate money for its operation in 1826. In 1970, it became part of the state system of colleges and universities. In that year it enrolled 500 students, studying in a handful of buildings. Since then enrollment has climbed steadily to over 11,000 students, and the campus has grown to nearly 120 buildings. In the 1970's, a number of historic buildings were destroyed or moved to make way for new mediocre buildings, somewhat softened by twenty years of lush plantings. A much-needed Program in Historic Preservation has finally been created by the College.

→   Walk through the Triumphal Arch and around to the right of Randolph Hall, passing the Kathleen Lightsey Garden, through the gates that lead to St. Philip Street, to the rear of Randolph Hall. Turn left onto the wide brick path (called Greenway but unmarked). Just before the gates that lead into the campus is:

65 **2 GREENWAY:** (Mathematics Department) The presence of historic houses brings a high degree of civility to the campus. The Martindale Bell house was built c. 1817 by James Martindale, a planter. In 1844, it was bought by Sally Johnson, a "free person of color" who had four slaves and was a "pastry cook." Her descendants owned it until the college acquired it in 1972.

6 Greenway

11 College Walk

66 **6 GREENWAY:** The Wagener House, c. 1817, was the scene of a confrontation between local preservationists and a College bulldozer. On Friday, February 12, 1971, the News and Courier reported that "demolition of four antebellum structures on the site of the proposed ... library has begun." The Preservation Society of Charleston protested since the College had promised to preserve this building (called "probably the only true example of the West Indian house remaining in the city") by moving it. An agreement was finally worked out, but a fine Greek Revival house and other antebellum houses were destroyed during the College's expansion.

67 **10 GREENWAY:** (Now the Honors Center) The Aiken House was built by William Aiken, Governor of South Carolina, 1844-46, along with a twin house, c. 1841, similar to the houses comprising Aiken's Row on Wragg Mall. Unfortunately, the twin was demolished to make room for the new library building in 1971. The News and Courier reported that 6 and 10 Green provided the College with more square footage at less cost than would a new building.

→ Continue walking straight ahead toward Coming Street.

68 **11 COLLEGE WALK:** The large yellow house on your right is the Wilson-Sottile House, built in 1891, designed by Richmond architect S. W. Foulk for Samuel Wilson, an entrepreneur. Wilson ran a grocery business (The Tea Pot at 306 King Street), was president of the Dime Savings Bank, the

Charleston Bridge Co. and the New Charleston Hotel Co. The design of his home is one of the finest examples of Queen Anne/Shingle Style Victorian in Charleston. It was once the home of Albert Sottile, the theater magnate.

→ Continue on straight ahead.

69 **14 GREENWAY**: Mrs. Walter Knox, a wealthy widow, built this c. 1846 "Tuscan Villa" with a bracketed Italianate cornice and an octagonal cupola, a style rare in Charleston. In 1870, the house was bought by Albert Osceola Jones, a black reconstruction politician.

→ Exit the campus through the gates and turn left onto Coming Street. Turn right onto Bull Street.

BULL STREET was named for William Bull, a native South Carolinian who was the last to fill the Royally-appointed office of lieutenant governor.

70 **2, 4, 6, 8 BULL STREET**. Four Victorian houses, c. 1907, known as the "Four Sisters."

12 Bull Street

18 Bull Street

71 **12 BULL STREET**: Hugh P. Cameron, a crockery merchant, built this house in 1851 on a site once owned by the Blacklock family. It is a very unusual form for a Charleston house, with its double piazzas facing the street, twin parlors behind them, and the entrance tucked off to the side. The house was remodeled in the 1890's in the then fashionable Colonial Revival mode. Presently the Caroline and Albert Simons, Jr. Center for Historic Preservation.

72 **18 BULL STREET**: This nationally important, Adamesque mansion was built in 1800 by William Blacklock, a wine merchant who once owned

18 Bull Street

the whole north side of this block. The architect is unknown, though the design has been attributed to Gabriel Manigault. It was built in the period of prosperity which followed the Revolution. By 1932, this incredible Adamesque mansion had become a boarding house. It narrowly escaped demolition in 1958. Many nearby homes were in ruins. The Old and Historic District was enlarged in 1966 to include Harleston Village and in 1969, the Blacklock House was bought by Richard H. Jenrette of Charleston and New York, head of Donaldson, Lufkin and Jenrette. In Charleston, he is better known for his restoration of great buildings, such as the Roper mansion on East Battery. After restoring the Blacklock House, Jenrette gave it to the College of Charleston. The College did further restoration work.

73 **24 BULL STREET**: Richard Jenrette also saved this handsome Greek Revival house built by Benjamin Lucas, a builder and building inspector, c. 1858. The house had been retained by Lucas descendants until the 1930s, when it was divided into eleven apartments. In the restoration, Jenrette made it into five large living units.

→ Cross Pitt Street.

74 **43 BULL STREET**: (The yellow house mid-block on the left, set back from the street) The lavish used of iron gives this house the flavor of New Orleans. Built by a King Street merchant, 1849-52, it was once the home of Joseph Fromberg, a lawyer who advocated the chain gang for drunken drivers.

75 **48 BULL STREET**: This plantation-style town house of a Goose Creek planter was built when Harleston Village was still open country. Threatened with demolition in 1964, it was converted into apartments.

76 **51 BULL STREET**: Holy Trinity Reformed Episcopal Church was built by African Americans in 1880. Many descendants of charter members still attend today.

48 Bull Street

77 **56 BULL STREET**: Denmark Vesey is believed to have lived here c. 1821-22. Vesey won a lottery in 1800, bought his freedom and became a prosperous carpenter. He was the alleged leader of an aborted slave insurrection in 1822.

78 **66 BULL STREET**: For over 175 years, this handsome single house has had few alterations. In 1969 it became the home of J. Douglas Donehue, a newspaper man, now contributor to National Public Radio. The rear of the property once overlooked Bennett's Mill Pond.

79 **76 BULL STREET**: The house dates from c. 1813 and became the home of Hugh Swinton Legare in 1821. Lawyer, editor and U. S. Secretary of State, Legare, had he lived, might have been the Whig candidate for President in 1844. According to *News & Courier* reporter W. H. J. Thomas, Legare's library, at the west end of the basement floor, was a gathering place for many of the best minds in antebellum Charleston.

76 Bull Street

80 **84 BULL STREET**: (NE corner of Bull and Rutledge) French Count Eugene Joseph Huchet moved here in 1857. He is said to have lost his fortune in a single day's trading in cotton. His daughter, who claimed to be the only living countess in South Carolina, died in 1932, leaving the house as a home for "white females of moderate financial consequences." Now it is clearly the home of an avid gardener.

→ Continue west on Bull, crossing Rutledge Avenue.

81 **96 BULL STREET**: Note the Adamesque frieze of swags under the cornice, a trademark of the Bennett family of builders. This house dates from c. 1815. Other Bennett houses include 104 and 128 Bull Street. A fourth notable Bennett house at 112 Bull was demolished.

→ Across the street, the stucco house behind the iron fence is:

99 Bull Street

82 **99 BULL STREET**: A famous Charleston murder occurred here when this was the home of Capt. Warrington Dawson, editor of the News and Courier. Dawson was shot to death in 1889 by Dr. Thomas McDow. A young French governess, who worked for Dawson, testified that the handsome young doctor had made inappropriate advances toward her. Dawson visited McDow in his office at 101 Rutledge and attacked him with his cane. McDow pleaded self-defense and was acquitted. Note the graceful ironwork.

83 **100 BULL STREET**: The career of Honore Monpoey is typical of many self-made members of the planter aristocracy. Monpoey, who built his home c. 1820, began as a grocer and later a factor. He prospered and became the owner of a couple of plantations on the Ashley River.

84 **101-107 BULL STREET**: An architectural anomaly of Charleston is this row of townhouses which look as if they belong in New York, Baltimore or Philadelphia. It is believed that Sarah Smith, who built them in 1849, was from Baltimore. The fashion for row houses, which was also popular in Bath and London, never caught on in Charleston. The city's own creation, the single house, with its piazzas placed to capture the late afternoon southwestern breezes and to shade from the sun, is more suitable to Charleston's climate. During the Civil War, the row became known as the "Bee Block", as the William C. Bee & Co. stores moved here. Blockade runners kept the stores supplied.

101-107 Bull Street

104 Bull Street

125 Bull Street

85 **104 BULL STREET**: Built by Thomas Bennett before 1802 and once home of Nicholas Harleston. A small portion of the Bennetts' favorite Adamesque frieze of swags survives on the west facade.

→ Cross Ashley Avenue. On your left is:

86 **125 BULL STREET**: Built in 1867 as the first free secondary school for the black community. T. M. Stewartt, a Liberian Supreme Court Justice and Judge Richard E. Fields were educated here. Today it is the College of Charleston's Avery Research Center for African American History and Culture.

AFRICAN-AMERICAN HISTORY

Charleston is central to the history of African-Americans. The first slave ship arrived here in 1672 and by 1719, some 1500 Africans had been brought to Carolina. Charleston was one of the few southern cities with a sizable community of free blacks, many of whom owned slaves and formed organizations such as the Brown Fellowship Society. Until the mid-20th century, the city was the most integrated of any major American city in terms of population distribution. Every historic neighborhood in Charleston has buildings that are significant to Black History. There is the Aiken Rhett House Museum (Mazyck Wraggborough), the Denmark Vesey House and the Old Marine Hospital (Harleston Village), Jones' Hotel (Broad Street), the Richard Holloway House and the Lewis Gregory House (Radcliffeborough), the Old Slave Mart (French Quarter), Cabbage Row (Charlestowne) and churches in Ansonborough, Harleston Village, Radcliffeborough and Mazyck Wraggborough. Many of the city's most charming carriage houses once contained slave quarters. The Visitor Center has information about walking tour guides who specialize in African-American history.

87 **128 BULL STREET**: Another graceful Adamesque Bennett mansion, this one by Joseph Bennett, brother of Governor Thomas Bennett, Jr. Note the frieze motif of swags.

88 **129 BULL STREET**: The Ashley River and the Bennett mill were just beyond when Rebecca Drayton, second wife and widow of John Drayton of Drayton Hall, built her home here before 1822.

128 Bull Street

→ Return to Ashley Avenue and turn right.

89 **107 ASHLEY AVENUE**: The planter mansion of Thomas Corbett, who built c. 1829 on land his wife inherited from her father, John Harleston. Note the handsome entrance with an elliptical fan window.

→ Turn around and walk north on Ashley Avenue, crossing Bull street.

90 **113 ASHLEY AVENUE**: Paul Hamilton Hayne, the poet, was born here in 1830. His parents bought the house in 1825 from Thomas Bennett, Sr., who built it c. 1800.

→ At Halsey Street, Cannon Park is on your right.

CANNON PARK: The park is named for Daniel Cannon, who developed saw mills in the area. A cavernous meeting hall—the Thomson Auditorium—was built here in 1899 to accommodate several thousand old soldiers for the United Confederate Veterans reunion. The hall continued to serve as a convention center until 1907 when it became the Charleston Museum. Founded in 1773, the Charleston Museum is the oldest in America. Soon after the Museum moved to Meeting Street, the Auditorium burned, leaving behind only the steps and columns of the portico.

Columns at Cannon Park

→   Turn left onto Halsey Street and continue through the playground to Governor Bennett's house with its Palladian window at the gable end.

91 **69 BARRE STREET**: When built, Gov. Thomas Bennett, Jr.'s home overlooked rice and saw mills and Bennett's mill ponds. This handsome Adamesque mansion was nearly lost to the city in 1976, when the Medical University of South Carolina was about to demolish it. The Preservation Society was granted a delay, and the house was moved across Calhoun Street to its present site. Bennett was a member of the South Carolina Legislature,

69 Barre Street

Governor of South Carolina 1820-1822, and active in running the family lumber and rice mills. Gov. Bennett had two English gardeners, one of whom developed the yellow Noisette rose named Isabella Gray. The Noisette rose was hybridized in Charleston.

→   Turn right (north) on Barre Street and walk to Calhoun Street, then left on Calhoun to 286.

92 **286 CALHOUN STREET**: The Jonathan Lucas, Jr. House, c. 1808, is an important example of Adamesque style in Charleston. It is even greater as a symbol of rice and the Lucas family, which established rice milling as a major industry in America and Europe. It is often remarked that Charlestonians are similar to the Chinese because they both spend their lives eating rice and worshipping their ancestors. (And they speak a foreign language.) The rice king of Charleston, Jonathan Lucas, Sr., built the first water-powered and tide-powered mills in this country on the Santee River. The technical advance in rice milling, which the Lucas family introduced, established rice as the mainstay of the Lowcountry economy. Jonathan Jr. expanded the business, and in 1822, was invited by the British government to develop rice milling techniques

286 Calhoun Street

268 Calhoun Street

there. By the early 1820s he and Governor Thomas Bennett Jr., his chief competitor, milled 70 percent of the rice brought into Charleston for sale. The family influence increased even further when Jonathan III, who remained in Charleston to manage the family's mills in South Carolina, married the daughter of Governor Bennett.

RICE

Rice was considered holy, according to Samuel Gaillard Stoney, who observed that no other food in the American colonies enjoyed the status rice did in Charleston. "Rice in Charleston is more an institution than a cereal," he wrote in 1937. "Until you subscribe to that belief, you will never altogether understand the history of the town...You will find on every proper Charleston dinner table a spoon that is peculiar to the town. Of massive silver, about 15 inches long and broad in proportions, it is laid on the cloth with something of the reverential distinction that surrounds the mace in the House of Commons at Westminster." The first rice in America was planted here, and by 1690 it was being exported. It is believed that African slaves brought with them the art of cultivating rice, and their immunity to malaria made it possible for them to keep the plantations going in the summer while the planters took refuge in the city.

93 **274 CALHOUN STREET**: The Margaret Cannon House was built by Daniel Cannon for his daughter in 1802. Cannon was a lumber man in partnership with Thomas Bennett, Sr.

94 **268 CALHOUN STREET**: Formerly the home of Edward Sebring who built in 1838-1846, on what was then the shore of Bennett's Mill Pond. In 1882, it was sold to Charles Aimar, the druggist, whose family owned it for six generations. According to tradition, Sebring, in a fit of abstinence, sealed up fine wine in the house, for which the Aimar family searched in vain.

Coffee Break: Charlestowne Café and Coffeehouse, 261 Rutledge, occupies space in one of the most-disliked new buildings in Charleston, a structure very much at odds with the historic district architecture and inappropriate even on Calhoun Street, which has been defaced by many other equally mediocre Modernist buildings. However the coffee shop is a most comfortable and inviting place for a coffee break and a light meal. If you walk further east and go right on Bull Street, there is the Bull Street Gourmet, 60 Bull, at the corner of Smith Street. There is a Starbucks at 168 Calhoun Street.

172 Rutledge Avenue

Radcliffeborough

Rhett Butler did not live South of Broad. According to legend, he lived here, in Radcliffeborough. In the early 19th century, wealthy members of the planter and merchant aristocracy began to build impressive mansions in this bucolic suburb, and by the 1820s, Radcliffeborough had become one of the best addresses in Charleston.

Originally much of the land was owned by Thomas Radcliffe, a Scottish merchant, who had it surveyed in 1786. After Radcliffe was lost at sea, development was continued by his wife Lucretia. She was one of Charleston's social elite, known for entertaining elegantly at her mansion on the NW corner of Meeting and George Streets, a few blocks from Radcliffeborough. One 19th century diarist recalled a party there attended by "all the town," referring to the 80 people who sat down to dinner, not the 15,000 who lived in Charleston. The Radcliffe mansion was later demolished, but the elaborate drawing room woodwork was salvaged and installed in the second floor of the Dock Street theater.

Radcliffeborough did not get the national press attention given to Ansonborough, but it went through a similar decline and rebirth. By the late 1960s, it was a slum, its grand antebellum mansions falling down. It began a quiet renaissance in the early 1970s. The city began to promote housing revitalization through low-interest loans and subsidies, and the neighborhood's improving conditions attracted private investors.

→ Begin the walk at Calhoun Street at Pitt Street.

1 214 CALHOUN STREET: (At the NW corner of Pitt Street and Calhoun) Frederick Shaffer, merchant, used 18 slaves to maintain his home, which he built soon after 1834. It is similar to antebellum Beaufort mansions, its piazzas ornamented with fluted Doric colonnades across the front. In the late 19th century it was owned by cotton merchant Isaac Bardin. The house is associated with an unsolved Charleston murder of 1899. Thomas Pinckney, Jr., a young attorney regarded as "a most charming gentleman," was found shot to death in the graveyard of the Bethel Methodist Church. He was said to have been visiting a Miss Bardin on the night of his death.

→ Across the street, (although the south side of Calhoun Street is part of Harleston Village) at the SW corner of Pitt and Calhoun streets, is:

214 Calhoun Street

57 Pitt Street

2 57 PITT STREET: Bethel Methodist Church which has a correct six-column Doric portico, was built, and probably designed, by James M. Curtis. Curtis was a member of a family of master builders who designed and built churches on Edisto, and he built the handsome Italianate/Greek Revival mansion at 20 Charlotte Street.

→ Across from the church, the three-story pale yellow house is:

3 **207 CALHOUN STREET**: A residential character prevailed on this block when Richard Brenan, a wealthy merchant, built his home c. 1817, one of the earliest in the area. It is distinguished by elegant quoins, a classical entrance and delicate Tuscan piazza columns. Brenan also built, c. 1817, on an adjacent lot (56 Pitt Street) "one of the major houses of the area." In 1981, over the protests of preservationists, it was demolished for the parking lot.

→ Walk west on Calhoun street.

4 **221 CALHOUN STREET**: Calhoun Street was once lined with gracious residential buildings. This historically significant single house was recently restored, but insensitively -- its former graceful Palladian window in the third floor gable end was not restored. To see what a difference an accurate restoration would have made, see its twin at 96 Smith Street. Built by Richard Holloway, master carpenter and wealthy entrepreneur, the house is an example of

221 Calhoun Street

19th century free black enterprise. It would be an excellent building for an African-American house museum.

AFRICAN-AMERICAN ENTREPRENEURS

During the antebellum years, there were a number of wealthy free black entrepreneurs, such as Jehu Jones, who ran a fashionable hotel on Broad Street, considered the city's best in 1820. According to the News and Courier, there were close to 5,000 free persons of color in 1860 and of these, some 353 paid real estate taxes and 190 were slave holders. Nine free blacks had real estate holdings of $10,000 or more, including Jones with $40,000. Richard Holloway, a master carpenter, owned some twenty houses by 1842, most of them in this area. Holloway built 221 Calhoun Street and its twin at 96 Smith Street (around the corner) in the early 19th century. 94 Smith Street, built for Morris Brown, founder of the African Methodist Episcopal Church in Charleston, may have been built by Holloway. In 1977, the BAR denied an application to demolish this house. Holloway and Jones were among the early members of the Brown Fellowship Society, established in 1790 by members of St. Philip's Episcopal Church. (It was one of the oldest free black associations in

America, restricted to fifty members, all "free brown men.") A benevolent society, it provided support for needy orphans and adults.

→ Directly across the street is:

5 **222 CALHOUN STREET**: Old
Bethel Methodist, 1797, is the
second oldest church building in
the city. In 1880, the building was
given to the black members of the
church and rolled across the street
on logs to its present location. Its
dignified portico has four fluted
columns with modified Tower-of-
the Winds capitals.

222 Cahoun Street

ARCHITECTS' DETOUR: Continue
walking west to Smith Street and go
left to 89 Smith Street. The Doric por-
tico was probably built in the late 1830's and is, according to Dr. Robert
Russell, "one of the purest examples of Greek Revival applied to a dwelling
in Charleston." He believes this portico, as well as 6 Thomas Street, may have
been designed by Robert Mills. Note the tripartite windows which appear
in both houses as well as in Ainsley Hall House in Columbia, designed by
Mills in 1823.

89 Smith Street

↪ Return to Pitt Street and turn left.

PITT STREET: In the 1960's, slum conditions threatened the survival of this block. The finest antebellum home—#83, listed as notable in a 1944 survey of the city's architecture— was, in fact, demolished for a parking lot. However, by 1978, nine houses were being restored. One of them had been abandoned for years and was occupied by rats. The new owner, using forty pounds of poison, collected two trash cans full of dead rats.

6 **71 PITT STREET**: Among the notable antebellum Mid-century Eclectic homes restored in the 1970's. Note the trefoil cluster columns of the entrance and large Greek revival piazza.

7 **72 PITT STREET**: The John Fitzmorris house was built before 1852 with Greek Doric columns on the piazza and a handsome Palladian window in the gable end. For many years there was a grocery store on the first floor. Note the round plaque, the Carolopolis Award.

73 Pitt Street   79 Pitt Street

8 **73 PITT STREET**: A restored single house, having an ornate cornice with Italianate filigree brackets, a Palladian window in the gable end, and fluted Doric columns on the piazza. The house dates to c. 1840, with alterations c. 1870.

9 **79 PITT STREET**: Dates to 1890, with Italianate styling—note the elaborate parapet with decorative brackets and the gracious entrance with sidelights, large console brackets, paneled pilasters, and an oval transom light.

THE CAROLOPOLIS AWARD

The Carolopolis Award is presented annually by the Preservation Society of Charleston for notable preservation efforts. The awards have been presented since 1959 to recognize those who uphold the standards of the

City of Charleston seal, "She cares for her buildings, manners and laws." The number of the small round plaques on houses in Radcliffeborough is a sign of the restoration progress made here.

10   **82 PITT STREET**: Notable for its fine brickwork, this Greek Revival home was built by Joseph and Septimus Sanders, bricklayers, c. 1842. It stands in what was formerly the garden of #84.

11   **84 PITT STREET**: A planter from Christ Church parish built his large town home, c. 1827, with a high brick basement, Doric columns on the piazza and a stately street entrance with Greek Revival pilasters. Coming's Creek once ran through this site.

→   Walk left onto Vanderhorst Street.

VANDERHORST STREET (pronounced Van Dross in Charleston) is named for Arnoldus Vanderhorst, the second Intendant (mayor) of Charleston.

84 Pitt Street

12   **55, 57, 59 VANDERHORST STREET**: Almost identical Italianate Victorian houses with bay windows are new construction (1987). A student high rise dormitory was proposed for the site, but was opposed by the next door neighbors who eventually bought the lot and built the houses that would look pleasant from their point of view. Randolph Martz, the architect, said that some interior amenities were sacrificed for the exterior embellish-

55 and 57 Vanderhorst Street

ments. The houses, built one at a time because of the lack of capital, sold quickly for modest prices. The impact on the streetscape, and the future of the neighborhood, of the original dormitory high rise proposal is not difficult to imagine.

64 Vanderhorst Street

13 **64 VANDERHORST STREET**: (NW corner at Thomas Street) John Bickley, who was a lumber factor and owned a rice plantation, built his town home c. 1815. The piazzas on three sides reflect the rural quality of the site which was near Coming's Creek. Bickley's gardens were extensive and elaborate. Note the beautiful Adamesque doorway with an elliptical arched transom and sidelights framed by engaged Tuscan columns. The graceful segmental arches of the piazza with acanthus leaves applied over each column also appear on the house at 13 Thomas and on the piazza of the Gov. Thomas Bennett, Jr. mansion at 69 Barre Street.

→ To the left is:

14 **66 VANDERHORST STREET**: A Victorian fantasy, dating to c. 1890, with an ornate gable, tower and an Eastlakian piazza.

→ Return to Thomas Street.

15 **6 THOMAS STREET**: (At the NE corner) The house dates to 1832, built by a planter and cotton factor. Robert Mills may have designed it, according to architect Randolph Martz, who cites similar floor plans to other Mills buildings, the tripartite windows, the continuous sills, the three arched openings across the front (similar to the First

6 Thomas Street

5 Thomas Street

Baptist Church) and the twin octagonal rooms on the main floor. In 1856, it became the home of Robert Barnwell Rhett, state legislator, Attorney General, Congressman and U. S. Senator. He advocated states' rights and was known as the "Father of Secession." The handsome iron fence, facing Vanderhorst, has corn and anthemion finials. The home is said to have two ghosts—a couple who move furniture and dance at night.

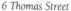 **5 THOMAS STREET**: Another 1890's Queen Anne with then fashionable German siding, a romantic tower at the SE corner, Eastlakian spindle work on the piazza, arched entrance and oculus windows.

17 **12 THOMAS STREET**: (SE corner at Warren Street) James Legare, a wealthy planter, built this house soon after 1836 in the Greek Revival style. One of the larger homes of the area, it was vandalized in the 1970's, and the owner wanted to demolish it and build multi-family townhouse units, which would have seriously diminished the character of this antebellum streetscape.

18 **13 THOMAS STREET**: (SW corner) Benjamin Faneuil Dunkin, chancellor of the Equity Court of Appeals, bought the entire block bounded by Thomas, Warren, Smith and Vanderhorst in 1823. Dunkin, who lived in a larger house at 89 Warren, apparently built this house as an investment, 1823-1828. It was restored in 1973. Note the delicate acanthus leaves applied over each column, the graceful segmental arches of the piazza and the Adamesque entrance.

19 **14 THOMAS STREET**: St. Mark's Episcopal Church was built 1876 to the designs of Louis J. Barbot. It is a simpler version of the Greek Revival temple which Barbot and his partner John Seyle designed earlier on Spring Street (now the Karpeles Manuscript Museum). It has served black Episcopalians for more than a century. The parish was organized in

1865, and according to Stockton, St. Mark's had the second largest membership of any church in the Diocese of South Carolina in 1888. The central stained glass window on the north side is attributed to Tiffany.

20 **15 THOMAS STREET**: Similar to a house built at 86 Warren. Both homes, built by brothers-in-law from Massachusetts, display features traditional to New England, such as the shiplap board facing, an Ionic corner pilaster, the broad cornice and recessed entrance.

→ Continue along Thomas to Radcliffe Street.

St. Marks Episcopal Church

RADCLIFFE STREET is named for Thomas Radcliffe, the Scottish merchant who once owned most of the land. Many of the antebellum homes on the street were built in the Mid-century Eclectic style and include Greek Revival and Italianate detailing. It is surprising to see so many modest homes in this fashionable antebellum neighborhood. According to Russell, the Radcliffe family "cashed out" about 1840 by re-platting Radcliffeborough with smaller lots priced to sell quickly.

To the right, you can see the domed octagonal belfry of the Central Baptist Church. Built in 1891, designed by John P. Hutchinson, a black architect, it is one of the first churches to have been founded by and built solely for the African-American community in

Central Baptist Church and St. Patrick's

Charleston. In the distance, St. Patrick's Roman Catholic Church of 1886 by Patrick Charles Keeley.

Coffee Break: Charles' Grocery, to the right, at the NW corner of Jasper and Radcliffe Streets.

21 **57 RADCLIFFE STREET**: (SW corner of Radcliffe and Thomas Streets) Known as the "West Indian" house because of the roof pitch and the elevated main floor, this is one of the oldest houses (c. 1816) in the neighborhood. There used to be a piazza which extended out over the sidewalk.

→ Walk to the left along Radcliffe Street.

22 **76 RADCLIFFE STREET**: On a street where so many fine old 19th century houses have been defaced by inappropriate changes, it is a pleasure to see a new house which is an asset. It was designed in 1989 by Randolph Martz, a local architect who is admired for his creativity in designing new buildings that fit gracefully into the historic architectural fabric. Other works by Martz are at 7 Savage Street, 116 Coming Street, at 55-59 Vanderhorst Street, 23 Elliott and 71 King.

At the SE corner of Smith and Radcliffe Streets, a surviving corner grocery store building. Over 85 such store buildings survive in the city, a reminder of pre-supermarket days.

23 **78 RADCLIFFE STREET**: (Northeast corner at Smith Street) This handsome frame house with a semi-octagonal bay, when built between 1852-1872, was on a very large lot bordering a pond to the west. It was the home of S. C. Congressman Thomas Miller, who had lived much of his life as a white man, but during Reconstruction, decided he could best serve the black community as an African-American. His epitaph in Magnolia Cemetery reads "It was not that he loved the white man less, but that the black man needed him more."

→ Continue on Radcliffe Street to Rutledge Avenue.

Coffee Break: Three excellent options for lunch are Hominy Grill, 207 Rutledge (Lowcountry cuisine), Lana, 210 Rutledge (a Mediterranean menu) and Five Loaves, 43 Cannon Street (soups, sandwiches).

24 **174 RUTLEDGE AVENUE**: (NE corner of Radcliffe) This exceedingly long house was probably built as a single house and transformed into an asymmetrical Queen Anne with curves, flourishes, a turret and a semi-octagonal wing.

25 **179 RUTLEDGE AVENUE**: (Across the street) One of Charleston's finest Victorians. Begun in 1876 by a wholesale hat merchant, the mansion was completed by George Wagener, the grocery wholesaler and phosphate industrialist. Architects Abrahams and Seyle gracefully adapted the Victorian fashion to Charleston traditions.

→ Walk to the left (south) on Rutledge Avenue. Immediately on your left you will see:

26 **172 RUTLEDGE AVENUE:** This extraordinary Neoclassical villa was built c. 1816 by Patrick Duncan who made his fortune as a tallow and candle maker. During the Civil War, it was the home of George Trenholm, said to be the model for Rhett Butler in *Gone with the Wind*. Trenholm, known as a courageous risk taker, was the Treasurer of the Confederacy and his shipping firm was the largest blocade runner of the war. In 1909, the villa became Ashley Hall, a private school for girls, whose most famous alumnae is Barbara Bush.

172 Rutledge Avenue

A TANTALIZING ARCHITECTURAL MYSTERY

Some of the finest architecture in Charleston is by architects of considerable sophistication whose names have been lost in the passing of the years. Who designed the Patrick Duncan house? Russell considers it "one of the greatest Neoclassical villas in America." The accuracy of the Neoclassical reference and the spatial complexity of the plan are similar to work being done in New York at the time (c. 1816), but no one known to be in Charleston was designing anything similar. The design has been attributed to William Jay, an architect from Bath who lived briefly in Charleston and practiced in Savannah. Jay's work featured some of the details here, such as the impressive porticos, curved lines and ornamental iron balconies.

ARCHITECTS' DETOUR: Walk west on Doughty Street to Ashley Avenue, then right to 178 Ashley, where there is a magnificant Greek Revival mansion built by a wealthy planter, John Hume Lucas in 1850. The columns of the front portico and the giant order columns of the piazza have the popular Tower-of-the-Winds Corinthian capitals. The Palladian majesty of this mansion is missed by most visitors as this once fashionable area has been fractured by poorly designed new construction.

→ Walk back to Radcliffe Street. Turn right and right again onto Smith Street. Continue along Smith Street until you come to Warren Street.

27 **89 WARREN STREET**: (SE corner at Smith) Chancellor Dunkin House, 1823-29, with octagonal bays and long piazzas, originally overlooking Coming's Creek. Benjamin Faneuil Dunkin, a Chief Justice of the South Carolina Supreme Court, moved here in the early 19th century from Boston and was a member of the prominent Faneuil family.

28 **86 WARREN STREET**: (First house on the left) New Englander Lawrence Edmonston, a brother-in-law of the builder of 15 Thomas (which is next door), built his home in much the same New England mode. The Charleston double piazza has a gracious colonnade of fluted Ionic columns. Clearly, a dedicated gardener lives here now.

89 Warren Street

64 Warren Street

→ Continue along Warren, crossing Thomas Street.

29 **73 WARREN STREET**: Handsome Bracketed-style Victorian with paired brackets decorating the cornice and gable, a bracketed hood at the entrance and arched windows in the gable end.

30 **67 WARREN STREET**: (The large pink house) The most fanciful and exuberant house on the block, a Queen Anne Victorian with fashionable German siding. Note the romantic octagonal tower with a curved roof, a profusion of diamond-shaped ornaments, fancy gable and Eastlakian spindlework on the piazzas. The house is a side-hall plan house (a variant of the Charleston single house) with the western double piazza enclosed.

31 **64 WARREN STREET**: The earliest home on the block, built in 1816 when the building lots were huge and this neighborhood was Charleston's chic address. Plantation-style houses were popular before the area became densely populated.

32 **60-52 WARREN STREET**: These five single houses look as if they might well have been built about the same time. Actually, #60 was built c. 1840, over a hundred and fifty years before #56 and #54 (1990). Charleston's unique single house style has endured because it is so eminently suited to the climate and narrow city lots. Its prevalence carries the city's sense of place and rhythm of the streets. Single house background buildings such as these that relate to each other with side piazzas and classical colonnades form the fabric of the city.

→ Walk right onto Coming Street.

33 **135 COMING STREET**: (SW corner Warren and Coming Streets) Built c. 1830 by William Wightman, a jeweler, who bought the west side of Coming Street between Warren and Vanderhorst. Dr. Maynard E. Carrere, who practiced acupuncture successfully and was a surgeon at the Confederate Hospital, moved here in 1863. In 1897, this became the home of Mayor J. Adger Smyth. The neighborhood declined in the 20th century and in 1972, preservationists persuaded the city not to demolish this important home.

34 **126 COMING STREET**: The Cathedral of St. Luke and St. Paul is the largest Episcopal church building in South Carolina. It was designed and built by James and John Gordon who also did the Second Presbyterian Church on Meeting Street. St. Paul's, 1811-1816, was known as the "Planters Church", built to be convenient for wealthy planters settling into the fashionable suburbs.

126 Coming Street

→ Continue south on Coming Street, crossing Vanderhorst.

35 **123 COMING STREET**: (Southwest corner at Vanderhorst) A Greek Revival single house, built by Jacob Newton Cardozo, a prominent Jewish journalist, with a handsome entrance on the second floor, barely visible from the street. A tripartite window on the front gable has a surround of fluted molding with cornerblocks. Three garret dormers on the south slope of the roof have fluted pilasters, fine details on a house that was originally built as a rental.

36 **116 COMING STREET**: In 1995, Randolph Martz designed the classical facade for a house that was oddly split, with two windows on one side and a half porch on the other.

37 **110 COMING STREET**: (The pale beige house with quoins) An Early Classical Revival style single house of 1820-1840. It was built as part of a trio of nearly identical large homes which were rated as notable in Charleston's 1944 architectural survey. Unfortunately #102 and #106 did not survive.

38 **107 COMING STREET**: (NW corner at Duncan) An 1851 Greek Revival home, which, according to legend, was the home of a "free person of color" whose slaves lived in the small house in back which fronts on Duncan Street.

→   Walk to the right onto Duncan Street.

DUNCAN STREET is a street in transition, with restorations in progress. It was named for John Duncan, a merchant, who in 1806 acquired the area bounded by Pitt, Vanderhorst, Coming and Calhoun Streets, and had it platted as Duncan's Square.

2 Duncan Street

39 **2 DUNCAN STREET**: Believed to be the kitchen house of 107 Coming. Built before 1830 and once a Sweet Shop, it was minimally restored in 1988.

40 **2 DESPORTES COURT**: The recently restored birthplace of Lewis Gregory is a museum of the National Spiritual Assembly of the United States and Canada. Gregory, an AfricanAmerican who grew up here, was one of the original members of Baha'i, an international movement advocating the brotherhood of man. This was the area where many free blacks built their homes. The city of Charleston has designated the house a museum and paved what had been a sandy alley.

41 **18 DUNCAN STREET:** This recently restored single house would have disappeared long ago had it not been for Mrs. Ransom Hooker, who rescued it in 1968. Mrs. Hooker had chaired the housing committee of the Women's City Club of New York, and when she moved to Charleston, she continued her civic activism by restoring four houses here that had become wrecks. She told the *News and Courier* she had bought them against everyone's advice and was making six to nine percent on her investment. Thanks to Mrs. Hooker, Duncan Street today continues to contribute to the historicity of the area. When #20 collapsed recently, preservationists insisted upon a reconstruction.

Coffee Break: Starbucks is two blocks east, at 168 Calhoun Street. Charlestowne Café and Coffeehouse in the Francis Marion Hotel at King and Calhoun is three blocks to the east. Kudu Coffee House, 4 Vanderhorst Street, is open daily, has a pleasant courtyard where you can also have light meals.

THE LOWCOUNTRY

Litchfield plantaion

Introduction by Robert Russell
Addlestone Professor of Architectural History
College of Charleston

•

Diana of the Chase, Anna Hyatt Huntington, 1922, left

The exceptionally fine plaster ceiling at Drayton Hall, a Historic Site of the National Trust for Historic Preservation.

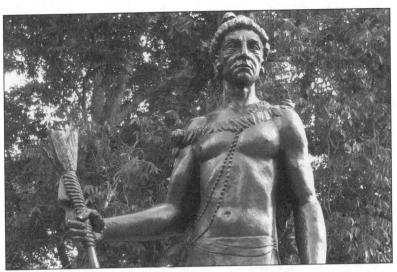

Cassique of the Kiawah, 1670. The Kiawah tribe was friendly to the settlers and led them to their first site on Charles Town Point. Sculpture by William Hirsch, 1971

INTRODUCTION TO THE LOWCOUNTRY

by Robert Russell, Addlestone Professor of Architectural History, Program in Historic Preservation, College of Charleston

PLANTATIONS

Lowcountry South Carolina was, to a remarkable extent, a plantation culture. Yet it was not only a plantation culture, for all the plantations remained in a kind of fixed orbit around a center, which was Charleston. The attraction between this center and its edges was economic, social, familial, and strong enough to resist separation. This centripetal pull of Charleston is the chief difference between South Carolina plantation life and that of, say, Virginia, and it explains many things about country life in the Lowcountry.

The huge amounts of land that were available to colonists, and the early encouragement of slave owning by the colonial government, virtually guaranteed that fabulous fortunes were made, first in cattle, and almost immediately afterward in rice, which came to be called Carolina gold. Rice was being cultivated already in the 1680s. In 1740 Eliza Lucas Pinckney started to experiment with indigo and solved most of the problems with its production within a few years, so that by the 1750s Carolina plantation owners were making fortunes from this crop as well, which

Interior of St. James Santee chapel of ease

could be grown on land that was unsuitable for rice cultivation. Thus almost all available land could be put to profitable use.

This profitable country was, however, unhealthy for its European inhabitants, and it soon became standard practice for plantation families to come to Charleston during the feverish months of the summer. They came back to town again during the social season in January and February, and so it made sense to keep houses in both the town and the country. This is one of the reasons most Carolina plantation houses were relatively modest. Unlike the independent fiefdoms which were Virginia plantations, Carolina planters remained closely linked, by bonds of blood and status, to the culture of Charleston. Even when there was a closer town, such as Georgetown, or — to a lesser extent — Beaufort, Charleston always remained "town" in the minds of the planter class.

But getting to town was not always an easy thing, so a social and political structure was created that aided the country life of the planters. By the middle of the eighteenth century, 'chapels of ease' were being constructed to supplement the parish churches which had been erected starting in 1706 when Anglicanism was established as the church in Carolina. The parishes were enormous, much too large for planters in the far reaches of them to contemplate travelling to the parish church on a Sunday. The chapels of ease were built for the ease of the planters, who could be served closer to home by travelling clergymen.

The plantations which once lined the waterways draining the Lowcountry, from the Pee Dee in the north to the Savannah in the south, can be better understood rather as outposts of Charleston society than as self-sufficient frontier settlements.

Few places in North America give such a vivid picture of the spectacular speed with which the colonists conquered the wilderness and set about imitating the cultural aspirations of the old country as the sites of the early English settlements on the west bank of the Ashley river. Just

The gardens at Middleton Place

a few minutes outside of Charleston, Charles Towne Landing State Historic Site marks the site of the first permanent European settlement in the Carolinas. A full scale replica of a 17th century trading ship, the Adventure, is under construction, scheduled to be completed sometime in 2007, near where the original settlers landed at Old Towne Creek in April of 1670. The palisade walls have be recreated at the original site, near a crop garden showing the plants that were under cultivation. In the near future, buildings from the first settlement will be recreated, showing what Charles Towne looked like c. 1675. There are several archeological sites being excavated.

A few miles further out the Ashley River Road stands Old St. Andrew's parish church. One of the ten original parishes established in 1706, the church dates, in its nave portion, to that year. It was expanded with a pair of transepts and a new chancel in 1723. But even the oldest part of the building shows how far the colonists had advanced a bare generation after they had arrived.

Another couple of miles along the road, and you come to Drayton Hall, a unique and justly famous plantation house. 'John Drayton's palace,' as it was called by neighbors, is scarcely a typical Lowcountry plantation. Started in 1738, it represents the farthest reach of the whiggish Carolina plantation aristocracy in their desire to bring the order and taste of the mother country to the new world.

The gardens of Middleton Place, Henry Middleton's plantation a few miles further up the River Road, represent the same striving to surpass the source, only here it is landscape, rather than architecture. But already by the middle of the eighteenth century (the gardens were begun c.1741) the source seems not to have been an English one, but instead Henry Middleton's brother William's plantation, Crowfield, in Goose Creek, and its famous gardens of the 1730s and '40s, now, alas, lost.

The surviving, and recently restored, parish church of St. James', Goose Creek demonstrates yet again how concerned the Carolina colonists were to replicate the highest style examples they knew. This c.1708 church uses, it is true, a distinctly old fashioned model, but it does a spectacular job in creating architectural elegance on the edge of the new world.

All in all, there are few journeys which can be undertaken that give, in as compact a space as the few miles between Charleston and Summerville, such a vivid picture of how important it was for Carolina settlers to recreate — as quickly as possible — the grandeur and elegance and tradition of the world they had left behind. It is an added treat that the Ashley River Road provides one of the most scenic drives in the Lowcountry.

THE NORTHERN RIVERS AND GEORGETOWN

The numerous rivers to the north of Charleston offered many opportunities to establish substantial plantations to those who were willing to put forth the effort. So many of the Huguenot families that arrived in South Carolina beginning in the 1680s settled in this region that it developed a distinctly Gallic flavor. The major parish of the area was named for St. Thomas and St. Denis (the latter the patron saint of France), and so many Huguenots settled along the Santee river that it came to be known as French Santee. Hampton plantation, for example, was first built c.1735 by a Huguenot named Serré. Serré's daughter married Daniel Huger (U-gee) Horry (O-ree), and after she died he

Interior of Hampton Plantation

married Harriott Pinckney, daughter of Eliza Lucas Pinckney, of indigo fame. Thus the house passed into the Pinckney family, and thus you have a taste of Lowcountry genealogy.

Farther north, lands were being granted in the Winyah area, just south of present-day Georgetown, starting as early as 1705. A new Anglican parish, St. George Winyah, was established in 1722 to serve a settlement which seems to have been founded only a couple of years before. In 1729 Georgetown was platted and lots were put up for sale. The new town was intended to be a center for trade and, when necessary, defense, and a place for the building of churches and a school, although these institutions were slow to get started. For instance, while the new parish had been created in 1722, it was not until 1736 that a subscription to build a church was undertaken, and it was not until 1745 that the cornerstone of the building was actually laid. And this was the first permanent public building in the new settlement.

The explanation for this slowness can be found in the fact that, for Georgetonians, the streets laid out in a grid facing the bay were primarily indicative of a trading center and gathering place, more or less located where the rivers of the region emptied into Winyah Bay. For them, 'town' meant Charleston, not Georgetown. This made perfect sense, since a good many of the first buyers of the lots in the new town were Charlestonians who seemed to have looked upon this whole venture as a speculative enterprise. Certainly Georgetown was never intended to replace Charleston as either a trading or a cultural center. Rather, its inhabitants looked to the flourishing capital for ideas and institutions. The leading men of the town read the Charleston newspaper, and the Winyah Indigo Society was formed in 1755 as the local version of the Charleston

Georgetown commercial building on Front Street, 1842

Library Society, which made it the chief intellectual effort of the northern plantation region.

The architecture of the town was, not surprisingly, strongly influenced by Charleston, although the famous Charleston single house did not migrate to Georgetown. Robert Mills, the native Charlestonian and South Carolina's most famous architect, designed the Georgetown Courthouse in 1822 while he was employed as the State architect and engineer. One of sixteen county courthouses that Mills designed in the decade of the 1820s while he was employed by the state, the Georgetown Courthouse is one of the handsomest and most interesting of these buildings to survive. The channeled masonry base of the portico creates a screen for the double stairway leading to the courtroom located on the upper floor. It is unclear whether this feature was original to the Mills building, or if it was a modification of the early 1850s by George Walker, another Charleston architect; either way it creates a powerful and memorable image.

Edward B. White, Charleston's most active and important architect of the 1840s, was responsible for the handsomely reticent Winyah Indigo Society Hall of 1857. It is clear that Charleston architects were only too willing to work in Georgetown, and that the local planter aristocracy sought architects from 'town' when important structures were desired.

It was not until a new mercantile middle class came to Georgetown from New England in the middle of the eighteenth century that a potential alternative to the dominance of Charleston became available. And it was not until the descendents of this class actually came to power after 1876 that the potential alternative became an actual one.

One last Yankee invasion is recognizable in the early twentieth century. Bernard Baruch, though a native South Carolinian, led the way soon after the turn of the century, after he had made a fortune in the stock market. By 1905 he had bought up all of the plantations on the Waccamaw Neck, to the east of Georgetown, and started calling his

The live oak alley at Brookgreen Gardens

accumulated 17,000 acres the Hobcaw Barony, though it was substantially more extensive than the original colonial barony of that name had been. In 1930 Archer Huntington and his sculptress wife Anna Hyatt Huntington bought several plantations north of the Hobcaw Barony and put them together with the name of Brookgreen. Thus began one of the most fascinating and memorable spots on the entire East coast.

What began as simply a winter retreat fronting on the Atlantic, has turned into the most extensive outdoor collection of American figurative sculpture in the world. As the Huntingtons elaborated their gardens (presently comprising 300 acres with over 2000 native and adapted species), Mrs. Huntington began to use the outdoor 'rooms' of the garden as display areas for her sculpture and for that of other sculptors whose work she admired. Over 500 works, by hundreds of sculptors, are displayed at Brookgreen Gardens, and serve as a salutary reminder of the powerful tradition of figurative sculpture which has persisted in this country. This one site would be more than enough of a reason to make the trip up the coast from Charleston.

Flying Wild Geese, Marshall Fredericks, 1967

Pegasus, Laura Gardin Fraser, 1946 - 51

SAVANNAH

"Savannah is a lovely city, not made so by architectural beauty, for there are very few fine houses here. What constitutes its beauty is the manner in which the city is laid out." So wrote Sara Hathaway of New York, when she visited Georgia in 1833. She was right. It is no exaggeration to say that old Savannah is the most beautifully laid-out town in America.

Comparisons between Charleston and Savannah are inevitable. Barely 100 miles apart, they are the two great cities of the Carolina and Georgia Lowcountry. Charleston was over fifty years old and was already a city of great wealth when Savannah was founded. Charleston's wealth was based on rice and indigo and slaves. Savannah was slow to develop and remained little more than a dreary and dirty frontier village during the 18th century. Thirty five families had arrived in the new colony in the winter of 1733, and by 1794 the total population was not above 2,500 souls. However, one of those souls was Eli Whitney, a recently arrived New Englander, Yale graduate and the inventor (in 1793) of the mechanical cotton gin. This one machine revolutionized the American cotton industry and marks the beginning of the period of Savannah's greatest prosperity, a prosperity based on cotton and slaves.

No one foresaw cotton in the early 1730s when plans for settling the new colony were being formulated in England. Georgia was to be a philanthropic enterprise, with more than a few utopian overtones. General James Oglethorpe was the driving force behind the granting, by King George II, of the lands south of the Savannah river to 21 trustees for 21 years. Oglethorpe was a reformer, appalled by the conditions in English prisons, and felt that somehow a new place for imprisoned debtors and the poor in general to go would be an improvement on the current state of social affairs in England.

Oglethorpe managed the settlement of the Georgia colony as if it were a military campaign, and expected the transplanted urban poor who made up the bulk of the first settlers to accommodate themselves to a spartan and rigid regimen. Each family was granted a town lot, a five-acre garden lot at the edge of town, and forty-five acres to farm in the country. This land could not be sold or mortgaged, and could only be passed on to a son. Slaves and rum were prohibited, and all settlers were required to plant hundreds of mulberry trees in order to feed the silkworms that were to be — according to Oglethorpe — Georgia's road to prosperity.

These initial regulations nearly wrecked the colony. By the time that Oglethorpe left Georgia to return to England in 1743 it was reported that there were more houses than people in Savannah. Of the six thousand or so colonists who had arrived in Georgia up to this point, no more than a thousand remained. The rest had moved on to colonies where it was easier to make a go of things.

Despite all the problems experienced in the early days of the Georgia colony, Oglethorpe left one enduring legacy: the plan of Savannah. Based on the repeatable unit of the ward,

Oglethorpe's plan for Savannah

the Oglethorpe plan was the guide for Savannah's expansion from its founding in 1733 until the eve of the Civil War. By 1856 the original four wards had expanded to twenty four. The late nineteenth-century enlargement of the city followed a completely different pattern, handsome enough in its own way, but very different from the first hundred and twenty years of the city's growth.

The remarkable similarity between a plan for an ideal city in Pietro Cattaneo's mid-sixteenth-century treatise on architecture (*I quattro primi libri di architecttura, 1554)* and Oglethorpe's design of a Savannah ward has led most scholars to posit a direct influence. But even if this is so, Oglethorpe actually put the plan on the ground as the basis for a city, something no one had ever done before.

The Savannah ward is centered on a square. These are stunningly beautiful, shady green park-like places now, but for a long time they were little more than barren spaces, dusty in dry weather and muddy in wet. Fronting onto the square to the east and west are four large 'trust' lots, intended for public buildings of some significance: churches, the courthouse, etc. To the north and south were four pairs of blocks intended for residential lots. Each of these blocks was divided into five lots. A pair of blocks thus had ten lots, and was named a 'tything.' The two blocks of a tything were separated from one another by an alley, and the tythings were separated by streets: wide ones cutting through the center of the ward, and narrower ones dividing the tythings from the trust lots. Wide streets separated each ward from the others around it.

Contemporary urbanists have nothing but praise for the way that this arrangement allows a gradation of social and economic hierarchy of building sites, all the way from the big, public uses of the trust lots, to the most desirable (and expensive) corner lots fronting on the square itself, to the humble, back-alley tenements. Oglethorpe, with his preoccupation with social equality, clearly did not intend this to be, but it is the way that things worked out, and it has worked well.

Sara Hathaway was a little harsh in her judgment on Savannah architecture. There are some very fine specimens indeed, though there were still a lot of humble, frame buildings standing when she visited the city in the 1830s. Many of those have been replaced by typical Savannah brick blocks of row houses in the antebellum years. These structures, three or four stories high and sometimes stretching for an entire block, provide solid and handsome walls for the outdoor 'rooms' of the squares.

Since there were not enough big public buildings to fill all the trust lots of the wards, the grandest houses in town began to be built on these sites in the early years of the nineteenth century. A number of these were designed by William Jay, an extremely talented, if erratic, young English architect who arrived in this country in the 1817 and attempted to carve out a niche for himself in both Savannah and Charleston. He was unsuccessful and returned to England in 1822, leaving behind a still under-appreciated legacy of Regency mansions.

Unlilke Charleston, Savannah had the misfortune of not developing an adequate supply of local architectural talent. Most of the identified designers working in Savannah came there from somewhere else, generally New England or the Middle Atlantic states. After Jay, the most significant of these was Irish-born Charles B. Cluskey in the 1840s and the New Yorker John Norris in the 1850s.

The fountain in Forsyth Park, Savannah

Also unlike Charleston, Savannah did not simply step out of time in the later nineteenth century. With the arrival in the city of the first two horse-drawn streetcars in 1869, Savannah continued to grow to the south, away from the river and the older parts of town. This area, the Victorian District, extends to Victory Drive, and contains a great deal of charming building. It also has Forsyth Park, one of the earliest of the grand urban public parks which began to appear in American cities around the middle of the century and of which New York's Central Park is the most famous.

Old Savannah has fared badly through much of the twentieth century. A number of the old squares have been butchered, not to say destroyed, by aborted highway building schemes, parking structures and other unsympathetic architectural interventions. The old city market hall in Ellis Square, for example, was demolished to make way for a concrete parking deck. Scarcely a single one of the twenty four wards does not have some jarring mediocre modernist insertion in its fabric.

As the twenty-first century dawns, Savannah is much more aware of what it has and what it has lost. There is serious talk of demolishing the Ellis Square parking garage and rebuilding the square. It looks like Savannah will have a future as well as a past.

King Tisdell cottage, 514 East Huntingdon Street, Savannah. A Museum of Lowcountry African American culture.

BEAUFORT

In 1844 the British geologist Sir Charles Lyell visited Beaufort and described it as "a picturesque town composed of an assemblage of villas shaded by a verandah surrounded by...live oaks and orange trees..." He was describing the grand houses that had been erected in the town starting in the 1780s and '90s as a result of the prosperity brought by the shipbuilding industry and the introduction of cotton cultivation to the sea islands, but his description would apply just as well to the houses which were to be built in the town in the following decade to show off the prewar cotton wealth which flowed into Beaufort in particular abundance during the 1850s.

Beaufort was the site of the first European landing in the Carolinas, although the settlers did not stay. There was an abortive Scottish settlement in the area in the 1680s, but the present town dates from 1711. This still makes it the second oldest town in South Carolina. Located on Port Royal island, amidst numerous other islands and waterways, Beaufort seems destined to have remained small.

Like Georgetown to the north, Beaufort was the local shipping point for a coastal plantation society devoted initially to rice growing and indigo production. Unlike Georgetown, Beaufort also came to be the center of the sea island cotton industry. Add to rice and cotton the shipbuilding industry that developed here after the Revolution, and you have a very wealthy town indeed.

But in its early days, Beaufort was a tiny and unimpressive place. In 1733 a visitor reported that "the houses are all of timber and very few have glass windows or brick chimneys." Soon after this, the colonists began to build with tabby, a sort of Lowcountry concrete made of crushed oyster shells, lime, sand and water, all shoveled into wooden frames to hold it until it set.

While there are a few buildings in Beaufort entirely built of tabby, the usual manner of construction was to make a high basement of the material, and then build a frame or brick house on top of that. For such a small town, Beaufort has a remarkable collection of surviving houses that embody, for many people, the storyland ideal of antebellum southern plantation gentility. Certainly Hollywood seems to think so, for Beaufort houses appear frequently in the movies.

The architectural characteristics of these sea island mansions are similar to the sort of houses that are often called 'plantation houses' in Charleston. They are raised on a high basement, generally with two stories above, the stories ringed with porches on the front and sides. The biggest difference between Charleston and Beaufort houses can be found in the amount of space around the latter. Lyell's characterization of them as 'villas' is apt: Beaufort remained in many ways an antebellum suburb of both Charleston and Savannah, tied to both cities by family links and trading connections and, after 1817, by steamship routes.

It still provides a beautiful and elegant place to go to see grand houses in a decidedly un-urban setting, and the detour to Beaufort from the Charleston — Savannah road is a memorable one.

Beaufort style house

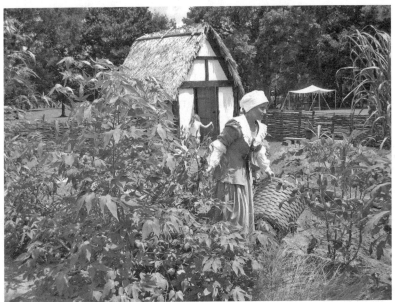

The Crop Garden at Charles Towne Landing, showing the crops the settlers depended upon.

EARLY CHARLESTON AND THE ASHLEY RIVER PLANTATIONS

Rice and indigo grown on Lowcountry plantations made Charleston, by 1740, the wealthiest colony of the New World. No visit to Charleston is complete until you visit the site of the first settlement in 1670 and the plantations along the Ashley, from which much of Charleston's wealth was generated.

At Charles Towne Landing, you will gather a sense of how quickly the colony prospered. In a relatively short time, the colonists moved from the primitive huts reconstructed here, into mansions unsurpassed in grandeur anywhere in the colonies. Drayton Hall, for example, begun in 1738, with its elaborate interiors, was the first mansion in America with a Palladian portico. Middleton Place presents a view of a major rice plantation with the earliest landscaped garden in America. Magnolia Plantation, a Drayton family home, is the oldest major public garden in America and one of the most beautiful in the world. This side trip also includes two of South Carolina's oldest churches.

→ Take US 17 South over the Ashley River Bridge, going right onto SC 61 almost immediately, leading to SC 171. Charles Towne Landing will be on your right.

CHARLES TOWNE LANDING: The ship Carolina arrived here in 1670 with about 100 settlers, establishing Charleston Charles Towne Point, the first permanent English settlement in South Carolina. Here you can see the original site of Charleston splendidly spruced up in a new park on the original site, opened in August of 2006, featuring nature walks, an Animal Forest that includes native birds and animals (birds, snakes, wolves, bison and a bear), a recreation of the palisade wall, computer-driven multi-media shows and the recreated ship Adventure. Many more exhibits are planned for the future. Admission is $5.00 for adults, $3.00 for kids and $3.25 for SC seniors.

→ Return to Rt. 61 (Ashley River Road, recently designated a National Scenic Byway) and go north, right, to St. Andrews Church, 4.5 miles on the right.

Coffee Break or Lunch Break: The Bluerose Café, 652 St. Andrews Boulevard, 225-2583, opens at 7am for breakfast and lunch. Their specialty is fish and chips. Daily specials might include a tasty grilled salmon. You could also pack a picnic (see the restaurant guide, page 270 for places that provide good food to go). Picnic tables are available at the plantations and Charles Towne Landing. Magnolia Plantation sells hot dogs and hamburgers. Middleton Place has an excellent restaurant. If you take the architects' detour to the St. James Goose Creek church, you will pass through Summerville where there is Woodlands (125 Parsons Rd. 875-2600).

ST. ANDREW'S PARISH CHURCH: Dating to 1706, with 1723 modifications, it is the oldest church in South Carolina. The economy of the parish was based on indigo. After the Revolution, when the indigo bounty ended, St. Andrew's fell into disrepair. After Rev. Grimke Drayton, owner of Magnolia Plantation, died in 1891, the church was closed for many years.

→ Continue on Rte. 61 to Drayton Hall, Magnolia Plantation and Middleton Place, all on the right hand side within a few miles of each other.

St. Andrew's Parish Church, 1706

Drayton Hall, 1738, Historic Site of the National Trust for Historic Preservation

DRAYTON HALL: Built in 1738, the oldest and most important Georgian Palladian mansion in America, was miraculously spared during the Civil War. According to legend, federal troops avoided the architectural gem because Dr. John Drayton posted yellow flags signaling it to be a hospital for smallpox victims. The Hall was built by Royal Judge John Drayton, who owned over 500 slaves and was one of the wealthiest men in the colony. Drayton Hall has been painted only twice, leaving the intricate molding unusually distinct. Like so many of Charleston's outstanding architectural landmarks, Drayton Hall was created by skilled craftsmen with access to pattern books, mostly from England, that depicted significant European buildings. The influence of classical styles is scorned by "Modernist" architects, but through the centuries, the guiding hand of tradition has shaped our most beloved architectural landmarks. So it is with Drayton Hall. Just as Palladio looked to Roman buildings, Charleston's builders looked to Palladio and to the English architect Inigo Jones, and later on, to the pattern books of Robert Adam. At Drayton, the famous portico closely resembles a plate of Villa Pisani in Palladio's *Quattro Libri* of 1716. The mantel and overmantel in the Great Hall is from William Kent's *Designs of Inigo Jones*, 1727.

Over mantel in the Great Hall at Drayton Hall

Magnolia Plantation

The sense of authenticity of Drayton Hall is very moving. The National Trust for Historic Preservation, which owns Drayton, has made a conscious effort to preserve this authenticity by conservation rather than renovation. The building has no plumbing, wiring or air conditioning. One has the feeling that the Drayton family, which occupied the Hall for 230 years, has just moved out. There are guided tours of Drayton Hall, which is open to the public. (843-766-0188, www.draytonhall.org)

MAGNOLIA PLANTATION: No serious gardener should leave Charleston without visiting Magnolia, whose gardens, begun in the 1680's, are the oldest in America and have been called South Carolina's greatest treasure. The Baedecker Guide of 1900 listed Magnolia as one of America's three top attractions, along with Niagara Falls and the Grand Canyon. Magnolia's fame derived from the changes made by the Rev. John Grimke Drayton, who studied for the ministry in England. When he inherited Magnolia, he introduced the more informal English style of gardening. Rev. Grimke brought the azalea to America in the mid-19th century and opened the gardens, lavishly planted with camellias and azaleas, to the public in 1870. Magnolia was the first home of the Draytons, an aristocratic Norman family that emigrated to Charleston by way of Barbados. The original plantation house was burned during the Civil War. The present house was

Wild turkey at the petting zoo at Magnolia Plantation

Middleton Place

furnishings. Open daily with guided tours of the house. In addition to the gardens, with something blooming year-round, there is an 18th century herb garden, a horticultural maze, enclosed tropical garden, petting zoo, Nature Train ride of the plantation grounds and a Nature Boat trip through old flooded rice fields which are now a waterfowl refuge. The azaleas bloom spectacularly in March and April, depending on the weather. We urge you to allow time to visit the Audobon Swamp Garden. This 60-acre garden in the swamp is considered one of America's most significant horticultural treasures -- "It is a magical place," said Dr. Ellen Henke, known on TV as "America's Plant Doctor."(1-800-367-3517, www.magnoliaplantation.com)

MIDDLETON PLACE is famous for having the oldest land-scaped gardens in America, modeled after the creations of Andre Le Notre for Versailles. Begun in 1741, it took 100 slaves a decade to create the garden's many terraces, paths and formal grandeur that has survived for over 250 years. It contains America's oldest camellias, which were planted in 1786 by the French botanist André Michaux.

The Wood Nymph by Rudolf Schadow, c. 1814 at Middleton Place

The Middletons were major players in American history. Edward Middleton emigrated from England to Barbados and to Charleston in 1678. The first Henry Middleton represented South Carolina in the First Continental Congress and was elected its president in 1774. Arthur Middleton was a signer of the Declaration of Independence. The second Henry Middleton was Governor of South Carolina, a United States Congressman and the United States Minister to Russia. It was this Middleton who expanded the gardens in 1786 with the help of his friend André Michaux, who brought exotic plants to Middleton Place. Williams Middleton, his son, was responsible for adding the azaleas. During the Civil War, Middleton's main house and flanker buildings were burned. The south flanker, however, was restored and is today a house museum containing many important family possessions.

In the 1930's, some 35,000 azaleas were planted in Middleton Place, and in 1941 the Garden Club of America called it "the most interesting and important garden in the United States." The gardens have been planned so that there is something in bloom all year. Don't miss the Stableyards with demonstrations of plantation activities, farm animals and agricultural displays. Open daily with guided house tours. (843-556-6020, www.middletonplace.org)

→   To return directly to Charleston, turn left onto Rte. 61. To visit St. James Goose Creek church (1708), turn right onto Rte. 61. (This will take you through Summerville. See below.) Turn right off Rte. 61 onto Rte. 165, Bacon Bridge Road leads you north to S. Main Street (Rte. 17A). Go right. This will take you through old Summerville Business District. Stay on 17A to Interstate 26 and go east toward Charleston. Exit at 205A (the second exit) onto Rte. 78 going west. Rte 78 will cross Nad Road. Go left. Stay on Nad, which will cross Rte. 52. (If you missed Nad Road and get to Rte. 52, go north and you will cross Nad again.) Turn right off of Nad Road onto Snake River Road. Turn right onto Vestry, a small hard-to-see dirt road. St. James Goose Creek is on the left in about 75 yards. We strongly urge you to go to www.mapquest.com and plot this route. It's worth the trip but very easy to get lost.

SUMMERVILLE: On the way to Goose Creek, you will drive through the historic business district on Old Main Street. Summerville was settled in 1785 by planters who came to escape swamp fevers in the summer. While most of South Carolina languished after the Civil War, Summerville prospered as a summer resort, especially as a health resort for those suffering from lung diseases. The town saw a steady influx of residents from the north who built elaborate raised cottages with large wraparound porches in a mode known as "Summerville style".

ARCHITECTS'/HISTORIANS' DETOUR: St. James Goose Creek church dates to 1708 and is one of the most interesting English churches and one of the best preserved. The parish included many wealthy planters

St. James Goose Creek Church, 1708

from Barbados. The roof style relates to West Indian architecture. Note the elaborate entrance entablature with flaming hearts to symbolize love and sacrifice. The pediment features a mother pelican and her young, emblem of the Society for the Propagation of the Gospel in Foreign Parts. The arched windows have unusual cherub-head keystones. Very detailed architecture for such an early church. General William Moultrie and his family are buried here. The church is not open to the public, but the grounds are.

And now back to feast in Charleston. In the past decade, the city has become a center of food in the southeast. With over 130 restaurants in the historic district, there is a wide variety of cuisines. See the restaurant guide on page 270. If you did not reserve dinner before you left this morning, do so now, as the better restaurants tend to be packed.

Front Street, Georgetown

Brookgreen Gardens, Georgetown and the Plantations

Brookgreen Gardens, on the site of one of the largest 18th century rice plantations, in 1931 became America's first public sculpture garden and is a National Historic Landmark. Today, with over 540 realistic works by American sculptors, it is the largest figurative sculpture garden in the United States. Less than 90 minutes from Charleston, Brookgreen alone would be worth the journey. Today, as we are seeing a classical revival in the arts, Brookgreen's mandate to collect and exhibit only works in the classical tradition makes the sculpture garden a particularly relevant experience. The figurative tradition never vanished completely during the era of Modernism, as the masterworks of such sculptors as Marshall Fredericks, Carl Milles and Charlestonian Willard Hirsch make vividly clear.

Between Charleston and Brookgreen, you will encounter charming small towns, the home of the first African-American congressman, "slave streets", important antebellum architecture, and South Carolina's finest example of a wood-frame Georgian plantation house. The contributions of the French Huguenots become clearer after a visit into the Santee River area. French names are common, because Gallic Protestants settled here as early as 1689. Most of the surviving portraits of Carolinians of the first quarter of the 18th century are of such French Santee Huguenot families as the Mazycks, Gaillards, Manigaults, Ravenels, Horrys, Porchers and Hugers.

In 1790 a British surveyor noted that the Santee River French have "out stript our English, who brought with 'em larger Fortunes, though (as it seems) less endeavor to manage their Talent to the best Advantage." The early Huguenots carved out plantations in the wilderness and attempted to cultivate grapes, olives and silk worms but soon switched to rice and indigo.

We have laid this trip out as if it could be done in a single day, and if you are a Type A personality, it might be. If you linger along the way, you could easily spend several days here, simply returning to Charleston each evening for dinner in a excellent restaurant when you've seen enough.

→   Go north on Meeting Street, right on 17N to cross the Arthur Ravenel Bridge over the Cooper River. Stay in the right lane as you leave the bridge heading toward Mt. Pleasant on N703, Coleman Blvd. At the first stoplight, there is an exit for Patriot's Point, built in 1975, featuring the WWII aircraft carrier Yorktown. Cross Shem Creek Bridge, bearing right at the fork onto Whilden Street. Turn right onto Hibben Street and park. The old village of Mount Pleasant is mostly residential and does not welcome organized tours. The best way to see the village is on foot. Most of the houses are 19th century, although the village was settled in the 18th. There is a small downtown centered on Pitt Street.

MOUNT PLEASANT: The most historically important building, Hibben House, 111 Hibben Street, was originally a modest plantation home of Jacob Motte, who also lived in one of the finest homes in Charleston

Hibben House

(69 Church Street). Motte was the Public Treasurer, a position second in importance only to the Governor of the Colony. As Charleston had no banks until the 1790's, the Public Treasurer served as the local banker. During the Revolution, William Moultrie erected a rampart in the front yard of Hibben House, fired on two British ships, driving them from the Charleston Harbor. After the fall of Charleston, Cornwallis used the house as his headquarters. James Hibben, the founder of Mount Pleasant and state senator 1800-1815, bought the plantation in 1803, dividing it into lots. One lot went to his daughter Sarah Margaret, who married the Rev. Daniel DuPré. The DuPrés lived in Mount Pleasant during the winter and maintained a summer home in McClellanville, which is the oldest surviving house there. Hibben House has been significantly altered, with columns added in the 19th century and side wings recently, over the objections of preservationists.

The Mount Pleasant Presbyterian Church, on Hibben and Church Streets, was built in 1854 and served as a Confederate hospital during the Civil War. It later housed the Laing School for freedmen.

→ When you return to your car, drive back to Coleman Blvd. Go right. The boulevard becomes Ben Sawyer and continues over the bridge to Sullivan's Island. After crossing the bridge onto Sullivan's Island, go right on Middle Street. Fort Moultrie is on the left in about a mile.

Lunch: On Coleman Blvd, just before you come to the bridge to Sullivan's Island, there is Momma Brown's with a full buffet of Lowcountry soul food. In Mt. Pleasant on 17 North, Gullah Cuisine also serves a fabulous Lowcountry buffet. Although some locals have been put off by the modest exterior, Food Network, Southern Living and The New York Times have been impressed by the food inside. Further north, at 4808 Highway 17N, there's another unpretentious culinary gem—See Wee, also a favorite of R.W. Apple of the Times ("Man can they fry," he exudes.)

FORT MOULTRIE: The fort defended Charleston during the Revolutionary and Civil Wars and is now a national park. The defense of the fort in 1776 under General William Moultrie was the first decisive patriot victory of the Revolution. The current fort was built in 1809. The site includes the grave of Osceola, who in the 1830's led the Seminole people of Florida in resistance against relocation to a reservation. Osceola was imprisoned here in 1837, where he died the following

Osceola's Grave, 1838

year. Edgar Allen Poe was stationed here and used Sullivan's Island as a setting for The Gold Bug. There is speculation that Annabelle Lee was a local girl and that Charleston was the fabled "Kingdom by the Sea."

→ Avoid the highway sprawl of 17N by returning along Middle Street past the beach houses of Sullivan's Island to the Isle of Palms. Go left on 517N to the bridge over the marsh then right on 17N to McClellanville (28 miles.) Go right at the caution light onto S. Pinckney Street.

MCCLELLANVILLE: This quaint village was originally called Seashore and was a beach resort for nearby rice planters of the mid-18th century. It is named after the McClellans of Point Plantation. The oldest house is the DuPré House, built in 1790 and reconstructed at 423 Pinckney Street in 1861.

Pinckney Street at Society Street. The New Wappetaw Presbyterian Church is at the right.

The streets are lined with live oaks, Victorian summer houses, and a number of handsome churches. White Gables, 528 Pinckney Street, a six-room Country Victorian was built in 1897. The James Hibben Leland House on Oak Street, c. 1858, was originally a modest Huguenot summer cottage and the scene of many parties and annual balls. On DuPré Road there is an important AME church, c. 1890, built by Paul S. Drayton, the son of a former slave. Drayton built most of the McClellanville homes of 1885-1896 as well as the Victorian Gothic St. James-Santee Chapel of Ease on Oak Street. (A Chapel of Ease was used by planters in the summer to avoid the long trip to the main church in the summer heat.)

White Gables, 1897, 528 Pinckney Street

GARDENERS' DETOUR: About 15 minutes beyond McClellanville, there is Roycroft nursery, famous for its extensive collections of daylillies in unusual shades.

AME church, c. 1890, by Paul S. Drayton

Ancient oak on Pinckney and Oak Streets. At right, the United Methodist Church

→ Return to 17N, go right, and continue on 17N, crossing the Sampit river, where you will see the steel and paper mills which, unfortunately, loom over historic Georgetown. Turn right on Front Street and park near the Visitor Center, 1001 Front Street, which has information and a free map of the Historic District.

GEORGETOWN: The extensive historic district is listed on the National Register of Historic Places. Georgetown was founded in 1729 and is the third oldest city in South Carolina, after Charleston and Beaufort. It is impossible to understand the history of Charleston and the planter aristocracy, whose life style and mansions defined southern gentility, without knowledge of the significant role played by Georgetown's plantations. Indigo, the source of a coveted blue dye, made the town rich in the mid 18th century. After 1760, however, a shift began in economic power. Indigo exports leveled off. Rice became the more lucrative crop. Charleston rice factors became the principal figures in marketing Georgetown's rice crop, and the Charleston port, always larger, undermined the growth of the Georgetown port.

By 1840, Georgetown, with over 175 rice plantations, produced nearly half the total rice crop of the United States and created huge fortunes for the rice planters. Georgetown planters wanted a Charleston showplace in which to entertain. By the 1850's, most planters spent much of the year in their Charleston mansions, clustered in Mazyck Wraggborough, Radcliffeborough, Harleston Village and Hampstead, and depended upon overseers to manage the plantations dur-

Joseph Hayne Rainey found ncar Waterfront park

ing the social season. So many Georgetown planters attended church in Radcliffeborough that St. Luke and St. Paul's was considered a Georgetown institution. Many members of Georgetown rice families were married there and, by the names in the graveyard, we know they were buried there.

Southern civic pride being what it is, both Charleston and Georgetown claim the area's most distinguished and wealthiest family names, such as Read, Ward, Alston, Izard, Hume, Lucas, Trapier, Poinsett, Manigault, Pinckney, Mazyck and Middleton. Both are correct since these families maintained homes in Georgetown and Charleston.

1 **THE ROBERT STEWART HOUSE,** 1019 Front Street, was built c. 1750 by the planter as his town home. (Not open to the public.) It is here that George Washington spent a night on his 1791 southern tour after being entertained by the Masons and the Winyah Indigo Society. Daniel Tucker, who owned Litchfield and Retreat plantaions, bought the house in 1787, updating it with Adamesque lintels, keystones and semicircular rooms. The house was later owned by Benjamin Allston, Sr. (1765-1847). It remained in the hands of his descendents, the Pyatt and Parker families, until 1979.

2 **KAMINSKY HOUSE MUSEUM,** 1003 Front Street. Built c. 1769, it was originally owned by Paul Trapier III, a prominent businessman known as "the King of Georgetown." House tours begin on the hour and last an hour.

The Kaminsky House Museum, c. 1769

→ Walk north on King Street. (There is no street sign at the beginning of King Street. It is directly across from the Visitors Center and Rainey Park.)

Coffee Break: Kudzu Bakery, 120 King Street, has delectable pecan pie, cakes, sandwiches, homemade relishes and jellies.

→ Go right on Prince Street.

Along Prince, between King and Cannon Streets, you will pass buildings from every era of Georgetown's history, many with explanatory plaques. The blue markers with dates refer to numbers on the Visitor Center map. Among the highlights along Prince Street are:

3 **JOHN ARTHUR HOUSE,** 921 Prince Street, c. 1740 and now the Dupré House B&B, named for a later owner Mary Magdalen Dupré. The second floor overhang on the west facade is typical of New England homes of the late 17th century.

4 **JOSEPH HAYNE RAINEY HOUSE,** 909 Prince Street, home of the first African-American elected to the United States Congress, serving four terms. He was an advocate of civil rights for blacks. Rainey was born into slavery in 1832, but his father bought the family's freedom. This pre-Revolutionary home is a single house, similar to the popular Charleston style.

Joseph Hayne Rainey House, c. 1760

5 **WILLIAM DOYLE MORGAN HOUSE,** 732 Prince Street, (at the NE corner of Broad) c. 1880, a romantic Victorian with double piazzas, fluted columns. Morgan was mayor of Georgetown, 1891-1906, introducing a modern water and sewer system, electric lights, sidewalks and a deeper harbor.

Georgetown County Courthouse, c. 1824

6 **GEORGETOWN COUNTY COURTHOUSE,** Prince and Screven Streets, an early example of the Greek Revival style, was designed in 1824 by Robert Mills of Charleston, who also designed the Washington Monument. The double stairway behind the screen is very beautiful and unique among Mills's courthouses (He built about 16 county courthouses between 1820-1830.)

Winyah Indigo Society, 1857 by E. B. White

7 **WINYAH INDIGO SOCIETY,** 1857, 509 Prince Street, at Cannon Street, is an example of Greek Revival style. Georgetown benefitted from the influence of Charleston and Europe. The Winyah Indigo Society, organized in 1755 was inspired by the Charleston Library Society, founded in 1748. The Society provided Georgetown with a library, a school and a social and intellectual center. The first president was Thomas Lynch, who was also a member of the Charleston Library Society. In 1857, Georgetown rice planter Francis Withers donated land and money for a new building, designed by Charleston architect E. B. White. The Winyah Indigo Society continues to function as a community center.

8   **FRANCIS WITHERS HOUSE,** 202 Cannon, c. 1815, at the NE corner of Prince Street, is an excellent example of an Adamesque home, built by a rice planter.

→   Go right on Cannon Street. Cross Front Street.

9   **RED BRICK WAREHOUSE,** 16 Cannon, is historically significant. It was here that Theodosia Burr Alston is believed to have waited with her husband before she boarded the ship Patriot in 1812 and was lost at sea.

10   **DR. CHARLES FYFFE HOUSE:** Across the street is a handsome Georgian house, built on a high Palladian basement by a Scottish doctor, c. 1765. Dr. Fyffe lost the house during the Revolution, as he remained loyal to Great Britian.

Dr. Charles Fyffe House, c. 1765

→   Return to Front Street. Turn left.

11   **MARY MANN HOUSE,** 528 Front Street, c. 1775, has a fine Georgian portico with double piazzas. The house was built with lumber from Mansfield, the family plantation. Theodosia Burr Alston danced in the ballroom before her ill-fated voyage, according to local legend.

Mary Mann House, c. 1775

12   **THE KAMINSKI BUILDING, 633 FRONT STREET,** 1842, with a handsome castiron front by Daniel Badger of New York, added in 1865 by a dry goods and hardware dealer. Heiman Kaminski bought it for his hardware business in 1869.

13 **THE RICE MUSEUM,** 1842, built in the Greek Revival style, was once a market and town hall. The exhibit depicts the growing and milling of rice.

Front Street is a charming historic restored downtown. Allow time to explore the many shops. Augustus Carolina Interiors, 830 Front Street, for instance, is well worth a visit if you are shopping for fine house and garden furnishings.

The Kaminski Building, 1842

Lunch: *The Rice Paddy, 732 Front Street. Excellent seafood, nice setting overlooking the river. A local favorite.*

HISTORIANS' DETOUR: Mansfield Plantation, an unusually intact plantation including a slave village, is now a bed and breakfast and may be seen by appointment only. Call 800-355-3223 or www.bbonline.com/sc/mansfield

Slave street at Mansfield Plantation

PRIVATE PLANTATIONS: Privately owned plantations are periodically open to the public on special tour days. It is possible then to visit such gardens as this 18th century showplace (on page 238) begun by Mrs. Benjamin Huger II. For information on visiting private homes and plantations, call the Georgetown Chamber of Commerce. (800-777-7705 or 843-546-8436)

→ Return to 17N and continue on to Hobcaw Barony, which is four minutes north of Georgetown.

Private plantation near Georgetown

HOBCAW BARONY: Today, as former plantations are converted into beach resorts with condos and golf courses, a preserve such as Hobcaw Barony is ever more precious. It consists of a 17,500 acre estate assembled by Bernard Baruch in 1905. Baruch's imposing columned brick home of 1930 was filled every weekend with house guests, including such notables as President Franklin D. and Eleanor Roosevelt, Henry and Clare Booth Luce, Hedda Hopper, Jack London, H. G. Wells and Sir Winston Churchill (a close friend with whom Baruch exchanged over 700 letters.) Hobcaw Barony was inherited by Baruch's daughter who established a trust with the mandate to conduct research and educational programs that contribute to our understanding of coastal ecosystems. On Tuesday and Thursday, there is a three hour tour of the Baruch house and a slave village. Other days, there is a 20 minute video. (843-546-4623. www.hobcawbarony.com)

→ Continue on 17N to Huntington State Park. You will pass Pawley's Island on your right.

PAWLEY'S ISLAND: Pawley's is a family beach with a small historic district of 19th century summer houses of rice planters such as the Westons and the Allstons. The old houses were built with porches facing south (instead of toward the ocean) to capture the sea breezes, which mattered more than an ocean view.

Lunch: Louis's at Pawley's is open from 11am-11pm. Louis used to be one of the stars of the Charleston culinary scene. Don't miss the opportunity to sample some of the best food in the southeast. Louis Osteen won the "Best Chef in the Southeast" award from the James Beard Foundation in 2004. A Sunday brunch of southern favorites costs only $10. On US 17 at the Hammock Shop. 843-237-8757 or www.louisatpawleys.com

HUNTINGTON STATE PARK is a public beach with a most exotic museum house, once the summer home of Archer and Anna Hyatt Huntington, important figures in the development of American art. Atalaya (Spanish for watchtower) is believed to have been built without architectural drawings. Supposedly the local builder followed Archer Huntington around and built according to his verbal instructions. "Archer has decided to build something," his wife wrote in her diary in 1930. "What he has in mind would probably be a hair raiser to an architect." This romantic Moorish medieval fortress contains the studio of Anna Huntington, a notable sculptor whose work fills Brookgreen Gardens. What look today like guest rooms were actually rooms for horses and bears Anna used as models. A trustee of Atalaya recently noted that "Atalaya is in a state of controlled and maintained decadence. It's really elegant in that state." The Huntingtons' winter home in New York City is today the National Academy Museum and School of Fine Arts.

Atalaya

BROOKGREEN GARDENS was once a large prosperous rice plantation, developed in 1738 by William Allston. In 1791 George Washington spent a night here as the guest of the widow of William Allston, remarried to Dr. Henry Flagg. In 1880, the plantation was owned by the Wards. Joshua Ward, called "King of the Rice Planters" in Georgetown, became famous for Carolina Gold, a big-grain high-yield rice that made him a millionaire at a time when that sort of wealth was rare.

In the 1930's, Archer and Anna Huntington, he of railroad money, bought 9,000 acres that included Brookgreen and three adjoining plantations and created a formal garden containing the largest permanent outdoor exhibition of American figurative sculpture. Many sculptures are by Anna Huntington, whose works are also in collections abroad and in 200 American museums including the Metropolitan Museum in New York. She was noted for her classical animal and equestrian sculptures. Fighting Stallions, which stands at the entrance of Brookgreen, is probably her most well-known work. Brookgreen, the first sculpture garden in the United States, features such American Renaissance artists as Augustus St. Gaudens, Daniel Chester French, Frederic Remington and Frederick MacMonnies. In many museums, the 20th century is represented mostly by abstract sculptures--at Brookgreen it is all realism and in

Fighting Stattions by Anna Hyatt Huntington at the entrance to Brookgreen Gardens.

The majestic lions of Brookgreen Gardens

a magical garden setting. One of the "garden rooms" includes a butterfly house and sculptures especially enjoyed by children. There is also an aviary and a wild-animal-feeding tour. Gardeners will find over 2000 of the different species that thrive in the Lowcountry. (800-849-1931 or www.brookgreen.org)

→ Return to Charleston on 17S, watching for signs to the sites, which will all be on your right.

HOPSEWEE PLANTATION: Built in 1735 by Thomas Lynch, Sr., one of the wealthiest indigo planters on the Santee River, a delegate to the first Continental Congress, president of the Winyah Indigo Society. Thomas Lynch, Jr., a signer of the Declaration of Independence, and also a delegate to the Continental Congress, was born here. The Lynches spent much of the year in their town home in Ansonborough. Open to the public (843-546-7891).

HAMPTON PLANTATION: South Carolina's finest example of a frame Georgian plantation house is also significant to national and architectural history. Originally built in 1735, Daniel and Harriott Horry added the portico in 1790. It is the first such Adamesque portico in the south and one of the earliest examples in America of the giant portico in a private home. The prototype is believed to have been created by the Adam brothers for David Garrick's villa on the Thames, also named Hampton. As a girl, Harriott and her mother, Eliza Lucas Pinckney, lived in England for six years in the 1750's. It is said that Mrs. Pinckney did not miss a play in which Garrick was acting. Surely, she did not miss the acclaim accorded his Adam portico either. The Horrys' portico was completed in time for the visit of George Washington in 1791. Mrs. Horry invited the neighbors and welcomed Washington with a grand breakfast served upon her green and white Wedgewood set in the 700 square foot two story ballroom. Two years after his visit, Washington was a pall bearer at the funeral of Mrs. Pinckney. Mrs. Horry's brother, Thomas Pinckney, was appointed by Washington as the first United States diplomat to Great Britian. Lafayette, Francis Marion, Daniel Webster, Edgar Allen

Hampton Plantation. Washington Oak is to the left, so called because Mrs. Horry said it blocked her view and Washington said that it should not be cut.

Poe and Robert E. Lee were also guests here over the years. Hampton later belonged to the Rutledge family and was the home of Archibald Rutledge, the state's first poet laureate. Now owned by the National Parks System, it is open to the public. (843-546-9361)

ST. JAMES SANTEE CHURCH: One of the most graceful of the lowcountry parish churches, c. 1768, with brick columns, St. James exhibits an unusual architectural sophistication. Indeed, the church reflects the tastes of its wealthy congregation of planters, mostly of French Huguenot descent. A traveler of 1805 noted that, "within their houses you meet great hospitality, the polish of society, and every charm of social life and abundance, food convenience and luxury." A few years earlier, George Washington had visited the parish and noted in his diary that "the inhabitants are wealthy, gay and hospitable."

St James Santee Church

Lunch: *The Crab Pot serves southern seafood, She Crab Soup, and fabulous hush puppies enlivened with onion. On US 17 at McClellanville. 843-887-3156. In McClellanville, T. W. Graham & Co. at 810 Pinckney Street serves local seafood.*

SWEET GRASS BASKETS: Preserving an ancient art, Lowcountry basket makers continue to produce beautiful quality baskets and sell them in stands which line US 17, just north of Boone Hall.

BOONE HALL PLANTATION: Nine slave cabins, c. 1790-1843, survive on this former cotton plantation. The house was built in 1935. In 1817, Major John Horlbeck planted one of the largest pecan groves in the world here, still producing pecans commercially. There is a beautiful rose garden, and the live oak entrance allee, c. 1843, has been frequently photographed for movies and television.

CHARLES PINCKNEY NATIONAL HISTORIC SITE: One of the seven plantations belonging to Charles Pinckney, who lived most of the time in Charleston. The c. 1828 cottage, built directly on the site of Pinckney's plantation house, contains an excellent history exhibit. Pinckney played a major role in drafting the United States constitution, was a four-term governor of South Carolina and ambassador to Spain. George Washington had breakfast here under the trees. Open to the public. (843-881-5516, www.nps.gov/chpi)

GARDENER'S DETOUR: Abide-a-While nursery, on US 17 about five minutes further, has a wide selection of plants for sale.

Streetscape at I'On

→ Go right off US 17 S at Bowman Road (at the stoplight). Turn left onto Mathis Ferry Road. Turn right into the neighborhood at Eastlake Road, or if you miss that, at the roundabout.

I'ON: The Community of I'On is an important example of the New Urbanism that is reviving inner cities and bringing urban civility and a sense of community to sprawling suburbs all over America. This growing movement began with Seaside, Florida, built in 1981, planned by architects Andres Duany and Elizabeth Plater-Zyberk and described by Newsweek Magazine as "probably the most influential resort community since Versailles." New urbanistic communities are designed to foster a sense of neighborhood, relying on traditional urban street grids, sidewalks and civic spaces instead of huge private lawns. I'On is named for the 19th century planter and legislator Jacob Bond I'On, who is buried nearby. It is best to park your car and walk through the neighborhood. I'On vividly demonstrates the importance of harmonious architectural fabric and quality construciton and the creativity possible within the classical language of architecture. The I'On design code is based on Lowcountry architectural traditions which persisted through the centuries until the advent of mid-20th century Modernism. The sophisticated classicism of architects designing for such communities as I'On and Newpoint (see page 251) is in great demand today. The mixed-use zoning, high density, pedestrian friendly and architecturally harmonious cities such as Charleston, Beaufort, New Orleans and Savannah have been models for New Urbanistic communites all across America. The inclusion of a commercial area reduces the residents' dependence on automobiles. The South Carolina Department of Natural Resources honored I'On with a Stewardship Award. I'On was named "Best Community in the Nation" by the National Association of Home Builders and Builder Magazine.

After a day on the road, you will surely be ready to relax and have a fine meal in one of Charleston's many excellent restaurants. We hope you made a reservation. If not, see the restaurant guide on page 270, which includes phone numbers.

The Edward Means house at Pinckney and King Streets.

BEAUFORT

Beaufort (Bew-fert), familiar to many Americans as the setting of such movies as *Forest Gump, The Great Santini* and *The Prince of Tides,* is the second oldest town in South Carolina. Founded in 1711, on Port Royal Island, Beaufort is named for Henry, Duke of Beaufort, a Lord Proprietor.

Early settlers planted rice and indigo, but it was Sea Island cotton, produced on Port Royal and nearby islands and considered to be the finest in the world, that brought Beaufort incredible wealth from 1790 until 1860. One 19th century historian described the town as the "wealthiest, most aristocratic and cultivated town of its size in America."

It was the fashion for planters to maintain a grand home in Beaufort, often with a large ballroom for dances and lavish entertaining, sited back from the street on a large lot. A home in the unique "Beaufort style" faces south toward the water, with two-story porches to capture summer breezes and winter sunshine. It was designed to be airy and cool, set on a high, often arcaded foundation, embellished with classical details, a high ceiling, a low pitched roof and often a T-shaped plan--a central core plus side extensions.

The grandeur of Beaufort's antebellum years has been carefully protected by historic preservationists. The whole town is listed as a National Historic Landmark District. The only way to properly savor Beaufort's charm is on foot, strolling through peaceful streets lined with live oaks, Spanish moss and colonnaded mansions.

→ Take 17 S out of Charleston to Gardens Corner and go SE on Rte. 21. The drive takes about 1 1/4 hours. As you enter Beaufort, stop at the Visitor Center at Boundary and Carteret Streets for brochures and a town map. Continue down Carteret, turning right on Bay Street, where there is parking. Begin your walk at Bay and Charles Streets.

Bay Street. The "Tabby Manse" of 1786 is at the far right.

1 BAY STREET MANSIONS: Between Charles and Monson, an assemblage of grand homes, overlooking the marsh, reflect Sea Island cotton wealth.

2 1211 BAY STREET: The "Tabby Manse" of 1786 is considered one of the finest early Beaufort homes. Built by planter Thomas Fuller, the walls are entirely of tabby, which is a combination of broken oyster shell, sand and lime. Note the graceful Adamesque portico. There are five homes in Beaufort with this same kind of elegant entrance.

→ Go right on Monson Street and right on North Street, to Church Street.

3 ST. HELENA EPISCOPAL CHURCH: Built in 1724 by a parish established in 1712, it is one of the oldest living churches in the United States. There have been many alterations, such as the removal of the steeple in 1866 and its replacement in 1942.

→ Go right on Church Street, turning left on Craven Street.

4 1113 CRAVEN STREET: Built in 1813, altered c. 1861, an excellent example of the "Beaufort style" with a Palladian basement, colonnaded porches. The

St. Helena Episcopal Church

Secession House is where Robert Barnwell Rhett drafted the first Ordinance of Secession in 1860.

Secession House, 1113 Craven Street

5 **1009 CRAVEN STREET:** Built c. 1820, it was the home of Thomas Rhett and his wife Caroline Barnwell, a daughter of Edward Barnwell, one of the most important Sea Island cotton planters. With fluted Doric colonnades, this is another gracious example of "Beaufort style."

→ Walk right on Charles and left on Bay Street.

6 **812 BAY STREET:** The John Cross Tavern building, with thick tabby walls, is one of the oldest buildings in Beaufort. In 1736, John Wesley, a founder of Methodism, stayed here.

The Rhett House, 1009 Craven Street

7 **802-806 BAY STREET:** The Habersham House, c. 1800, is believed to be the only three-story tabby house left in America. It has been restored with shops in the ground floor.

The Habersham House, c.1800, left and the John Cross Tavern building, 1736, right.

8 **801 BAY STREET:** John Mark Verdier, a merchant, built his home in 1790 with a stately Adamesque portico. In 1825, General Marquis de Lafayette addressed a crowd from the front steps. During the Civil War, it was a Union headquarters. Now owned by the Historic Beaufort Foundation, it is open to the public. (843-524-6240)

John Mark Verdier house, 801 Bay Street, 1790

9 **601 BAY STREET:** A summer home built by cotton planter Lewis Reeve Sams, built in 1852, in the "Beaufort style" with fluted Ionic and Doric orders on the double piazza.

601 Bay Street, 1852

→ Go left on New Street to Port Republic Street. At the SW corner is:

10 **8214 NEW STREET:** Thomas Hepworth, chief justice of South Carolina, built his home in 1717 with musket slits in the foundation so the family could protect themselves from Indians. This is the oldest surviving house in Beaufort.

→ Continue on New Street, turning right on Craven Street., which has many Victorian houses.

11 **411 CRAVEN STREET:** "The Castle", c. 1850, is one of the grandest homes in the area, known as "the Point." It was built by Dr. Joseph Johnson, a serious horticulturist who laid out the lush gardens, which included olive trees imported from the Holy Land. You can glimpse the Castle through the live oak trees and Spanish moss. The Rev. Richard Fuller, one of the most important Baptist theologians of the 19th century, also lived here.

→ Turn left on East Street

12 **412 EAST STREET:** Frances Parker, one of South Carolina's most renowned gardeners, lives here. Call 843-524-6232 for an appointment to visit her garden.

→   Walk right on Federal Street..

13   **302 FEDERAL STREET:** William Fripp, who owned nine plantations and 313 slaves, built "Tidewater" in 1830 as his summer home. Such house names were adopted in the 1930's. A two-story portico faces the river. Note cottage garden border.

→   Go left on Pinckney Street.

14   **604 PINCKNEY STREET:** The brick summer mansion, with fluted Doric columns, of planter Edward Means, built c. 1853. Its beauty so impressed a war correspondent for the *New York Daily Tribune* in 1861, that he wrote, "the house of Colonel Edward Means would be the handsomest in any town in the North."

→   Walk right on King Street, left on Short Street, passing more of the grand summer houses on the Point, going right on Laurens.

15   **I LAURENS STREET:** "Tidalholm", built by the planter Edgar Fripp, was featured in *The Big Chill* and *The Great Santini*. Fripp built it as a summer home in 1856.

16   **201 LAURENS STREET:** Berners Barnwell Sams, a cotton planter, built his home of tabby. It was the scene of masked balls with elaborate costumes and dancing until dawn. Facing the Green, a private park, the Sams house has been in the same family for generations. Note the pattern garden.

→   Continue along Laurens Street, going right on East Street, left on Prince Street.

17   **511 PRINCE STREET:** The 1834 home of Henry McKee is also closely associated with Robert Smalls, who was born into slavery here in 1839. In 1862, Smalls hijacked a confederate ship and delivered it to Federal forces. He bought his childhood home in 1863, and after the war was a successful politician, serving five terms in the US Congress. When she was old and ill, McKee's widow wandered into

Robert Smalls House, 511 Prince Street, 1834

the house, thinking it was still her home. Smalls installed her in her former bedroom and cared for her until her death.

→ Walk left on New Street.

18 **601 NEW STREET:** The First African Baptist Church was built in 1865. Smalls was a member here for over ten years.

→ Go left on King to 501 King Street.

19 **501 KING STREET:** The William Wigg Barnwell House, built in 1816, and an outstanding example of Adamesque architecture, was slated for demolition in 1973. It was moved to this location and restored by Jim Williams, Savannah antiques dealer and preservationist, chronicled in *Midnight in the Garden of Good and Evil.*

501 King Street, 1816

→ Return on King to Carteret Street. Go left on Carteret to Craven Street and go right..

20 **713 CRAVEN STREET:** The Arsenal, built in 1795, now houses the Beaufort Museum. When the English laid out the town, they envisioned this intersection of Craven and Carteret as the town square.

→ Go left on Scott Street. Go right on Bay Street, and return to parking lot.

Lunch: *Plums, 904 1/2 Bay Street. Firehouse Books on Craven (fabulous coffees, wraps, salads). Kathleen's, 822 Bay Street (do sit outside). Bistro, 205 West St. On Sunday the Beaufort Inn, 809 Port Republic Street, has an excellent brunch, 10am to 2 pm. Reservations recommended (843-521-9000). Bistro 205, 205 West Street, serves seafood, sushi and duck, using local ingredients prepared by a Belgian chef.*

Newpoint streetscape with two houses designed by James Strickland, at left and one by Eric Moser, at right.

ARCHITECTS'/GARDENERS' DETOUR: Newpoint is actually a must-see for anyone troubled by suburban sprawl and the absense of a sense of community which characterizes so much of America today. Newpoint is an exemplary neighborhood inspired by the New Urbanism of Andres Duany and Elizabeth Plater-Zyberk--we hope you visited I'On in Mt. Pleasant. Both visionary and award winning projects, developed by Vince Graham, have been attracting new residents from all over America because of their high quality of life. A sense of community is promoted by the new/old principles of urban design. Houses are close to each other and close to the sidewalk, creating a "street wall", providing a comfortable sense of enclosure to invite strolling. Front and side verandas are within conversational distance. There are nine neighborhood parks. Be sure to visit The Green, modeled on Charleston's Battery, lined with imposing mansions. Alleys, similar to those in Savannah, hide garbage cans and parked cars. Design codes mandate visual harmony – a harmony deliberately disrupted by 1950's Modernism, which continues to be a problem in almost every town and city. But not in Newpoint, which showcases some of the most talented young architects in America: the New Classicists. The architectural historian Vincent Scully noted that "The most important development of the past three decades has been the revival of the classical and vernacular traditions of architecture." Among its many honors, Newport received an AIA award for Design Excellence in 1995. It continues to use high quality materials and construction.

Newpoint is just a few minutes away from downtown Beaufort, across the bridge to Lady's Island (driving directions, p. 252). There are some 127 single family home sites in Newpoint and a small commercial district with a general store, which enables residents to shop for meals and incidentals without driving. Newpoint has attracted full-time residents who are clearly passionate gardeners. Allow time to stroll, experience the harmonious architectural ambience and view the many gardens visible from the street.

→ Take US 21 (Carteret Street) to Lady's Island and turn left at the first light, then left onto SC 802. About 1.5 miles, go left at the old brick columns that mark the entrance to Newpoint.

HISTORIANS' DETOUR: To reach one of the nation's most significant sites for African American history, follow highway 21 south through Beaufort and on to St. Helena Island. Take a right at Martin Luther King. Jr. Drive and continue until you see the Penn School Historic District. Penn Center was the first school for former slaves. Today Penn Center is an important community and educational center and a museum of Gullah culture. It is about 7 miles from downtown Beaufort. Penn Center was established in 1862 by Unitarian missionaries. A group of Pennsylvanians provided the first building in 1864. During the 1960s Dr. Martin Luther King, Jr. and members of the Southern Christian Leadership met here. There are many programs celebrating the history and culture of the Sea Islands. The Center was designated a National Historic Landmark in 1974. Phone 843-838-2432. www.penncenter.com

THE MOST ROMANTIC RUINS IN AMERICA

Sheldon Church (Prince William's Parish Church) was built in 1745 under the direction of Gov. William Bull and was considered second in importance only to St. Philip's in Charleston. An English priest said at the time, it was "by many esteemed a more beautiful building than St.Philip's. It is far more elegant than St. Michael's." Many members of the Bull family worshipped here, and were buried in the churchyard. The church was burned by the British during the Revolution, rebuilt and then burned by General Sherman.

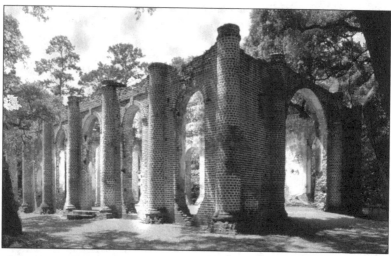

The ruins of Sheldon Church, burned first by the British and then by Federal troops.

Professor Robert Russell considers the ruins to be the most romantic in America. They are about 17 miles north of Beaufort.

→ Take US 21 North for 16 miles, then US 17 South for 1/10th mile. Go right on SC 21 for a few miles to the ruins on your right. Return to Charleston on 17N.

As Charleston has become such a culinary center, it is wise to make a dinner reservation before setting out on a side trip. If you did not do this before leaving this morning, see the restaurant guide on page 270 for possibilities and phone numbers

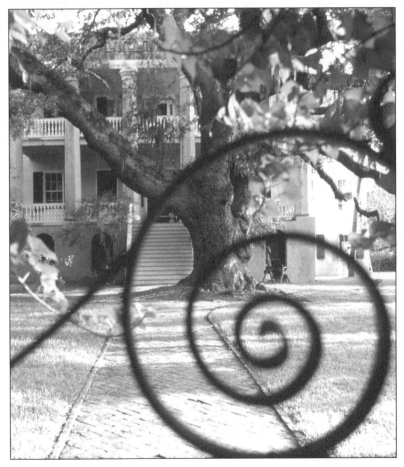

The house known asThe Castle on Old Point in Beaufort

Forsyth Park

Savannah

The most notable feature of Savannah is the city's spacious squares, roofed with sprawling live oaks, curtained with Spanish moss, surrounded by houses lavishly ornamented with architectural details and elaborate ironwork. Twenty squares survive. Four were destroyed to accommodate cars.

General James Oglethorpe and his Trustees, who founded Savannah in 1733, conceived of a New World Utopia that would benefit the worthy poor – an agricultural colony that would provide England with such imports as silk and wine. The Trustees deliberately selected debtors and the indigent, hoping that a fresh start might set them on their feet, but the new colonists from England proved to be ill-suited to the rigors of frontier life. Utopia did not materialize. Savannah was still a struggling community when George Washington visited in 1791. In Charleston, Washington had been housed in a mansion, but in Savannah, a modest frame inn was all the town could provide.

Savannah's gracious plan may have been derived from military architecture, reflecting her position as a military outpost and Oglethorpe's
military background. Another possible source is a 16th century Italian
treatise on an ideal city, which would have appealed to Oglethorpe's
idealism. Whatever the source, Savannah's grid of squares is a brilliant
urban design.

By the end of the century, idealistic pioneering was overtaken by
merchants from England, Scotland and the northern states who developed
Savannah as a major port for cotton. Eli Whitney, a New Englander, per-
fected the cotton gin in 1793 on a Savannah River plantation. By 1818,
Savannah had been transformed from a poor frontier town into the sixth
largest city in America, with exports of more than $14 million.

→   From Charleston, (trip is just under two hours) take US17 South (Savannah
Highway) to Interstate 95 South. At exit 5, take US17 South into the city. Take the first
exit off the Savannah Bridge. Follow signs to the Visitor Center, which has brochures
and maps. Exit the Visitor Center onto Fahm Street and turn right onto Bay Street.
Go left onto Barnard Ramp which leads down to River St. and a parking lot.

1   **RIVER STREET AND
FACTORS WALK:** The most
touristy area of Savannah
is along River Street down
by the Savannah River. The
tourist shops and restaurants
occupy significant 19th century buildings designed by
New York architects Charles
Cluskey and John Norris for

Warehouses on River Street.

wealthy cotton factors. (Norris's best known work in Savannah is
Mercer House, featured in *Midnight in the Garden of Good and Evil*,
known here as "The Book.") Factors Walk is at the top of the bluff.
(The Hyatt Hotel has an elevator on the eastern side.)

2   **CITY HALL:** At Bay and Bull Streets, with its grand golden dome,
designed in 1905 by Hyman Whitcover, clearly inspired by the
Chicago World's Fair of 1893 and the City Beautiful Movement.
City Hall is carefully sited to provide a spectacular vista for Bull
Street, the most important street of the historic district. This grand
avenue, between City Hall and Forsyth Park, is punctuated by elegant
squares, lined with imposing domestic and commercial architecture,
graceful Bishop's Crook streetlights. It is named for Col. William Bull,
who helped Oglethorpe site and plan Savannah in 1733. Charleston
also honors and claims Bull, who lived there in a Georgian mansion,
c. 1720, at 35 Meeting Street.

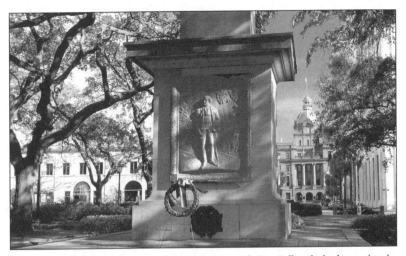

Nathanael Greene Monument at Johnson Square, with City Hall in the background to the right, looking north on Bull Street.

3 **THE COTTON EXCHANGE:** 100 East Bay, is a handsome Romanesque design of 1887 by Boston architect William Gibbons Preston, who also designed the old Chatham County Courthouse at 124 Bull, 340 Bull Street, 225 E. Hall St., 223 Gwinnett St.

The Cotton Exchange, 1887, by William Gibbons Preston

→ For a look at the heart of Savannah, walk down Bull Street to Forsyth Park and back. Buildings we mention will always be to your right. We urge you to take at least some of the detours we describe on the walk. You need not be a serious student of architecture to appreciate the beauty of Savannah's streetscapes.

JOHNSON SQUARE: Laid out in 1733, named to honor Robert Johnson, Governor of South Carolina, who had helped the Georgia colony (South Carolina provided food and protection until 1737). The first 40 houses of the new settlement were built in this area, which was also the commercial heart of Savannah, as it still is today. The Nathanael Greene Monument was designed in 1830 by William Strickland, noted Philadelphia architect.

HISTORIANS'/ARCHITECTS' DETOUR: Walk right on W. Congress St., just south of Johnson Square to Franklin Square. The First African Baptist Church, 23 Montgomery Street, was built by slaves in 1859 and is one of the oldest African-American congregations in America.

A block further west, at 41 Martin Luther King Blvd., is the William Scarbrough House, a neoclassical villa designed in 1818 by William Jay, the great Regency architect from Bath. Note the recessed arched windows which are a characteristic of Jay's work. Later the building was used as a school for children of African descent. Today it is the

First African Baptist Church,1859

Ships of the Sea Museum, with a lovely formal garden. (912-232-1511).

WILLAM JAY

William Jay of Bath, England, worked for John Nash in London before coming to Savannah in 1817. He transformed this frontier town into a city with mansions and public buildings reflecting the more sophisticated styles of Regency Bath and London. Jay also maintained an office in Charleston, where he designed two buildings, possibly more. He founded the South Carolina Academy of Fine Arts with

William Scarbrough House, by William Jay, 1818

Samuel F. B. Morse, Charles Fraser and others. In 1820, Jay was appointed architect to the Board of Public Works in South Carolina and is known to have executed a series of designs before being replaced by Robert Mills. Some buildings attributed to Mills may essentially be Jay designs.

→ Return to Bull Street through the City Market area, where there are shops and restaurants.

Lunch, Coffee Break: *The Lady & Sons, 102 W. Congress Street. 912-233-2600. Traditional Southern food. Reservations recommended. Cosentino's Trattoria, 44 MLK Blvd. for Italian food. Café Ambrosia, 202 E. Broughton, Savannah Coffee House Café, 7 E. Congress Street, and Gallery Espresso, 234 Bull Street for coffee and light meals.*

4 **BROUGHTON STREET,** like so many American shopping streets, destroyed itself by "Modernizing" in the 1960's. The bleak, unornamented facades did not invite shopping and strolling. Today, restoration and replication, important economic revitalization tools, are helping the street make a comeback similar to the rebirth of King Street in Charleston. Be sure to see the Marshall House Hotel, 1851, at 123 Broughton, which recently removed the blank stucco wall that had been slapped over its gracious 19th century facade. The elaborate balcony was replicated from an old photograph.

WRIGHT SQUARE is the second oldest square, also laid out in 1733. It honors Georgia's last Royal Governor, Sir James Wright.

5 **THE U.S. POST OFFICE,** 127 Bull Street, was built in 1898 under the supervision of Charlestonian William Aiken, who trained with Henry Hobson Richardson. The Post Office is a distinguished example of American Renaissance classical eclecticism.

US Post Office on Wright Square, 1898

ARCHITECTS' DETOUR: Go right on West York at the southern end of Wright Square to Telfair Square for another example of the sophisticated architecture of William Jay--a mansion designed for the Telfair family in 1818. General Lafayette dined here in 1825. Now a museum, it is open to the public. (912-232-1177) The interior is a rich display of such Jay features as recessed arched niches, curved walls and ornate cornices. As you return to Bull Street along W. York, you pass a contro-

Telfair Museum by William Jay, 1818

versial site. The much-hated modern "bathroom tile buildings", which caused the loss of a much-loved 1889 building, are now scheduled to be torn down for a handsome contextual federal building designed by the contemporary classicist Robert A. M. Stern, one of the most important architects in the current classical revival.

6 **INDEPENDENT PRESBYTERIAN CHURCH,** Bull and W. Oglethorpe, was originally built in 1817 to the plans of John Holden Greene of Rhode Island, who won the design competition. It has a soaring steeple and fine proportions modeled after London's St. Martin-in-the-Fields. The church burned in 1889 and William Gibbons Preston directed the building of a replica. How many architects today would be so modest? Preston was an important architect of the late 19th century, noted for his Romanesque designs.

Independent Presbyterian Church

CHIPPEWA SQUARE, laid out in 1815, contains a bronze statue of James Oglethorpe, designed by American Renaissance architect Henry Bacon and sculptor Daniel Chester French, who also collaborated on the Lincoln Memorial in Washington, D. C.

7 **THE FIRST BAPTIST CHURCH,** 223 Bull Street at Chippewa Square, built in the Greek revival style in 1833, has six massive columns with modified Tower of the Winds capitals.

8 **MOSES EASTMAN MANSION:** W. McDonough and Chippewa Square, designed in 1844 by Irish-born New York architect Charles Cluskey for a silversmith from New Hampshire. With its graceful elevated columned porticos, the Eastman house provides an important anchor for the square. Each square was laid out with several large sites , trust lots, for such important buildings.

Moses Eastman Mansion,1844 by Charles Cluskey, on left, next to the First Baptist Church, 1833

ARCHITECTS' DETOUR:
Go right on Perry Street
to Orleans Square. You
will pass many hand-
some town homes. Note
the Second Empire dou-
ble house at 105-107 W.
Perry, designed 1872 by
DeWitt Bruyn, an associ-
ate of John Norris, who

Perry Street

came to Savannah in 1860. At 230 Barnard is a Greek Revival masterpiece with Tower of the Winds capitals, designed by Charles Cluskey in
1844 for Aaron Champion, a bank president. The Second Empire roof
was added later. Return to Bull Street and go right.

Lunch: Six Pence Pub, 245 Bull Street.

Sgt. Jasper monument in Madison Square

MADISON SQUARE, laid out in 1839, named for President James Madison,
is dominated by a statue of Sergeant William Jasper who was killed in
1779 during the siege of Savannah. There is a similar statue of Jasper in
White Point Gardens in Charleston.

9 **SORRELL-WEED HOUSE:** W.
Harris and Bull, designed by
Charles Cluskey in 1840 for
Francis Sorrell, a cotton merchant. The recessed arched
windows and shallow elliptical
arch of the parapet reflect the
influence of William Jay. The
house has notable ironwork.

Sorrell-Weed House on Madison Sq., 1840

Cluskey is credited with introducing the tripartite window system to Savannah, as well as for establishing the mid-19th century Savannah house type until the arrival of late 19th century eclecticism. Another example of Cluskey's work may be seen at 14-18 W. Harris Street--paired houses which also feature tripartite windows.

10 GREEN-MELDRIM MANSION: Built on a trust lot on Madison Square at W. Harris Street, a Gothic villa designed in 1853 by John Norris, using opulent materials for a creative design. Green was a cotton merchant who

Green-Meldrim Mansion by John Norris, 1853

had materials for his home shipped from England. The Green House is said to be the most expensive antebellum mansion in Savannah. Later it became the home of Judge Peter Meldrim, a former mayor. General Sherman was headquartered here in 1864 when he presented Savannah to Lincoln as a Christmas present. The Green-Meldrim house is open to the public and has a surviving 19th century garden. (912-233-3845)

11 ST. JOHN'S EPISCOPAL CHURCH: 329 Bull Street, dates to 1853 and was designed by Calvin Otis from New York. Its neo-Gothic style may have inspired the Green-Meldrim mansion design.

12 MASONIC TEMPLE BUILDING: 341 Bull Street, designed by Hyman Whitcover, who also designed City Hall. This 1912 design features a graceful curving corner, arches and a rusticated base, altogether an urbane presence on Madison Square.

Lunch: *Gryphon, 341 Bull, Mrs. Wilkes' Dining Room, 107 W. Jones, famous for authentic southern food (opens at 11am; go early to avoid lines), and Firefly Café, 321 Habersham on Troup Square with outside tables and an eclectic inventive menu.*

MONTEREY SQUARE, laid out in 1847, features a Pulaski Monument to honor Count Casimir Pulaski, who was killed in the 1779 Siege of Savannah.

429 Bull Street, Mercer House on Monterey Square by John Norris, 1860

13 **423-425 BULL STREET:** A trust lot with paired houses by noted architect John Norris. Designed in 1858 with bracketed Italianate cornices and lavish ironwork. Savannah preservationist Lee Adler lives here.

14 **429 BULL STREET:** Another John Norris masterpiece, with elaborate lintels and brackets, designed in 1860 for Gen. Hugh Mercer and once the home of composer Johnny Mercer and later preservationist Jim Williams, who rescued some 70 buildings in Savannah. Williams is better known as the antiques dealer featured in "The Book."

15 **NOBLE HARDEE HOUSE:** SW corner of Gordon and Bull Streets, the mansion is a fine expression of the Italianate craze, with its bracketed cornice, decorative cast iron lintels, handsome ironwork. It was designed in 1860, altered in 1884. President Chester A. Arthur was once a guest here.

Noble Hardee House, 3 W. Gordon Street, 1860

16 **447 BULL STREET:** An Italianate American Renaissance mansion, designed in 1917 by Henrik Wallin, an architect who had been associated with Henry Bacon in New York. When the Historic Savannah

Forsyth Park. 1851

Foundation mounted a campaign to prevent demolition of the mansion, Jim Williams bought it for his antiques business.

FORSYTH PARK: Designed in 1851 by a Bavarian landscape gardener from the Nymphenburg Palace gardens near Munich. He brought sophisticated European ideas to Savannah.

ARCHITECTS' DETOUR: South of Gaston Street, the streets around Forsyth Park are lined with a remarkable assemblage of late 19th century architecture. Alfred Eichberg designed in 1888 Savannah's best expression of the Aesthetic Movement, also known as Queen Anne, at 118 West Hall. Detlef Lienau, an important Neo-Grec architect from New York, designed 501 Whitaker in 1876. Note also 225 East Hall by William Gibbons Preston, architect of the Romanesque Cotton Exchange on East Bay Street.

→ Return to Gaston Street and walk north on Bull.

17 **SCUDDER'S ROW:** On Gordon, just south of Monterey Square is an outstanding row of Greek Revival houses, characteristic of mid-19th century Savannah, built by John and Ephraim Scudder, active builders of the period.

18 **17 EAST GORDON:** Note the beautiful courtyard garden through the gate with urns, a fountain and topiary, popular in Savannah's tiny and usually formal gardens.

17 East Gordon, 1881

→ At Gordon Street on Monterey Square is:

19 **TEMPLE MICKVE ISRAEL:** Built in 1876 for the third oldest Jewish congregation in the United States, the only Gothic style temple in the United States, designed by New York architect Henry G. Harrison, and one of the city's finest examples of Victorian Gothic. It contains a museum devoted to the Sephardic community that arrived in Savannah in 1734. (800-728-6610)

Temple Mickve Israel, 1876

20 **2 EAST TAYLOR:** Handsome Italianate house built in 1880 for Hugh Comer, president of the railroad. Note the segmental arches, molded lintels and overhanging eaves with brackets, characteristics of the Italianate style.

21 **12-14 EAST TAYLOR:** Though built in 1867, the Second Empire mansard roof and projecting bays reflect an 1896 alteration.

East Jones Street

ARCHITECTS'/GARDENERS' DETOUR: Go right on Jones Street, one of the prettiest streets in Savannah. Notice the iron work at #14. Continue east to 220 which has a lovely fountain and iron gate. Return to Abercorn and turn right. On your right, as you enter Lafayette Square is 207 E. Charlton, built in 1858. The architect is believed to have been John Norris. This Greek Revival house was the childhood home of author Flannery O'Connor. Open to the public. (912-233-6014) At 330 Abercorn on a trust

220 Jones Street

14 Jones Street

lot is a flamboyant Second Empire, baroque, Italianate mansion of great charm, ornamented with quoins, balconies and mansard roof, designed by J. D. Hall in 1873. On the opposite side of the square, at 329 Abercorn is the Andrew Low House designed by John Norris in 1849. Greek details are combined with Italianate bracketed eaves. Low was a British cotton broker. In 1870 Robert E. Lee stayed here. Detlef Lienau remodeled the house in 1886. There is a handsome pattern garden. Open to the public. (233-6854)

→ Walk back to Bull Street along Charlton Street.

22 **340 BULL STREET:** Another example of Richardsonian Romanesque as designed by William Gibbons Preston. The building is owned by the Savannah College of Art and Design (SCAD) which has restored many important historic Savannah buildings.

23 **326 BULL STREET:** A Greek Revival mansion of 1834 with a popular bookstore at the street level.

24 **142 BULL STREET:** The Wayne Gordon House of 1818 was designed by William Jay for James Wayne, mayor of Savannah. Detlef Lienau added an attic story and curved piazza in 1886. It was the birthplace of Juliette Gordon Low, who founded the Girl Scouts, and is now a Girl Scout museum, open to the public. A formal garden is visible on Oglethorpe. (912-233-4501)

Lafayette Square

→ At Wright Square:

25 **124 BULL STREET:** The Chatham County Courthouse of 1889 set the fashion for Romanesque in Savannah when it was designed in 1889 by Boston architect William Gibbons Preston, who designed some 23 buildings while here, including the DeSoto Hotel, a romantic gem with turrets, arches and ornamental terra cotta, demolished in 1968 for the DeSoto Hilton, a grotesque misfit in this gracious city.

26 **122 BULL STREET:** The Evangelical Lutheran Church of the Ascension incorporates medieval turrets and Gothic arches. Designed in 1879 by George Clarke.

Lunch: 1790 Restaurant at 307 East President Street. The Tea Room, 7 East Broughton. SoHo South Café, 12 West Liberty Street. www.sohosouthcafe.com

---

ARCHITECTS' DETOUR: Walk across East President Street to Oglethorpe Square. The Richardson-Owens-Thomas House at 124 Abercorn Street was built for Richard Richardson, a banker and cotton merchant who was related by marriage to the architect William Jay. This Jay design is one of the finest Regency homes in America, rivaled only by the George Trenholm mansion in Charleston, which also

Andrew Low garden

The Wayne Gordon House, 142 Bull Street, by William Jay

Savannah College of Art and Design, 340 Bull Street, by William Gibbons Preston, 1893

Chatham County Courthouse by William Gibbons Preston, 1889 and the Evangelical Lutheran Church by George Clarke, 1875

may be a Jay design. There are slave quarters and a restored garden. Lafayette stayed here in 1825. Continue along East President to Columbia Square. At 123 Habersham Street is a flamboyant Queen Anne house, designed in 1893 by De Witt Bruyn. On the north side of the square, 324 State, is the

The Owen Thomas House by William Jay, 1817

Isaiah Davenport House, considered the finest federal house in the city, built by and for Davenport, who came to Savannah from Rhode Island. The Davenport House was threatened with demolition in the 1950's and rescued by ladies who had organized after the important City Market building was demolished. The preservation of this significant house led to the formation of the Historic Savannah Foundation in 1955. There is an 18th century style garden. Open to the public. (912-233-7787) Return west (left) on State Street, going right on

Abercorn to #23 on Reynolds Square. Known as the Pink House, the former home of James Habersham, Jr., c. 1789, is the oldest brick mansion in Georgia. It was restored by Jim Williams (of The Book) in 1968.

→ Return to Bull Street along St. Julian Street.

The Isaiah Davenport House, 1820

27 **CHRIST CHURCH EPISCOPAL** at Bull Street on Johnson Square was built in 1842 on a trust lot set aside by Oglethorpe for the colony's first church. This is the fourth church on the site.

28 **22 BULL STREET:** A neoclassical bank by Mowbray and Uffinger, designed in 1907, relating to the scale and style of Christ Church. Sophisticated architectural good manners.

29 **206 EAST BRYAN STREET:** Mowbray and Uffinger also designed this bank in 1911, with elaborate cartouches and capitols, a skyscraper that respects the classical traditions of Savannah, designed with a base, middle and top. Unlike the 1976 addition to the right. Modernist designs of the mid-20th century were deliberately hostile to their neighbors, obsessed with the "nouveaumania" of that time. Such architecture, disruptive to Savannah's gracious old streetscapes, severely diminishes the integrity of the older buildings. Savannah, like Charleston, needs to be more rigorous in reviewing new construction and in recognizing that the city itself is a work of art that merits restoration. "It is unbelievable that a few unknowledgeable people could allow such a completely out-of-scale, out-of-mileu structure," lamented longtime Savannah preservationist Leopold Adler II of a planned addition to the Telfair Museum. The original Mowbray and Uffinger banks offer a valuable lesson in architectural good manners when designing for a historic context.

30 **1-5 EAST BAY:** Another important John Norris design, the United States Customs House of 1848 with Tower of the Winds capitals on the six granite columns of the portico.

HISTORIANS' DETOUR: The Beach Institute is a detour you can make by car as you head back to Charleston. Go east (left) on Bay, South on Price to East Harris. The museum is on the SE corner. Built in 1867 as a school for free blacks, it is now an African-American museum with an exhibit of the astonishing works of folk artist Ulysses Davis. Continue down Price to your last stop in Savannah, the King Tisdell Cottage, a gingerbread cottage of 1896 at 514 East Huntingdon Street, a museum of Lowcountry African-American culture.
(Call 914-234-8000 to arrange a tour.)

Having feasted your senses on the romantic charms of Savannah's squares and the beauty of her 19th century architecture, you are undoubtedly ready for a gourmet feast in Charleston, which has become a culinary center in the southeast. See page 270 for the restaurant guide with phone numbers so you can make a reservation.

→   Exit Savannah by driving west on Oglethorpe, which leads directly onto the bridge and 17 North to Charleston, regardless of how it looks on the city map.

Cru Café is located in a Charleston single house, which includes seating on the piazza. Chef/owner John Zucker, one of the most talented chefs in town, serves eclectic cuisine that is inventive and always comforting.

Restaurants

CHARLESTON IS A "CULINARY STAR

An up-to-the-minute report on the changing restaurant scene in Charleston — where the locals go and where you can savor the best food in one of America's most important gastronomic centers.

Since we first published *Complete Charleston* in 1997, the culinary scene has undergone an extraordinary transformation. The food revolution reached Charleston in the mid 1990s, when restaurants featuring New Southern cuisine began to proliferate. In 1992 a travel writer observed that, "eating out in restaurants is a somewhat new trend in Charleston." However, Craig Claiborne, the late noted food critic, wrote later that same year that, "Charleston boasts more restaurants per capita than any city in America. And it has clearly earned preeminence as one of the great restaurant cities in the South. The old world ambiance, combined with fresh local ingredients and even fresher ideas from resident chefs and gastronomes, makes dining an irresistible affair." The culinary renaissance of Charleston occurred rapidly. Claiborne's observation is even more to the point today. The decade proceeded into a feeding frenzy. Charleston became one of the most important culinary cities in the whole country.

Eating well is a Charleston tradition. As early as 1745, visitors marveled at feasts prepared for them in Charleston homes. Bostonian Josiah Quincy wrote in 1773 of his pleasure at a "most elegant table" in the Miles Brewton house with "the richest wine I ever tasted." Puritan influences inhibited cooking in New England. Charlestonians, on the other hand, sought to emulate the aristocratic social life enjoyed on their extensive travels in Europe. Lavish dining was a mark of high status in Charleston.

Influences from the Caribbean, France, Spain, Great Britain, Africa and the Orient converged to create a unique cuisine during the 18th century. In part, the traditional food of Charleston might be considered a forerunner of the now trendy "fusion" cooking. Culinary historian John Martin Taylor (*Lowcountry Cooking* and *The New Southern Cook*) believes Charleston may be the first place in America to have developed a regional cuisine. Taylor has also pointed out that young salad greens, now known as mesclun, were staples in Charleston's colonial kitchen gardens. He notes, too, that stone-ground grits, garlic and the finest olive oils were also early staples just as they are today. The African contribution was particularly significant. "It was the African connection" states Karen Hess (*The Carolina Rice Kitchen*), "that accounted for the near mythic reputation of Southern cooking." Ingredients with an African connection include okra, yams, watermelon, black-eye peas, peanuts, sesame seeds and rice. One of the most famous local dishes is she-crab soup, created by William Deas, who was a butler for Mayor Robert Goodwyn Rhett. In *Two Hundred Years of Charleston Cooking* (1930), Deas was described as "one of the greatest cooks in the world."

As in modern "fusion" cooking, foreign culinary techniques in the 18th century were applied to local ingredients and exotic imports. Charleston being a port city, benne (sesame) seeds from Sierra Leone, Jordanian almonds, port and Madeira were staples in early local kitchens. Henry Laurens, eminent patriot and statesman, who had been imprisoned in London during the Revolution and released in exchange for Lord Cornwallis, was also seriously into gardening and good food. Laurens introduced the city to olives, capers, limes, ginger, French grapes, plums and pears in his four-acre Ansonborough garden. The Duke of Saxe-Weimar, visiting in 1826, was astonished by "the most beautiful tropical fruit."

But the 20th century brought some bleak dining years for Charleston visitors. According to a travel writer of 1939, travelers engaged in "a frantic search for civilized food, winding up in a chain drugstore." A visitor of 1947 noted that "the great cooking of Charleston has always been private, although there are tales of the old Planters Hotel and Mansion House."

CHARLESTON BECAME A FOODIE MECCA IN THE 1990S

Charleston's public culinary scene began its dramatic transformation in 1989 when Chef Louis Osteen opened his first Charleston restaurant and was soon acclaimed as "one of the most gifted chefs in America." He is credited with elevating grits to "haute status." Charleston is now a mecca for young talent from leading restaurants and cooking schools around the country. These chefs are frequently featured on national television and vie with each other for exalting the excellence and creativity of Charleston's restaurants.

Food critics and their followers have been flocking here. The city is now famous as a center of New Southern cuisine. Savvy foodies visit on a regular basis,

Bob Waggoner, chef of Charleston Grill, where you can depend on the fish being very fresh.

not only to feast their eyes on Charleston's Palladian splendor, but also to experience the cuisine of the city's famous restaurants. Two that opened in 1997 — **Charleston Grill** and **Peninsula Grill** — have received innumerable awards. Both restaurants feature ingredient-driven Lowcountry favorites, New Southern cuisine and American classics.

Shrimp and grits is a quintessential Lowcountry dish. Together and separately, they are a staple of Charleston menus. There are more restaurants serving haute grits in Charleston than in any other city of a similar size. If you thought grits were only a rather tasteless breakfast food, you have not experienced the stone-ground grits of Charleston's finest restaurants and the tasty varieties of the city's famed local sweet shrimp and grits. This is serious haute comfort food.

Charleston is inspiring dishes in great restaurants of other cities. For instance, lobster with grits, long a staple of **Charleston Grill** and **Anson** finally made it to New York. The dish inspired high praise from *New York Times* critic William Grimes. Lowcountry grits and polenta, which are being milled in Columbia, SC, by the owners of Anson, are showing up on the menus of the best restaurants all over America and were featured in *Saveur Magazine*. The Manager of **Anson**, dining recently in Wolfgang Puck's Post Rio, a popular restaurant in San Francisco, was delighted to read on the menu that the tuna was served with "Anson Mills polenta." A recent restaurant review in *The New York Times* recommended a side dish of "Anson Mills polenta."

R. W. Apple, Jr. of *The New York Times* is a regular in Charleston restaurants. Apple has deemed the breakfast at **Hominy Grill** "one of the best in America". He has also proclaimed that Hominy Grill, in his view, ties with Galatoires in New Orleans for the best food in the whole Southeast. On a recent visit to Charleston, Apple added **FIG** to his list of favorites: "Chef Mike Lata turns out a superb hanger steak...his luscious pudding made with Carolina Gold Rice puts other local versions to shame...FIG's strongest suit is vegetables...An adherent of the Slow Food movement, Lata knows when to gild and when not to...his roasted beets are sweet simplicity."

Food critic John Mariani wrote in *Esquire Magazine* that, "This impeccably maintained historic small city now ranks as a bellwether of good taste in America."

Mariani said he'd rather eat here than in Boston, Denver or Seattle. Catharine Reynolds, an editor of *Gourmet*, who covers the restaurant scene in Paris and New York, shared her list of favorites: **Cru Café, Cypress, Hank's, Hominy Grill,** and **Peninsula Grill**. The *Wine Spectator* notes that, "The charm, the history, the favorable climate, the hospitality and hot restaurant scene all add up to a terrifically alluring package.". *Sky Magazine* recommended **Hominy Grill, Jestine's, Hank's, Peninsula Grill, McCrady's, Cypress, Magnolias, Circa 1886, 39 Rue de Jean, High Cotton,** and **Charleston Grill**. *Gourmet* featured **Anson, Cru Café, Coast, FIG, Fulton Five, Modica, Hominy Grill, Il Cortile del Re.** and **39 Rue de Jean.** *Food and Wine* recommended **FIG** and **Fleet Landing**. *Southern Living* featured **Lana, Fulton Five, La Fourchette,** and **Il Cortile del Re.** Educational television recently featured the chefs of **Hank's, SNOB, Charleston Grill, Magnolias, Cypress** and **Oak Steakhouse.**

Nathalie Dupree, who sparked the New Southern cuisine movement with cooking classes, books and TV shows, chaired the first annual Charleston Food and Wine Festival and gave demonstrations.

THE CHARLESTON FOOD AND WINE FESTIVAL

In 2006 Charleston celebrated its culinary achievements with the city's first annual Distinctively Charleston Food and Wine Festival. Wine professionals and food celebrities from across America gave demonstrations, signed books, and conducted wine tastings. For four delicious days, it was possible to experience Charleston's finest cuisine — at special dinners and in Marion Square, where there were 70 vendors and many free samples. Organizers of the festival expected three thousand people. Actually over eight thousand people attended the various events.

The festival was chaired by the TV celebrity and author Nathalie Dupree, who now lives in Charleston. Dupree began the New Southern cuisine movement when she lived in Atlanta and founded a cooking school there. The Charleston festival was hailed by *The New York Times* — "A culinary star is born" headlined a two-page review of the festival, which marked Charleston's arrival in the gastronomic big time. "The festival went above and beyond what anyone could have dreamed," said Chef Bob Waggoner of **Charleston Grill**. It is to be an annual event. In 2007, it will be held March 1-4. For info: www.charlestonfoodandwine.com.

BISTRONOMIE IN CHARLESTON

During 2006, there were numerous press reports on a new trend in Parisian restaurants — certain bistros serving traditional food with a creative flair have become so popular they are upstaging the Michelin three-stars. These neo-bistros are replacing novelty cuisine, grand floral arrangements and frightfully expensive menus with a more casual atmosphere and an emphasis on the food itself. Prices are more reasonable. Chefs are focused on pleasing customers, not intimidating them. Yves Camdeborde, considered the godfather of the bistronomie movement in Paris, is currently the chef/owner of Le Comptoir du Relais, a tiny bistro with a gastronomic dinner on week nights that must be booked six months in advance.

Bistronomie is popular in Charleston, too, and many restaurants fit the mode. This renewed enthusiasm for traditional regional cuisine parallels the resurgence of passion for the classical tradition in the fine arts and architecture. Novelty for novelty's sake, as practiced by Modernist architects and nouvelle chefs, has run its course. Respect for history has always been intense in Charleston. The current Renaissance in classical painting, sculpture and architecture is closely related to the culinary Renaissance. Chef Frank Lee of **SNOB** points out that in Charleston the Renaissance of the arts, craftsmanship and food are all related. "It would not have happened

without preservationists and those with vision, such as Mayor Riley. Protecting our cultural heritage has enriched the whole area." Chefs such as Lee are applying their training in classical cooking techniques to local ingredients and celebrating the culinary heritage of Charleston.

The first two restaurants in the bistronomie style — **SNOB** and **Hominy Grill** — opened in Charleston in the mid-1990s at about the same time as Camdeborde's first restaurant in Paris, La Regalade.

The most talented chefs seek to enchant, not shock, the palate—with new takes on local classics, such as the okra and shrimp beignets at Hominy Grill.

Bistronomie chefs are guided by tradition, enhancing Lowcountry dishes with new flavors but with restraint. Emphasis is on the excellence of the ingredients, local as much as possible. The bistronomie style is a natural for Charleston where residents cherish tradition and good taste and are not impressed with the novel, the ostentatious or the weird. The best bistronomie chefs create dishes with the intent to delight, not shock — the okra and shrimp beignets at **Hominy Grill**, for instance. The shrimp and grits at **SNOB** have set a standard — stone-ground grits, of course, with the purest local shrimp. Discrete amounts of truffle oil may enhance sauces and mushroom grits cakes. Fabulous New Southern cuisine at modest prices can also be savored at **FIG, Joseph's, Cru Café, Fleet Landing,** and **Carolina's.** The newest star on the bistronomie scene is **Mercato,** where Chef Jacques Larson is focused on the cuisine of Italy, creating such memorable dishes as ravioli di Lowcountry. Other local favorites that focus on superior food in a casual setting and have reasonable prices include **La Fourchette, Hank's, Lana, Il Cortile del Re, Pane e Vino, 39 Rue de Jean, Sermet's, Coast, Chai's, Basil, Fish,** and **Fast and French.**

A new local favorite is La Fourchette, an authentic French bistro, which opened in 2006. Forget your diet. The frites, double-fried in duck fat, are not to be missed.

CULINARY TOURISM—DON'T MISS THESE STARS

Some fourteen restaurants in the Historic District (plus two nearby) feature chefs who have been honored by the prestigious James Beard Foundation in New York (as compared with only seven in the whole state of North Carolina and two in Savannah).

The James Beard Foundation was the brainchild of America's much-loved chef, the late Julia Child, who suggested, after Beard's death in 1985, that his townhouse in New York be preserved as a gathering place, fostering and celebrating culinary excellence in America. "The Beard House is like having Beethoven's house as a center for musicians, because Beard is as important to food people as Beethoven is to the music world," she said. Beard began to write for *Gourmet Magazine* in 1942 and by the 1950s, he was considered the dean of American cooking. Foundation awards are the "Oscars of the food world." In addition to awards, every month the Foundation invites talented chefs to prepare dinners at the James Beard House. Charleston is fortunate that so many of its local chefs have received this honor. It is the culinary equivalent of a debut at Carnegie Hall.

You will surely want to taste the creations of local chefs who have taken their Charleston expertise to the Beard townhouse in Greenwich Village and who have been lauded by the sophisticated palates of the New York food community: Mike Lata (**FIG**), Robert Carter (**Peninsula Grill**), Frank McMahon (honored while at Elliott's in Charleston, now at **Hank's**), Frank Lee (**SNOB, High Cotton**), Brett McKee (**Oak Steakhouse**), Donald Barickman (**Magnolias, Blossom Café, Cypress**), Bob Waggoner (**Charleston**

Grill), John Olsson (honored while chef of Le Plumet Royal in Princeton, now at **Meritage**), Brett Maynard (**Fulton Five**), Ciaran Duffy (honored while at Rainwater in Atlanta, now at **Tristan**), and Jacques Larson (honored while at Union Hall in Charleston, now at **Mercato**). The Beard Foundation has yet to discover one of Charleston's newest culinary stars—Tin Dizdarevic, who took over the kitchen at **Carolina's** recently. Dizdarevic was lured away from Tom Colicchio's Craftbar in New York. He's smoking pork bellies at Carolina's, adding a variety of vegetables and focusing on the best of the region's local ingredients. You can taste South Carolina's

Chef Robert Carter is one of a number of local chefs, who put Charleston on the national culinary map. From the moment he arrived as chef and co-owner of Peninsula Grill in 1997, the restaurant has been packed.

palmetto bass here. The Fruits de Mer is one of the best of the fresh local seafood dishes in Charleston. And don't miss the New Southern creations of Robert Stehling of **Hominy Grill**, who has been repeatedly acclaimed in *The New York Times*. **Lana's** John Ondo and John Zucker of **Cru Café** are chefs who are also creating very good buzz among local foodies.

OVER 130 RESTAURANTS IN THE HISTORIC DISTRICT

The pedestrian-friendly streets of Charleston, lined with beautiful classical buildings and the concentration of so many fine restaurants within walking distance of each other makes the city especially attractive to those seeking seriously good food. Many restaurants have the added charm of being located in buildings built nearly two centuries ago. The old warehouse district along East Bay has become a restaurant row. Market Street is filling up with fine dining restaurants. As you experience the incredible architecture of the city, you can also read menus and plan meals in advance. And after dinner, the magic of the evening persists — you can stroll leisurely back to your hotel room, continuing to enjoy the historicity and architectural treasures of the city. No need for taxis or designated drivers. There are over 130 restaurants in the historic district. This dense concentration makes Charleston unique among other food cities, such as New Orleans or San Francisco. Most are locally owned; many chef-owned. This and a growing emphasis on fresh local ingredients encourage high culinary standards. Menus have begun to credit local farmers for organic and heirloom produce.

GRITS, BEIGNETS AND BAGELS

Two of the brightest talents on the breakfast scene are Robert Stehling of **Hominy Grill** for traditional Lowcountry/New Southern cuisine and Joseph Passarini of **Joseph's**, if you crave beignets, awesome French toast and creative egg dishes. Both restaurants also do outstanding brunches. Be sure to allow time for a leisurely lavish Sunday brunch. Historically, breakfast was a substantial meal in Charleston. Breakfast daily is also served at **Diana's, Fast and French, Modica, Grill 225, Kennedy's, Kudo Coffee, Palmetto Café, Peninsula Grill, Port City Java, Sweetwater Café, Tristan,** and **Wentworth Grill.** And on Sunday, there is brunch at **39 Rue de Jean, Boathouse, Jestine's, High Cotton, Magnolias, Mistral, Sermet's,** and **Vickery's.** Bagel cravings may be satisfied at **Bruegger's, Modica, Café Café, Diana's, Kennedy's** and **Port City Java.**

CULINARY FOOD TOURS, COOKING LESSONS

Historians are taking food seriously, examining the new field of culinary tourism. Lucy M. Long (*Southern Folklore*, 1998) observed that food is central to the touristic experience, that "culinary tourism utilizes the senses of taste, smell, touch and vision and offers a deeper, more integrated level of experiencing" another place. So you can intellectually rationalize those delicious calories as serious research, serious touring. Leslie Brenner analyzes the food revolution and the phenomenon of chic food and celebrity chefs in *American Appetite*, noting that, "one reaches the ulti-

A foodie headquarters, Charleston Cooks offers classes and demonstrations and a shop of essential kitchen tools. After a demonstration, it is more like a restaurant, as wine and whatever was cooked is served.

mate level of sophistication if one knows restaurants in cities other than one's own." The word is certainly out about Charleston as a gastronomic center of the South. The better Charleston restaurants report that they have regulars who visit from Atlanta, Charlotte and New York.

Charleston Cooks, 194 East Bay Street, features an emporium of kitchen supplies and culinary events of classes and demonstrations. A pleasant lunch or dinner plan is to attend a demonstration. After the demonstration, guests are served a glass of wine and the meal that has been cooked. www.mavericksouthernkitchens.com

Edible Lowcountry provides tours and events for the serious culinary visitor. The organization also publishes a magazine devoted to the culinary scene in Charleston. www.ediblelowcountry.com

THE THREE O'CLOCK DINNER

It was the custom in Charleston, in pre-air conditioning days, to have dinner at three o'clock. A book with the same title by Josephine Pinckney describes these more gracious leisurely days. In fact, eating a major midday meal makes very good sense in these calorie-conscious times, as you can walk off the calories after. If you are visiting Charleston in the summer, it is particularly pleasant to linger over a lengthy meal at midday and walk about the city in the late afternoon. **Tristan, SNOB, Sermet's, 82 Queen, Lana, Joseph's, Cru Café, Little Thai Too, Palmetto Café,** and **Wentworth Grill** and **Grill 225** serve until three. A few restaurants produce serious meals almost all day: **39 Rue de Jean, Diana's, Fast and French, Fleet Landing, Jestine's, Jim 'N Nick's, Magnolias, Mistral,** and **Vickery's.**

FEASTING AS YOU STROLL

One of the great pleasures of Charleston is that you are never far from a restaurant that is open and serving exceptional food. It is a pleasure cherished by local residents and particularly important for visitors, as it is impossible to calculate how long a tour of a house museum or a walk through a neighborhood might take. In some cities, the finest restaurants tend to maintain rigidly conventional hours — Le Bernardin in New York, for instance, does not open a second before noon. But here in Charleston, you will find it much more relaxed, with hours hospitably geared to visitors and to children who might need a snack or a cool drink between usual meal times.

Some excellent restaurants serve non-stop all day. Chef/owner Donald Barickman of **Magnolias** explained, "Charleston is the kind of town where people aren't looking at their watch all day long. We want to be there when they need us." You can pop into Magnolias in mid afternoon to sample house-made potato chips with blue cheese and scallions, the seared yellow grits cake, or the Down South egg roll (do not leave Charleston without tasting this).

Also on East Bay is **SNOB** (lunch until 3, dinner at 5:30). The menu varies, but you might find shiitake mushrooms with foie gras mousse and spinach or an oyster stew. Good place to sample shrimp and grits. **High Cotton** opens at 5:30, with such possibilities as a terrine of foie gras, tasty fried oysters, or beer battered onion rings.

If you are doing the Waterfront tour, there is **Carolina's** nearby, which opens at 5 and has extraordinary shrimp and crab wontons, fried local oysters, and fried green tomatoes with pimiento cheese on the appetizer menu. **Oak Steakhouse** on Broad Street has a casual bar area, where you may sample such appetizers as steak tartare, grilled calamari, pan seared Hudson Valley foie gras with a truffle potato cake and a spiced poached pear.

On Market Street, **Peninsula Grill** opens at 5:30pm — feast away on wild mushroom grits, seared carpaccio of lamb, foie gras with Carolina peach jam and duck BBQ biscuit, fried oysters with a mango coulis. A few doors away, **Mercato**, which opens at 5, offers magical Italian-inspired creations, such as octopus and shaved fennel and delicious pizzas. If you have a craving for mussels at 4 o'clock and you are near Marion Square, pop into **39 Rue de Jean**, 39 John Street, which serves hamburgers and delicious French bistro food all day.

If you've just enjoyed the Greek Revival grandeur of Ansonborough and it is 5:30, you could recharge over the calamari with apricot sauce at **Anson** or a yummy fruits de mer (seafood tower) at **Hank's**. While you are doing the Radcliffeborough walk, you have an opportunity to enjoy the New Southern cuisine of **Hominy Grill** and the Mediterranean menu at **Lana**. They are both local favorites.

When you need that break from strolling through the eleven neighborhoods of Charleston's extraordinary historic district, when the Palladian grandeur and glorious gardens have overwhelmed your senses, let this be an opportunity to sample the food of a nationally-acclaimed chef. The appetizer and salad sections of the best menus offer an astonishing array of temptations, often large enough so that one or two make a meal. Dessert menus feature sinfully delicious creations. Southerners love sweet foods, even add sugar to some vegetables. Forget about dieting. Our coffee break suggestions include convenient places in the neighborhoods, ranging from corner grocery stores to meccas of haute cuisine. But wherever you are in the historic district, except on South Battery, it is but a short walk to nationally-acclaimed kitchens.

THE SIMPLE MEAL

There are times when you need a break from foie gras and elaborate creations. Charleston has a wealth of locally-owned, modest but excellent, charming little restaurants where you can have a light meal in a casual ambiance without spending a fortune. Chain restaurants do not thrive in a city that attracts so many culinary sophisticates and where local residents demand high standards. Hamburgers and good club sandwiches are readily available; however, while in Charleston, you might find it more fun to have a crabburger or a BST (bacon-salmon-tomato). Tasty simple meals are served at **Joseph's, Hominy Grill, Hank's, FIG, Fleet Landing, Jimmy Dengate's, Mercato, Fish, Pane e Vino, SNOB, Fast and French, Lana, Jim**

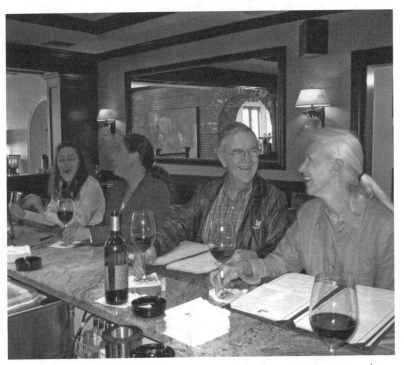

A not-very-well-kept secret is that the juiciest and tastiest hamburgers in town are served at the bar of High Cotton.

N Nick's, Kudu Coffee, Cru Café, Oak Steakhouse (which has wonderful fried chicken in a generous portion), Sermet's and La Fourchette.

For some of the best old-fashioned Southern food at modest prices, have at least one meal at Jestine's. Vickery's is popular with college students. 39 Rue de Jean serves good hamburgers with authentic French fries all day. High Cotton also serves delicious hamburgers at the bar, which opens at 4pm. Modica, an Italian café, offers a tempting array of paninis, soups, and salads and some of the best gelato in town, which is made fresh every day, as is the mozzarella cheese.

TASTY TAPAS

Tapas are creative small plates. Dining on just a few tapas, especially at night, is a smart way to keep calories as well as the budget under control. Meritage was the first tapas restaurant to open in Charleston with an eclectic menu of such things as won tons, lobster mashed potatoes, chicken livers, and rack of lamb. Chai's (which serves sophisticated Asian/American fusion dishes) and Raval (notable for good Spanish wines, outrageously good fried potatoes and an artisanal cheese plate) arrived recently. Pearlz, an oyster/seafood bar, is another good option if you seek a light dinner. The Thoroughbred Club inside Charleston Place, a cocktail/tea lounge, now offers tapas beginning at 4pm. If you prefer a quiet meal, go early. Tapas places tend to be very popular with a young crowd that may become noisy later in the evening. Many of the tapas plates, such as spring rolls, are designed for sharing. If you do not plan to share, make that clear when you order. Otherwise, the service can be haphazard, with a plate or two coming out sporadically rather than orders for everyone being filled at once.

BEYOND HAMBURGERS: CHILD-FRIENDLY RESTAURANTS

Charleston's famed hospitality extends well into the kitchens of the city's most upscale restaurants. Children will find themselves being pampered by celebrity chefs, many of whom will produce hot dogs, hamburgers and such while preparing foie gras extravaganzas for their parents.

Timing is everything. The best time to dine with children at Charleston's finest restaurants is early. Go when the restaurant opens, and you are more likely to get special service. High chairs and boosters are readily available. Some restaurants features items for children or can honor requests. Side dishes often include foods children like. **Anson** has a children's menu and can often accommodate special requests. **High Cotton** recommends its onion rings. **Hank's** offers chicken fingers. Grilled cheese sandwiches might be produced at **SNOB**. Bob Waggoner of **Charleston Grill** is especially pleased to welcome children. Waggoner says he was never served lamb as a child and believes it is an important part of a child's education to introduce them to restaurant foods they don't get at home everyday. He's noticed that when strangers are offering children new foods and asking how they like it, children often become more adventurous. But he promises to produce chicken fingers if necessary. There are also a few kitchens that stay open all afternoon; some serve lunch until three; some open for dinner as early as 5. **Fleet Landing** has a special kids' menu of grilled cheese, chicken fingers, fried seafood and fries. One of the most popular restaurants for families with small children is the **Boathouse**. There is no foie gras on the menu, but you can order excellent sushi and lobster. There are many child-friendly options, a relaxed setting and free valet parking. Some restaurants include both formal and informal dining areas, where children would be comfortable, such as **Carolina's** and **Oak Steakhouse**.

DINING AL FRESCO

There is a special magic about the European sidewalk café that has prompted restaurants all over the world to expand their service to tables outside. In Charleston, the narrow sidewalks have restricted this pleasure. However, many possibilities for dining al fresco do exist in secret gardens behind such restaurants as **Hominy Grill** and **Joseph's**. **Il Cortile del Re** has a romantic side courtyard of tables. **Fleet Landing**, which is built on a pier in the Cooper River, has 100 seats outside. **Tristan** has a pleasant terrace on

South Market Street. **Basil**, which is located on a wide sidewalk, has tables on the sidewalk. **Palmetto Café**, in a courtyard within Charleston Place, is one of the most charming places for lunch. **Chai's**, a tapas restaurant, serves in a side courtyard. The **Pavilion Rooftop** is popular for light meals and a view of the city. **Pane e Vino** serves authentic Italian trattoria food in a garden. At **Fish** and **Cru Café**, you can eat on a piazza. **Kudu Coffee** serves delicious coffee drinks and light meals all day and has a pleasant courtyard. **Vickery's** and the **Boathouse** have outside terraces. **82 Queen** serves meals in a quiet charming courtyard, is a pleasant space for a simple lunch. **Wentworth Grill** has 15 seats outside. However, the most Parisian experience is provided on the terrace of **39 Rue de Jean**. Here, the round tables and chairs are as authentically Left Bank as the food.

It is possible to dine al fresco in many somewhat secret gardens and courtyards. One of the most popular is Il Cortile del Re, where they serve authentic Italian cuisine in a side courtyard, barely visible from King Street.

EATING LOCAL

Organic food these days is being rivaled by the increasing demand for local ingredients. At the forefront of the movement in Charleston are such chefs as Mike Lata (**FIG**), Robert Stehling (**Hominy Grill**), Frank Lee (**SNOB**) and Tin Dizdarevic (**Carolina's**). More and more chefs are joining the movement and feature fresh local seafood and produce on their menus. Local shrimpers, for instance, provide a number of restaurants with shrimp that has never been flash-frozen or dipped in preservatives. These shrimp have a much sweeter taste than any you might have eaten in the finest restaurants in New York. It is smart to ask questions about the source of foods before you order.

One of the few sidewalks that are large enough for outside tables and chairs is by Basils, where you can savor delicious Thai food al fresco.

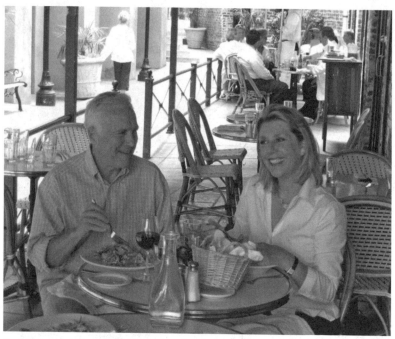

Parisian brasserie food, (also sushi and hamburgers) is served at 39 Rue de Jean. It is particularly pleasant to eat on their side terrace.

BON APPETIT

The following restaurant list is by no means complete. There are over 130 places to eat, from pizza places to multi-course fine dining restaurants, in the historic district, which is an area less than two square miles. We've listed our favorites plus others, which are popular with visitors.

As locals, we prefer restaurants that are reasonably priced, take cooking seriously, and are not noisy. We lived for many years in James Beard's neighborhood in New York City, which had New York's best food markets during the 1980s and a cluster of excellent restaurants, including The Coach House (where Beard was a regular) and La Tulipe (our favorite). Having experienced the food revolution there, it has been very exciting for us to watch the culinary transformation of Charleston. Local Charleston chefs have become obsessed with fresh ingredients, maintain restaurant herb gardens, get regular deliveries from nearby Wadmalaw farmers and import such delicacies as foie gras and baby lobster tails. We regularly visit New York and Paris and are proud to discover that Charleston's restaurants are keeping pace with the finest in both cities and are producing creations and regional specialties that are, in fact, unique.

From the beginning, Charleston cuisine has been a fusion of influences from many places. Charleston menus feature such delicious New Southern creations as ravioli di Lowcountry, collard-green egg rolls with tasso, red pepper puree and peach chutney. Local fish is enhanced with truffle oil or hoisin/ginger sauce, and mac' and cheese is infused with lobster and crab or truffles. Foie gras may be served with a hush puppy.

In addition to all the New Southern dishes, don't leave town without tasting such traditional Lowcountry specialties as crab cakes, she-crab soup, shrimp and grits, shrimp pilau, fried chicken, Frogmore Stew, red rice, artichoke relish, peach chutney, hoppin' John, okra, fried green tomatoes, pimiento cheese, fried catfish, red pepper jelly, hush puppies, corn bread, collard greens, yams, fresh local seafood, such as grouper, mahi mahi, shrimp and oysters, Huguenot torte, benne wafers and pecan pie.

Some restaurants discount wine or food on certain nights. On Sunday, for instance, the seafood tacos are only $3 at **Coast**, the tapas at **Meritage** are ½ off, and wine is discounted at **Carolina's**. When you reserve, ask about such special offers.

LOWCOUNTRY RESTAURANTS

ANSON, *12 Anson Street. 577-0551.* Dinner nightly at 5:30pm. Bar opens at 5. New Southern. Highly praised by *Southern Living* and *Gourmet Magazine*. Specialties include local grouper, cornmeal fried oysters, crab cakes with a sweet onion corn relish and spicy aioli, calamari with apricot shallot sauce, and crispy flounder. This is a good place to taste she-crab soup, a quintessential Southern specialty. Chicken breast is served with heirloom Carolina Gold Rice Pudding. And of course, there are Anson Mills grits served with shrimp. *Saveur Magazine* featured the grits and the polenta, which are being milled in Columbia, SC, and may be ordered from www.ansonmills.com. *Wine Spectator* has called Anson "the most romantic restaurant in Charleston" and "the city's best example of high class Lowcountry cooking." www.ansonrestaurant.com

BRUEGGER'S, *347 King Street.* Many varieties of old-fashioned kettle boiled bagels are baked daily on a stone hearth. Try an everything bagel with salmon and cream cheese.

BASIL, *460 King Street. 724-3490.* Lunch 11:30am-2:30pm. Dinner nightly at 5pm. Owner/chefs Chai and Henry Eang were born in Cambodia. Their restaurant is a star of Upper King Street. Excellent Thai cuisine created by a Thai chef. His signature dish is a red curry duck, which is deep fried and served with vegetables in a curry sauce. The Pad Thai is addictive. Reasonable prices and tables on the sidewalk. www.basilthair-estaurant.com

BOATHOUSE, *Chapel and East Bay. 577-7171.* Dinner daily from 5 on. Raw bar opens daily at 4pm. Sun. brunch 11am-2pm. Specializing in seafood, delicious lobster tails, and sushi-quality yellow fin tuna — try it with stone-ground grits and bleu cheese coleslaw (*Gourmet Magazine*

recently printed the recipe). Convenient if you are returning from a side trip, as there is a large parking lot. The restaurant is popular with families, has a casual setting and a diverse menu with fried seafood as well as sushi and lobster tails. www.crewboathouserestaurants.com

BURBAGE'S GROCERY, *157 Broad Street.* 723-4054. Open 8am-6:30pm M-Sat. This much-loved corner grocery is a great place to pick up a picnic. There are usually about a half dozen different sandwiches available, but you can call ahead for special orders. Their excellent Bar-B-Q has won many awards.

CAFÉ CAFÉ, *177 Meeting Street.* 723-3622. Daily from 7am. Bagels, croissants, wraps, salads.

CAROLINA'S, *10 Exchange Street.* 724-3800. Dinner nightly, from 5:30 pm. Some of the best and most reasonably priced food in Charleston can be savored here. Chef Tin Dizdarevic was lured away from Craftbar in New York in late 2005. Carolina's declined a few years ago. However, Chef Dizdarevic has revamped and invigorated the menu with fresh local ingredients. Heirloom South Carolina pork bellies are smoked in-house, and the restaurant is producing bacon and outrageously delicious pates. Lavender for a yummy panna cotta and other herbs are grown in the restaurant's herb garden. The popular won tons remain and are better than ever. The seasonal menu features impeccably fresh seafood, Palmetto bass, South Carolina quail, and Southern specialties such as crab cakes, a crabmeat grits cake, fried green tomatoes and pimiento cheese. While some restaurants may seek to dazzle you with fussy and weird flavor combinations, at Carolina's the emphasis is on the craft of cooking and the purity of the finest ingredients in the mode of the celebrated Tom Colicchio, chef/owner of Gramercy Tavern, Craftbar and Craft in New York. Colicchio has been hailed as one of the most influential chefs in the country, and that influence can be experienced at Carolina's. Wine by the bottle is reduced on Sunday and Monday before 8pm. www.crewcarolina.com

CHAI'S, *462 King Street.* 722-7313. Daily 5:30pm on. The owners of nearby Basil recently opened this tapas restaurant, which includes tables in a side courtyard. Crispy salmon is perfectly flash-fried, leaving it quite rare and served with a delicious seaweed salad and ponzu sauce. If there is a special of figs stuffed with gorgonzola with a balsamic port wine reduction sauce, it is a must. Yin and yang features vegetables tempura and grilled with roasted garlic oil. Excellent spring rolls. Other tiny tasty dishes include tuna sashimi, duck scallopini, oysters Rockefeller, papaya salad and a mini angus burger with shoestring fries. On Sundays, there are 30 wines reduced to $30 a bottle.

CHARLESTON GRILL, *244 King Street.* 577-4522. Dinner nightly at 6pm. New Southern/French. Bob Waggoner, considered one of the most talented chefs in the Southeast, cooked in respected restaurants in France before coming to Charleston in 1997. He trained with French super chefs, such as Pierre Gagnaire, and he operated his own restaurant in Moneteau, France. Charleston Grill has been awarded a coveted Four-Diamond Award from AAA and has received numerous other awards. Waggoner applies his expertise in classical French cooking to local traditional recipes and ingredients. A seasonal menu with fresh ingredients includes herbs from his garden on the terrace of Charleston Place and local farm produce. The James Beard Foundation praised Waggoner's use of traditional fare, "elegantly reimagined." The crab cakes are perfection. Normally Frogmore Stew, a spicy

This Gullah classic traditionally has corn on the cob and shrimp still in their shells. At Charleston Grill, however, the flavor is there, but the cobs and shells have been removed for you.

Lowcountry dish which originated on St. Helena Island, includes corn on the cob and unshelled shrimp. Nibbling on an ear of corn that has been floating in a stew is a bit messy. At Charleston Grill, it has been tidied up, and you will encounter shelled shrimp and corn that has been removed from the cob. Every Friday, Chef Waggoner changes five items on the menu. A sophisticated dessert menu includes a chocolate quintet for chocoholics. Dinner here can be pricey; however, main courses may be shared with no tacky plating charge. www.charlestongrill.com

CINTRA, *16 North Market Street*. 377-1090. Dinner nightly, from 5:30pm. Northern Italian cuisine by chef Thomas Clayton, including a butternut squash ravioli with fried sage, osso bucco, Tuscan bean soup with truffle butter and veal Marsala. Pastas are made in house and include veal cheek ravioli with wild mushroom jus, and gnocchi with truffled spring veggies. Banquettes, an open kitchen, gracious service.

CIRCA 1886, *149 Wentworth Street*. 853-7828. Dinner Mon.-Sat. from 5:30pm. Seasonal innovative menu by chef Marc Collins, who combines his classical French training with Lowcountry traditions. Dining room has comfortable booths, a romantic intimate ambiance. Expensive.

COAST, *39D John Street*. 722-8838. Dinner nightly at 5:30pm. A beachy décor within an old warehouse with exposed brick and wood floors. There are the usual fried offerings. More interesting choices would include the seafood tacos, the red snapper almondine with a white wine and lemon sauce, or lobster and crab au gratin. Popular with a young-ish set. Don't be put off by the noisy recorded music outside. It is possible to have a quiet meal if you go early and ask for a booth in the back room. Moderate prices, and the wine is discounted on Sunday. www.coastbarandgrill.com

CORDAVI, *14 North Market Street*. *577-0090*. Dinner Mon.-Sat. at 5:30pm. On Wednesdays from 9pm to midnight, there is jazz and wine at ½ price. Haute cuisine exquisitely presented. California/Lowcountry creations, including exotic ingredients. Can be expensive. A lengthy walk eastward on Market Street but worth it if you are want to sample some of the most innovative food in town — a haute chicken with mac and cheese of truffled orzo, foie gras in foam, a rare fish from Australia. The ricotta gnocchi, normally served with lamb, is addictive, and the restaurant is happy to grant a request for just that as an appetizer. www.cordavi.com

CRU CAFE, *18 Pinckney Street*. *534-2434*. Lunch Tues.-Sat. 11am.-3pm. Dinner Tues.-Sat., from 5pm. A small local favorite located in a Charleston single house with coveted seating on the piazza. It is possible to eat very well here without straining the budget or overdosing on calories. The menu includes small plates of yummy calamari with Asian slaw, truffled mussels or fresh mozzarella, tomato and sweet peppers, a tasty Chinese chicken salad. Popular main courses include ginger-seared salmon and lemon risotto and seared duck breasts with won tons. The Thai seafood risotto is memorable, with shrimp, mussels and generous chunks of salmon, tuna and grouper. The soups of the day have been unfailingly delicious. If you are in luck, that Lowcountry dessert Huguenot torte will be on the menu. There is nothing pretentious or weird at Cru — it is eclectic comfort food at its best. The ambiance is as comforting as the food. Chef/owner John Zucker studied at the Cordon Bleu in Paris and trained at Wolfgang Puck's Spago restaurant, where the freshest ingredients were a must as they are at Cru Cafe. Critic Catherine Reynolds (*The New York Times*) recommends that you "capitulate to a side of four-cheese macaroni as well as a molten chocolate torte." So do we. Reservations are a must. www.crucafe.com

CYPRESS, *167 East Bay*. *727-0111*. Dinner nightly, from 5:30. Asian/American fusion. Open kitchen, fancy lighting effects and formality downstairs. Upstairs, there is a more casual very elegant bar area. Both levels are expensive. However, you might snack lightly at the bar tables on such appetizers as spring rolls, butter poached lobster with a delicious truffled grits cake, and crab cakes. www.magnolias-blossom-cypress.com

DIANA'S, *155 Meeting Street*. *534-2434*. Daily, 6:30am on. Generous portions. Modest prices. Convenient for a simple breakfast or lunch.

FAST AND FRENCH, *98 Broad Street. 577-9797.* Opens 8am. M-Sat. for breakfast, serving lunch foods all day, dinner after 6pm. Closed Sunday. Casual French served at the counter. Noted for its tasty soups, pate, cheeses. Packed at lunch time and not so fast, but very pleasant Bohemian atmosphere in which to linger. A gem for providing snack foods all day (hot and cold, including vegetarian). Wine is 40% off if you order 3 bottles. Inexpensive. www.fastandfrench.org

FIG, *232 Meeting Street. 805-5900.* Dinner from 5:30pm Mon.-Sat. An instant hit with locals, many of whom are regulars and dine there nearly every night. Paper protects the linen table cloths here, a smart way to keep laundry bills down and prices reasonable. Casual bistro atmosphere, emphasizing fresh ingredients. R.W. Apple of *The New York Times* recently added FIG to his list of favorite restaurants in Charleston, recommending the hanger steak and the seafood stew. Unlike some celebrity chefs, Mike Lata actually does a lot of the cooking. He is one of the first chefs to become obsessive about using organic foods, heirloom vegetables, pastured pork, shrimp fresh off the boat, freshly-ground organic grits and corn meal. Pork is cured in house. The suckling pig is a house specialty. FIG is an acronym for "food is good." It definitely is at FIG. Chef Lata has influenced culinary trends in Charleston regarding vegetables, too. He has transformed neglected vegetables, such as cauliflower, fennel, rapini and beets into culinary treats. Lata came to Charleston in 1997 after working for Bacco in New Orleans and Ciboulette in Atlanta and was at Anson for several years. Specials on the blackboard change daily and are likely to include Florida pompano, local triggerfish, wild salmon, halibut and soft shelled crabs in season. The roast chicken here (free-range, organic and local, of course) served with wild mushrooms and a cream sauce is one of the best in the city. Tuesday is jazz night. If you seek a quiet ambiance, choose another night to dine here or come early. If you are trying to avoid sugar, a selection of artisanal cheeses makes a tasty dessert. The espresso here is exceptional. www.eatatfig.com

The blackboard at FIG is a constantly changing display of the freshest food in town. Chef Mike Lata is a leader of the Slow Food movement in Charleston, has transformed neglected veggies, such as beets and cauliflower, into talked-about gastronomic treats.

FISH, *442 King Street. 722-3474.* Lunch Mon.-Fri. 11:30am-2pm.; dinner at 5:30pm. On Wednesdays, there is ½ price wine until 8:30pm. Friendly ambiance in a restored 1840's single house. The emphasis here is on local seafood, local produce. Good fried oysters, soft-shelled crabs, beautiful presentations. A particularly Southern dish is local wreckfish caught on the "Charleston bump" and served with okra and black-eyed peas. Irresistible corn bread. www.fishrestaurant.net

FIVE LOAVES CAFÉ, *43 Cannon Street. 937-4303.* Open Mon.-Sat. 11am.-9pm. A casual neighborhood favorite in Elliottborough/ Cannonborough, which is just north of Radcliffeborough. Gourmet soups, salads, sandwiches, pasta, vegetarian friendly. Popular with college students; can be noisy. Wine is discounted on Tuesday and Friday.

FLEET LANDING, *186 Concord Street (at the eastern foot of Cumberland Street). 722-8100.* Lunch daily 11am.-4pm. Dinner nightly at 4pm. Brunch Fri., Sat. 11am-3. Seafood (all the Southern favorites plus a few surprises) is served here in a proper seafood atmosphere — right out on a pier overlooking the Cooper River in a restored State Ports Authority building. This is where the fleet sailors landed in Charleston in WWII.

Crispy flounder turns up on many Charleston menus. One of the best places to have it is at Fleet Landing, which has a most dramatic setting right on the river. Here, the flounder has been given an apricot glaze.

The prices are moderate. This family-friendly restaurant seats 250 with 100 seats outside on the pier. Fabulous huge hush puppies, filled with a seafood stew, a crispy flounder with an apricot glaze and fried green tomatoes. One of the tastiest dishes on the menu also happens to be perfect for those seeking low calorie or low fat food. It is a tilapia, which is moist and succulent, seared to a crisp in only a smidge of canola oil, and served with fingerling potatoes, sun-dried tomatoes, and charred asparagus. Can be noisy near the bar or on the southern deck, where there is piped music. The eastern deck at night is romantic, much calmer. www.fleetlanding.net

FULTON FIVE, *5 Fulton Street. 853-5555.* 5:30pm M-Sat. A cosy trattoria, seating only about 40 and serving Northern Italian cuisine. Chef Brett Maynard grew up in South Africa and Atlanta, trained at Bacchanalia in Atlanta and SNOB in Charleston. Good osso bucco, mussels, halibut with beans, wahoo, vitello tonnato, carpaccio of venison, grilled shrimp with prosciutto, ravioli with ricotta in a creamy walnut sauce and tiramisu. A seasonal menu — Chef Maynard is devoted to fresh local and organic produce.

GRILL 225, *225 East Bay.* 266-4222. Lunch daily 11:30am-3. Brunch on Sunday. Dinner nightly at 5:30pm. Steak and seafood in an elegant dining room just off the hotel lobby. www.grill225.com

HANK'S, *10 Hayne Street.* 723-3474. Dinner 5:30pm nightly. Popular seafood brasserie. The city's tastiest seafood is served here in an ancient warehouse. Owner Hank Holliday has recreated one of his fondest childhood memories, resurrecting seafood dishes from a popular restaurant of the 1950s. He has restored the warehouse to look properly old rather than too slick and newly restored. Hank's sets an example for sensitive restoration as well as excellence in seafood. The menu is varied. In addition to traditional Charleston favorites and seafood platters, there is an extensive raw bar and some of the most sophisticated food in Charleston. A seafood tower, which includes the freshest raw and cooked seafood, is a yummy way to begin a feast here and practically a meal in itself. The menu includes she-crab soup and many options for eating simply. Fresh fish,

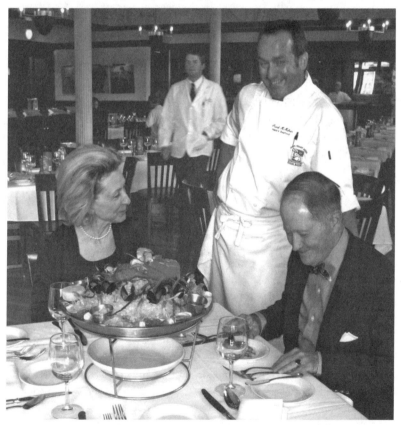

If it is seafood that you crave, Hank's is a must. Chef Frank McMahon trained at Le Bernardin in New York, which is considered the best seafood restaurant in the world. Chef McMahon's talents are especially evident in the specials. The seafood tower here is a sublime way to begin your meal.

grilled or sautéed, can be ordered with a variety of sauces. Wahoo, which can be dry and bland, is moist and flavorful here. Frank McMahon, one of Charleston's most talented chefs, learned to cook seafood to perfection as a sous chef in the renowned Le Bernardin restaurant in New York, which has been called the world's best seafood restaurant. The appetizers and daily specials are where you will find Le Bernardin-quality haute seafood and at much more reasonable prices. Appetizers might include scallops with truffle oil on mashed potatoes, an octopus crostini, a ceviche of scallops, cucumbers and truffle oil, or an addictive salmon tartare.. Truffle oil has become quite ubiquitous on the menus of many restaurants and is often used to excess, overpowering everything else. Chef McMahon knows just how much to add. Triggerfish was listed one night as having a mushroom sauce. What a delicious surprise to find it enhanced just perfectly with truffle oil. Chef McMahon's memorable New American creations are likely to include fish that you don't see on most menus — a cobia ("the New York Strip of the sea," says McMahon), John Dory, or a Costa Rican Corvina embellished with an almost-too-pretty-to-eat bouquet of slivered cucumbers, fennel and pea shoots. Reservations are essential here. www.hanksseafoodrestaurant.com

HIGH COTTON, *199 East Bay. 724-3815.* Dinner nightly at 5:30. Lunch on Sat.11:30am-2:30pm; Sun. brunch 10am-2pm.The bar opens at 4pm. (discounts on house wine M-F) and serves the best hamburgers in town. The main dining room has beautiful ceiling fans, exudes graciousnes and sophistication. The menu offers serious grilled meats, game, fish, good roasted duck, excellent venison, addictive fried oysters, a praline souffle. Beautiful presentations on trendy square dishes. www.mavericksouthernkitchens.com

HOMINY GRILL, *207 Rutledge Avenue. 937-0930.* Breakfast 7:30-11am M-F. Lunch 11:30am-2:30pm M-F. Brunch Sat and Sun 9am-2:30pm. Dinner nightly at 5:30. Lowcountry/New Southern. Chef/owner Robert Stehling uses only the freshest ingredients and like many of Charleston's serious chefs, he maintains an herb garden. Convenient if you're going on the Radcliffeborough walk, but well worth going out of your way. The restaurant is in a restored 19th century barbershop building in the not yet fashionable neighborhood of Cannonborough. Regularly praised by *The New York Times*. Reasonable prices, very popular with locals. Chef Stehling keeps standards high, is in the kitchen for most meals. He is in the forefront of the Slow Food movement in Charleston — "Local is more important than organic," says Stehling. The ambiance at Hominy Grill is low key, and the focus is the food — "It is riskier, but more fun," he says. "Americans are more educated about food now. If you are getting $30 a plate, it is a lot of pressure." Prices at Hominy Grill are modest, with small plates at $9.95 and main courses at $11.50-$16.95. The okra and shrimp beignets on the dinner menu are a quintessential New Southern dish you must not miss. www.hominygrill.com

IL CORTILE DEL RE, *193 King Street. 853-1888.* Dinner Mon-Sat. at 6pm. Traditional Italian trattoria cuisine, including wild boar with beans, lamb loin, mushroom ravioli and a memorable spaghetti ai frutti de mare (seafood pasta) and other Roman and Tuscan specialties. A good cheese selection. Reserve early for the few coveted tables in the romantic courtyard, where you will be transported to Florence. The tiramisu rivals any you will find in the Veneto.

JESTINE'S KITCHEN, *251 Meeting Street. 722-7224.* Open 11am Tues.-Sun. Closes 9:30pm Tues.-Thurs, at 10pm Fri., Sat. and 9pm Sun. Owner Dana Berlin features the recipes of Jestine Matthews, who was the family's cook. Don't miss the fried green tomatoes, meat loaf, collards, flounder. Traditional Lowcountry. Featured on Food TV Network and in *Gourmet Magazine.* Inexpensive.

JIM N NICK'S, *288 King Street. 577-0406.* Opens at 10:30am daily. It is part of a small chain, but you can sate a craving for hickory-smoked pork barbecue or ribs here. Good cheese biscuits. Huge portions. Moderate prices.

JIMMY DENGATE'S, *5 Cumberland Street. 722-1541.* Lunch 11:30am-2:30pm daily. Dinner Wed-Sat. 5:30-10pm. Jimmy Dengate's, an Irish pub that has been in Charleston for fifty years, is packed at lunchtime with locals who work and live nearby. Legendary fried chicken. Sides include collard greens, cornbread, red rice, string beans and Mac pie. Casual and inexpensive.

JOSEPH'S, *129 Meeting Street. 958-8500.* Open Mon-Sat. 8am-11am. Lunch 11:30am-3pm. Sunday 9am-2pm. Chef/owner Joseph Passarini trained at Brennan's in New Orleans, and the influence on the menu is obvious. Beignets, po' boys and bananas Foster as well as delicious sandwiches and light entrees, a perfect salmon with poached eggs on a croissant. Passarini concentrates on breakfast and lunch, two meals which most chefs neglect. This family-run restaurant is very popular with local residents. To get a table for lunch, go either early or late. Do try the crab cakes, the fried oysters with fried green tomatoes (on Sunday), roast beef with roasted peppers and balsamic syrup or mozzarella on a croissant. The spinach salad with fried oysters is addictive. You can watch chef Passarini perform in the open kitchen. Reasonable prices.

KENNEDY'S MARKET AND BAKERY, *60 Calhoun Street. 723-2026.* Open 8am-7pm. Mon.- Sat. Sandwiches, irresistible pastries, soups.

KUDU COFFEE HOUSE, *4 Vanderhorst Street. 863-7186.* M-Wed. 6:30am-7pm. Thurs.-Sat. 6:30am-10pm. Sun. 9am-6pm. Excellent coffees and snacks with a very pleasant outside courtyard. The music is low and gentle, the ambiance soothing. www.kuducoffee.net

LA FOURCHETTE, *432 King Street. 722-6261.* Dinner is served Mon-Sat. from 6pm on or at the bar, from 5pm on. The bistro authenticity here will transport you to the Left Bank in Paris. Owner Perig Goulet, who is from Brittany, greets everyone, keeps the ambiance joyful. Reasonable prices for such bistro classics as steak frites, mussels, blanquette de veau, cassoulet, Coquille St. Jacques et Crevettes, house-made duck pate. The frites, double-fried in duck fat, are the best in Charleston. Good French-press coffee. La Fourchette features fresh local ingredients, free-range organic chickens. Monsieur Goulet tries to make it all "taste exactly like what you have in France." He was pleased when French tourists ate there several times. "There is a need for this kind of traditional, not complicated, food," he says. Charleston residents agree and flocked here even before the rave reviews. Featured in "Undiscovered Charleston" in *Southern Living.*

LANA, *210 Rutledge Avenue. 720-8899.* Lunch 11am-3pm. Dinner 6pm on. Mon.-Sat. Happy Hour 5-7. Chef John Ondo's menu features Mediterranean fare with especially fresh, perfectly cooked seafood. You won't find hard over-cooked shrimp or scallops here. The lunch menu usually includes serious seafood, chicken and meat entrées. The

Lunch does not have to be just soup or a sandwich. Many Charleston restaurant serve seriously good hot meals midday, as well as great salads. Lana is a local favorite for both lunch and dinner. The cuisine is Mediterranean.

Puttanesca pasta is excellent. Wonderful bistro ambiance with booths and banquettes of eggplant plush, ceiling fans. Reasonable prices. A great neighborhood favorite. Unlike chefs of so many restaurants with an Italian-influenced menu, chef Ondo is savvy enough not to serve lemon peel with the espresso. In Italy, espresso never comes with a peel. The wine list is reasonably priced, and half liters are available, from $12. www.lanarestaurant.com

LITTLE THAI TOO, *350 King Street. 723-4990.* Lunch Mon.-Fri. 11:30-3pm. Dinner Mon-Fri. 5-10:30.. Sat-Sun 1-10:30. Happy Hour 5-7 with discounted drinks. Tasty curry puffs, excellent Pad Thai, spring rolls. Convenient for lunch. Reasonable prices.

MAGNOLIAS, *185 East Bay. 577-7771.* Daily from 11:30am. One of the pioneers of fine dining in Charleston, Magnolias opened in 1990 in an 1820's warehouse. "The New Southern dishes by Donald Barickman helped put the city — and the restaurant — on the 'gotta do' map," raved the *Atlanta Journal Constitution.* Since the restaurant does not close between lunch and dinner, you can sample some of the city's finest cuisine whenever you choose and avoid the busiest times. Good crab cakes, seafood over grits, Wadmalaw salads. It is worth abandoning Atkins for the homemade potato chips. If you want a small meal, stay with the creative appetizers, as the restaurant is not used to splitting entrees. Don't miss the egg roll with collard greens, fried chicken livers and pan-seared sea scallops on sweet corn hoe cakes. www.magnolias-blossom-cypress.com

MCCRADY'S, *2 Unity Alley. 577-0025.* Dinner at 5:30 nightly. Contemporary French/American. You can relish the historic vibes here — when George Washington visited Charleston in 1791, he was feted grandly in the same building, called then McCrady's Tavern. If you are wearing black, the hostess replaces your white napkin with a black one to protect you from lint. McCrady's started the national fashion for black napkins and was given credit for doing so by *Gourmet Magazine.* Chef Sean Brock is very keen on sous vide cooking and experimenting with unusual flavor combinations, such as foie gras and carob ice cream. Expensive. www.mccradysrestaurant.com

MERCATO, *102 North Market Street. 722-6393.* Dinner nightly from 5pm. Chef Jacques Larson has returned to Charleston after a stint at Mario Batali's Lupa restaurant in New York and a tour through Italy, where he cooked in a number of top northern Italian restaurants. The butcher paper, which protects the white linen tablecloths, is the Italian way to keep restaurant costs and prices down. Larson is curing pork belly for pancetta in the Mercato kitchen, inspired by the artisanal pork products he encountered in Italy. You will meet this pancetta in the pasta carbonara and other

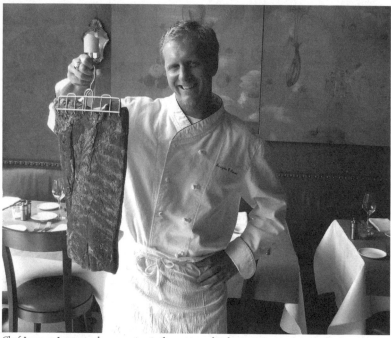

Chef Jacques Larson, whose passion is the cuisine of Italy, is curing pork in the kitchen to rev up his pasta carbonara and other dishes. Artisanal products, such as this house-cured pancetta, bring excellence to many dishes on the Mercato menu.

dishes. Artisanal sausages are being produced in house, just as they are in fine restaurants in Italy. Larson used to be the executive chef at Cintra in Charleston and has a loyal local following. Reservations are essential here. Mercato serves some of the best food in town and at moderate prices. Chef Larson produces magical dishes by his skills in the kitchen rather than trying to shock with weird novelty flavor combinations. Fennel, for instance, looks more like a beautiful flower when he shaves it to go with braised octopus in a red onion and citrus vinaigrette. It is almost too pretty to eat and is reason enough to eat often at Mercato. Do not miss the vitello tonnato with paper-thin veal, the crispy pizzas, an incredible house-made ravioli di Lowcountry (stuffed with collards and shredded ham hocks and served in a tasty broth), a crispy free-range organic chicken that has been grilled under a brick and is served with a peperonata of sweet peppers. The tiramisu surpasses any we had in Venice. This new star on Charleston's culinary scene is clearly in tune with the bistronomie trend, where the focus is on excellence and reasonable prices rather than novelty. There are wines at reasonable prices. Serious foodies know there is a wine glut and that good wine need not cost a fortune. www.mercatocharleston.com.

MERITAGE, *235 East Bay.* *723-8181.* Dinner nightly at 5pm. Multinational tapas, some 50 of them hot and cold. A grazer's heaven. The restaurant attracts a young, sometimes noisy crowd, especially on

Friday night after 9:30pm. Dine early for a quieter, almost somber ambiance, excellent food. Yummy lamb chops, crispy crab wontons, vegetable lasagne. Food is ½ off on Sundays.

MISTRAL, *99 South Market Street. 722-5708.* Daily from 11am on, with Sunday brunch. The location is very convenient, and the cozy bistro ambiance of banquettes and brick walls is enhanced by subdued background music of French vocalists. Mistral opened in Charleston in 1985. Lunch is particularly pleasant. Not a foodie destination, but serving very tasty rainbow trout meuniere, mussels and braised rabbit (the rabbits are delivered from an upstate farm twice a week). Moderate prices.

MODICA, *41A George Street. 723-8868.* Open at 9am. For an ice cream fix, this is the place to go. The gelato is made in house daily. The Moak coffee is imported from Italy and is made in an espresso machine that was hand-crafted in Sicily. Co-owner Vince Liviola claims they make the tastiest coffee outside of Italy. The owners are adherents of the Slow Food movement and use local produce on their delicious paninis. The meats, such as prosciutto, are all imported. The mozzarella is made fresh daily. If you like grilled cheese sandwiches, you will be transported by the four-cheese panini. In addition to all the gelatos, Modica creates a wonderful tartufo and an affogato cioccolato — espresso poured over chocolate gelato and topped with whipped cream. It is worth every calorie.

OAK STEAKHOUSE, *17 Broad Street. 722-4220.* Open daily at 5pm. Popular neighborhood restaurant serving so much more than steak. Yummy

One of the most beautiful restaurants, located in a restored 1850's bank building on Broad Street, is Oak Steakhouse. Chef/owner Brett McKee creates many delicious Italianate options besides steak. A thin crispy bread, made in house, is addictive.

buttermilk fried chicken, pasta Carbonara, fresh seafood such as tempura soft-shelled crabs. Chef/owner Brett McKee is one of the many local chefs who have performed at the James Beard House in New York. We often eat at the bar for a quick reasonable meal. Several locals dine there nearly every night. For a celebration dinner, reserve upstairs. There is a grand formal atmosphere upstairs with blue velvet curtains, gilded mirrors, and golden walls — one of the most beautiful dining rooms in the city. The mid-19th century building with high ceilings has been lovingly restored. The portions are generous, and chef McKee is very gracious about dividing main courses for diners without adding a tacky plating charge. www.oaksteakhouserestaurant.com

PALMETTO CAFE, *205 Meeting Street (inside Charleston Place)*. 722-4900. Breakfast 6:30-11am. Lunch 11:30-3pm. Mon.-Sat. Sun. brunch 8-1:30, lunch until 3. She-crab soup, a wonderful fennel bisque, beautifully composed salads, crab cakes, a calamari trio and sandwiches. This is a good choice if you want a serious meal for lunch. The menu may feature seared red snapper, beef tenderloin, grouper and lamb chops. The fish taco, a cylindrical layer cake of wondrous flavors is not to be missed. Chef Enan Parazo changes the menu seasonally. The inner courtyard is very pleasant. www.charlestonplace.com

PANE E VINO, *17 Warren Street*. 853-5955. Lunch Fri., Sat. 11:30-2pm.; dinner 6-10pm. Northern Italian regional specialties. Nice courtyard for a very pleasant inexpensive lunch or dinner. Wine is reasonably priced and is available by the carafe. No hard liquor is served, as the restaurant is located in the neighborhood of Radcliffeborough and seeks to discourage a noisy heavy-drinking crowd. There are small plates of sun-dried tomatoes and capers, roasted red peppers and hummus plus serious meals of grilled tuna, Roman-style cod, a tasty duck salad with baby arugula and a variety of pastas.

PAVILION ROOFTOP BAR, *225 East Bay*. 266-4218. Daily from 11:30am on. Appetizers and sandwiches with view of the city. www.marketpavilion.com

PEARLZ, *153 East Bay Street*. 577-5755. Daily. 4pm on. Oysters are the star here at this seasonal seafood/oyster bar. This is a good choice if you want a light dinner in a casual setting. www.pearlz.com

PENINSULA GRILL, *112 North Market Street*. 723-0700. Dinner nightly at 5:30pm. Breakfast 7am-10am. There are a few tables outside in the courtyard. New Southern cuisine in the hands of a master chef. Acclaimed as a best new restaurant of 1997 by Esquire's critic John Mariani, chef/partner Robert Carter has attracted a large local following. Reservations are a must here unless you wish to dine after 10pm. Classic sophisticated fare, featuring New Southern dishes. "A near-brilliant resurrection of the despised iceberg" pleased *New York Times* critic William Grimes. Delicious foie gras, venison chops, wild mushroom grits, lamb, Lowcountry Hoppin' John and lobster-basil hush puppies. Wisely, Chef Carter is not into novelty and trendy techniques, such as sous vide. He focuses on perfecting traditional dishes beyond delicious. Do not miss the seven-layer coconut cake, probably the most seductive dessert in town. www.plantersinn.com/peninsula/home.html

RAVAL, *453 King Street. 853-8466.* Mon.-Sat. 5pm. on. An upscale tapas bar. Spanish wines are the focus here. Crispy fried potatoes with a garlic-y aioli (patatas bravas) are a must. There is also tasty grilled shrimp, grilled ham and cheese, artisanal cheeses. Go early if you dislike noise.

SERMET'S, *276 King Street. 853-7775.* Daily 11am-3pm. Dinner is served 5pm. on. Sunday brunch. Mediterranean/American cuisine. Chef/owner Sermet Aslan creates interesting pastas, crab burgers, ginger-y salmon, grilled calamari. Young, casual clientele. Special menu for children. The Sunday brunch features crab cakes benedict. Inexpensive.

SLIGHTLY NORTH OF BROAD (SNOB), *192 East Bay. 723-3424.* Lunch M-F 11:30am-3pm. Dinner nightly, from 5:30pm. From the moment it opened in 1993, the "maverick" southern cuisine here has made SNOB (The name is an in joke, as SOB refers to those who live South of Broad) one of Charleston's most popular restaurants. Chef Frank Lee has continued to pack the restaurant, located in a 19th century warehouse. Lee is a South Carolinian, trained in classical French cooking. He creates dishes described by *The Los Angeles Times* as a "sly toss of Thai and Dixie ideas." Those who like to graze or who are counting calories will be delighted to see a variety of tempting small plates featuring roasted quail and maverick grits with shrimp (this is a must). Fabulous molten chocolate cake with ice cream. The restaurant is packed at lunch. It is wise to go early or late. The express lunch, which might include a delicious braised veal breast, soup or salad and coffee is only $9.95. www.mavericksouthernkitchens.com

STARBUCKS, *239 King Street and 168 Calhoun Street. 805-8007.* 6am-10 M-F. 7am-9pm Sat., Sun. The King Street location has lounging chairs upstairs.

SWEETWATER CAFÉ, *137 Market Street. 723-7121.* Not a foodie destination, but convenient and popular for breakfasts. Funky 50's coffee shop décor.

THOROUGHBRED CLUB, *inside Charleston Place. 722-4900.* Tea from 1-4pm. Tapas from 4pm on. A comfortable place for a snack of crab cakes, cheeses, a salmon mousse by Chef Enan Parazo.

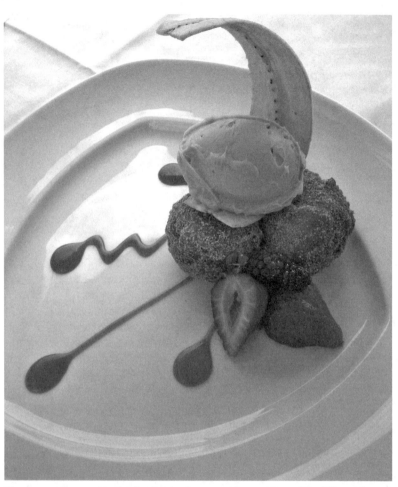

If you want a haute cuisine lunch at bargain prices, it is here at Tristan. The $15 prix fixe includes three courses of food that is almost too beautiful to eat, such as this dessert of banana fritters, which are tossed in cinnamon and sugar and served with a fried plantain, caramel sauce, and avocado ice cream.

TRISTAN, *55 Market Street.* *534-2155.* Lunch Mon.-Sat. 11:30am-2:30pm. Dinner nightly from 5:30pm. Sunday brunch 11am-2:30pm. Happy Hour weeknights 4-7pm. Chef Ciaran Duffy was honored by the James Beard Foundation while he was executive chef at Rainwater in Atlanta. Great prix fixe haute cuisine lunches — $15 for 3 courses, which might include kobe beef, ostrich, belon oysters or pork belly, dishes that are usually offered on the dinner menu as appetizers. There are cozy booths inside and tables on a terrace if you wish to eat al fresco. www.tristandining.com

VICKERY'S, *15 Beaufain Street.* 577-5300. Daily11:30am-1am. Lowcountry/Caribbean. Generous portions. Burgers, bean cakes and such. Popular with students. Very pleasant on the outside terrace.

WENTWORTH GRILL, *68 Wentworth Street. 534-9054.* Daily 7am-2:30pm, Dinner nightly, from 6pm on. Sunday brunch 11:30am-3pm. There are a few seats outside. Good salads, crab cakes.

39 RUE DE JEAN, *39 John Street. 722-8881.* Lunch 11:30am-3pm daily. Dinner daily 5:30-11pm. There is a limited menu all day until 1am. Great French brasserie fare — snails, mussels, frisee Lyonnaise, sole meuniere, braised rabbit, bouillabaisse, steak and frites — as well as some of the best hamburgers in town. The noise level can be high at the popular bar at night. If you seek quiet, ask for a table on the terrace. The ambiance is authentic, enhanced by the typical woven straw bistro chairs and round marble tables. There is a good house wine for $21 a bottle.

82 QUEEN, *82 Queen Street. 723-7591.* Lunch daily, 11:30am-3:30am. Dinner nightly at 5:30pm. Not a foodie destination; however, the courtyard is a pleasant place for lunch.

Charleston is a seafood city. There are more restaurants per capita than in any city in America, and most of them serve seafood. One of the most scrumptious seafood dishes in town is the braised octopus at Mercato. It is embellished with paper-thin shavings of fennel and a red onion and citrus dressing.

Ackerman, James S. *Palladio*, Penguin Books, New York, 1966.

Anderson, Charles *Charleston A Golden Memory*, Wyrick & Co., Charleston, 1992.

Austin, David *Shrub Roses and Climbing Roses*, Antique Collectors' Club, Woodbridge, England, 1992.

Bacon, Mardges *Ernest Flagg Beaux-Arts Architect and Urban Reformer*, MIT Press, Cambridge, Mass, 1986.

Baker, Paul R. *Richard Morris Hunt*, MIT Press, Cambridge, Mass., 1980.

Bivins, John and Thomas Savage "The Miles Brewton House", Antiques Magazine, New York, 1993.

Bowes, Frederick P. *The Culture of Early Charleston*, UNC Press, Chapel Hill, N.C., 1942.

Brandt, Nat *The Congressman Who Got Away With Mureder*, Saracuse Univ. Press, New York 1933.

Briggs, Loutrel *Charleston Gardens*, USC Press, Columbia SC, 1951.

Bryan, John M., Editor Robert Mills, Architect, The American Institute of Architecture Press, Washington, DC, 1989.

Bushman, Richard L. *The Refinement of America*, Vintage Books, New York, 1993.

Cameron, Louisa Pringle *The Private Gardens of Charleston,* Wyrick & Co., Charleston, 1992.

Carolina Art Association *Selections from the Collections*, Carolina Art Assoc., Charleston, 1977.

City of Charleston *King Street Facade Program*, City of Charleston, Charleston, 1980.

City of Charleston Tourism Commission *Information For Guides*, City of Charleston, Charleston, 1985.

Clark, Thomas *S.C. The Grand Tour 1780-1865*, USC Press, Columbia SC, 1973.

Cothran, James R. *Gardens of Historic Charleston*, USC Press, Columbia SC, 1995.

Courier *"Charleston in Olden Times"*, Courier, Charleston, 1868.\

Crevecoeur, J. Hector St. John De *Letters from an American Farmer,* E. P. Dutton & Co., New York, 1782.

Edmunds, Frances "The Adaptive Use of Charleston Buildings", Antiques Magazine, 1970.

Fletcher, Sir Banister *A History of Architecture*, Charles Scribner's & Sons, New York, 1938.

Francis, Dennis Steadman *Architects in Practice in NYC*, Committee for the Preservation of Architectural Records, New York, 1979.

Fraser, Charles *Reminiscences of Charleston*, Garnier & Co., Charleston, 1854.

Fraser, Walter J., Jr. *Charleston! Charleston!*, USC Press, Columbia, 1989.

Gayle, Margot *Cast-Iron Architecture in N.Y.*, Dover Publications, New York, 1974.

Hamlin, Talbot *Architecture Through the Ages*, G.P. Putnam's Sons, New York, 1940.

Hamlin, Talbot *Greek Revival Architecture in America*, Dover Publications, New York, 1944.

Handlin, David P. *American Architecture*, Thames & Hudson, London, 1985.

Hitchcock, Henry Russell *The Pelican History of Art*, Penguin Books, New York, 1958.

Jacoby, Mary Moore *The Churches of Charleston and the Lowcountry*, U.S.C. Press and the Preservation Soc., Columbia SC, 1994.

Kloss, William *Samuel Finley Breeze Morse 1791-1872*, Abrams, New York, 1988.

Kunstler, James Howard *Home From Nowhere*, Atlantic Monthly, , Sept. 1996.

Kuralt, Charles *Charles Kuralt's America*, G.P. Putnam's Sons, New York, 1995.

Landau, Sarah Bradford *Rise of the New York Skyscraper*, Yale University, New Haven, 1996.

Landau, Sarah Bradford *The Architecture of Richard Morris Hunt, chapter 3*, Susan Stein, Ed.U. of Chicago, Chicago, 1986.

Lane, Mills *Architecture of the Old South,* Abbeville Press, New York, 1984.

Lebovitch, William L. *America's City Halls,* The Preservation Press, Washington D. C., 1984.

Leiding, Harriet Kershaw *Charleston Historic and Romantic,* J. B. Lippincot Co., Philadelphia, 1931.

Leland, Jack. *62 Famous Houses of Charleston, South Carolina* Post and Courier, 1970

Longstreth, Richard *Main Street,* The Preservation Press, Washington D. C., 1987.

Mabee, Carleton *The American Leonardo A life of Samuel F. G. Morse,* Knopf, New York, 1943.

Maddex, Diane *All About Old Building,* The Preservation Press, Washington, D. C., 1985.

Marszalek, John *The Diary of Miss Emma Holmes 1861-1866,* Louisiana State Univ. Press, , 1979.

Mazyck, Arthur *Guide to Charleston,* Charleston, 1875

Mazyck, Arthur and Gene Waddell *Charleston in 1883,* Southern Historical Press, Easley SC, 1983.

McAlester, Virginia and Lee *A Field Guide to American Houses,* Alfred A. Knopf, New York, 1984.

Middleton, Margaret Simons *Affra Harleston and Old Charles-Towne in S. C.,* R. L. Bryan Co., Columbia SC, 1971.

Moise, E. Warren "The Confederate States Court for the District of S. C.", *Preservation Progress,* Charleston, 1996.

Nepveux, Ethel S. *George Alfred Trenholm,* Charleston, SC, 1973.

News and Courier "Do You Know Your Charleston?", News and Courier, Charleston, various dates.

O'Brien, Michael and David Moltke-Hansen *Intellectual Life in Charleston,* U. of Tennesses Press, Knoxville, 1986.

Pease, William and Jane *The Web of Progress,* U. of Georgia Press, Athens, 1991.

Pierson, William H. *American Buildings and Their Architects-Vol. 2,* Oxford University Press, New York, 1978.

Pinckney, Elise *Thomas and Elizabeth Lamboll: Early Charleston Gardeners,* The Charleston Museum, Charleston, 1969. and *The Letterbook of Eliza Lucas Pinckney,* USC Press, Columbia, 1997.

Post and Courier *The Battery,* Post and Courier, Charleston, 1977.

Powers, Bernard E., Jr. *Black Charlestonians,* Univ. of Arkansas Press, Fayetteville, 1994.

Prince, William Robert *Prince's Manual of Roses,* William Robert Prince, New York, 1846.

Ravenel, Beatrice St. Julien "The Public Buildings of Charleston", *Antiques Magazine,* , 1970.

Ravenel, Beatrice St. Julien *Architects of Charleston,* USC Press, Columbia, 1945.

Ravenel, Mrs. St. Julien *Charleston The Place and the People,* The Macmillan Co, New York, 1922.

Reed, Henry Hope *Palladio's Architecture and its Influence,* Dover Publications, New York, 1980.

Rhett, Robert Goodwin *Charleston, An Epic of Carolina,* Richmond, 1940.

Rogers, George C. *Charleston in the Age of the Pinckneys,* USC Press, Columbia, 1969.

Rogers, George C. *S.C. Chronology,* USC Press, Columbia, SC, 1973.

Rosen, Robert *A Short History of Charleston,* Peninsula Press, Charleston, 1982.

Roth, Leland M. *A Concise History of American Architecture,* Harper & Row, New York, 1979.

Roth, Leland M. *McKim, Mead and White, Architects,* Harper & Row, New York, 1983.

Ryan, Lee W. *French Travelers in the Southeastern United States l775-1800,* The Principia Press, Bloomington, Indiana, 1939.

S. C. Interstate and West Indian Exposition, *S.C. Interstate and West Indian Exposition,* Charleston, 1901.

Saunders, Boyd and Ann McAden *Alfred Hutty and the Charleston Renaissance*, Sandlapper Publishing, Orangeburg SC, 1990.

Savage, J. Thomas *The Charleston Interior*, Pace Communications, Greensboro, NC, 1995.

SC Department of Archives "Jehu Jones: Free Black Entrepreneur",

SC Dept of Archives and History, Public Programs Document Packet No. l, , .

Severens, Kenneth Charleston, *Antebellum Architecture and Civic Destiny*, U. Of Tennessee Press, Knoxville, Tennessee, 1988.

Severens, Martha R. and Charles L. Wyrick,Jr. *Charles Fraser of Charleston*, Gibbes Art Gallery, Charleston, 1983.

Simons, Albert "Architectural Trends in Charleston", Antiques Magazine, , 1970.

Simons, Albert and Samuel Lapham, Jr. *The Early Architecture of Charleston*, USC Press, Columbia SC, 1927.

Smith, Alice R. Huger and D. E. Huger *The Dwelling Houses of Charleston*, J. B. Lippincott, New York, 1917.

Spence, Dr. E. Lee *Treasures of the Confederate Coast*, Narwhal Press, Charleston, 1995.

Steele, John Carson Hay and James Moore Rhett *Charleston Then and Now*, R. L. Bryan Co., Columbia, SC, 1974.

Stern, Robert *New York 1900*, Rizzoli, New York, 1983.

Stevens, William Oliver *Charleston Historic City of Gardens*, Dodd, Mead & Co., New York, 1939.

Stockton, Robert P. Do *You Know Your Charleston?*, News & Courier, Charleston, SC, Various dates.

Stockton, Robert P. *The Great Shock*, Southern Historical Press, Easley, SC, 1986.

Stoney, Samuel Gaillard *Charleston Azaleas and Old Bricks*, Houghton Mifflin, Boston, 1937.

Stoney, Samuel Gaillard *Houses on the Tours*, Historic Charleston Foundation, Charleston, 1953.

Stoney, Samuel Gaillard *This is Charleston*, The Carolina Art Association, Charleston, 1944.

Summerson, John *The Classical Language of Architecture*, MIT Press, Cambridge, 1963.

The Brooklyn Museum *The American Renaissance*, Pantheon Books, 1979.

Thomas, W. H. J. *Do You Know Your Charleston?*, News & Courier, Charleston, SC, Various dates.

Thorndike, Joseph *Notable American Architects*, American Heritage, New York, 1981.

Tung, Anthony M. *Preserving the World's Great Cities*, Clarkson N. Potter, New York, 1998.

Verner, Elizabeth O'Neill *Mellowed By Time*, Tradd Street Press, Charleston, 1941.

Waddell, Gene *Charleston Architecture*, 1670-1860. Wyrick & Co., Charleston, 2003.

Waddell, Gene "An Architectural History of Kahal Kadosh Beth Elohim", SC Historical Magazine, Charleston, 1997.

Wells, John & Robert Dalton *The S. C. Architects 1885-1935*, New South Archhitectural Press, Richmond, 1992.

Whitelaw, Robert and Alice Levkoff *Charleston Come Hell or High Water*, Levkoff and Whitelaw, Charleston, 1976.

Willensky, Elliot *AIA Guide to New York City*, Harcourt Brace Janovich, New York, 1988.

Withey, Henry *Biographical Dictionary of American Architects*, Hennessey and Ingalls, Los Angeles, 1970.

24 Meeting Street, Charleston, designed in 1822 by the talented Regency architect William Jay

GLOSSARY OF ARCHITECTURAL TERMS
By Professor Robert Russell

ACANTHUS A plant with thick, fleshy, spiky leaves. The source of decorative inspiration for Corinthian and Composite capitals and other decorative moldings.

ANTHEMION Ornamental motif based on the honeysuckle flower and leaves. Common in Greek and Roman — and therefore in Charleston — architecture.

Acanthus leaf, above the column

Anthemion grill over a lintel

BALUSTRADE- A row of short pillars, or balusters, topped by a handrail and serving as an open parapet, as along the edge of a balcony, terrace, roof or staircase.

BASEMENT- The lowest story of a building. Usually distinguished from the upper floors by a different surface treatment. Basements in Charleston are rarely below ground level.

BAY- Any clear subdivision of an architectural space or of a wall, marked off by orders, windows, buttresses, vaults, etc.

BELT COURSE- A broad horizontal band on a building, usually marking the separation between floors. It may project, but does not have to. A belt course is distinguished from a string course by its breath.

BLIND ARCH- An arch attached to a solid wall, almost always as decoration.

BRACKET- A projection from a wall or pier to support an overhanging weight.

BULL'S EYE WINDOW- A circular or oval window.

CARTOUCHE A scroll-shaped ornament with curling edges; any tablet of ornamental form.

COLONNADE- A series or range of columns placed at regular intervals and connected by arches or an entablature.

CORINTHIAN- See ORDERS

Colonnade

CORNICE- The horizontal — and usually projecting — member crowning a wall or other vertical surface. Also, the uppermost member of a classical entablature.

CRENELATION- A notched parapet, consisting of alternating solids and spaces. Usually used to give an impression of military fortification.

CROCKET- A decorative feature common in Gothic architecture, consisting of leaf shapes or leafy balls, projecting at regular intervals from spires, pinnacles, canopies, gables, etc.

CUPOLA- An old-fashioned synonym for a dome. In Charleston a cupola is a small domed structure, on a circular or polygonal base, crowning a roof or turret.

DENTIL- A small rectangular block in a series, projecting like teeth under a cornice or forming a molding.

DOGTOOTH FRIEZE- A horizontal band of bricks set diagonally on their sides so that corners project. Also called a Sawtooth frieze.

DORIC- See ORDERS

DORMER- A window with its own gable set in the slope of a roof.

EGG AND DART COLUMN- A classical molding with egg-shaped ornaments alternating with others in the form of darts or tongues.

ENGAGED COLUMN- A column partly embedded in, or bonded to, a wall or pier.

ENTABLATURE- In classical architecture, the horizontal element resting on the Capitals and, at the gable end of a building, supporting the pediment. It is divided into three parts: the architrave on the bottom, the frieze and the cornice.

FACADE- The face or front of a building.

FAN WINDOW- A semicircular or elliptical window with radiating sash bars like the ribs of a fan, generally placed over a door. Also called a fanlight.

FENESTRATION- An architectural term referring to the number, size and placement of windows in a building.

FLUTING- Incised parallel vertical grooves of a curved section in a column or pilaster shaft.

FOLIATION- Architectural ornament, usually carved, derived from leaf forms.

FRIEZE- In classical architecture, the middle division of the entablature. Also a horizontal decorative band on a building.

GABLE- The triangular upper portion of a wall under the end of a pitched roof.

GAMBREL ROOF- A four-part ridged roof,with the two lower parts pitched more steeply than the two upper parts. Barns often have gambrel roofs.

GIBBS SURROUND- The surround of a doorway or window consisting of alternating large and small blocks. Named after the architect James Gibbs.

'GOTHICK'- An l8th century spelling of 'gothic', referring to a view of Gothic architectural decoration that saw it as essentially exotic and decorative, rather than the more serious and ecclesiastical Gothic of the l9th century. In Charleston 'gothick' decoration generally appears on dependencies.

GREEK WAVE- A horizontal decorative band consisting of a stylized, repeated wave-like pattern.

HIPPED ROOF- A roof with sloped instead of vertical ends. A hipped-roofed building has no gables and four distinct roof planes.

IONIC- See ORDERS

Gibbs Surround

Doric

Greek Ionic

LINTEL- horizontal member, carried on posts or walls, that spans an opening. In classical architecture the entablature is the lintel carried by the posts of columns.

LUNETTE- semicircular or crescent-shaped opening or surface.

MANSARD ROOF- A roof with two slopes, the lower being nearly vertical, and the upper almost flat. Popular in French architecture from the 17th century on, and in late Victorian architecture in the U.S.

MODILLION- The ornamental bracket or console, generally found in a series under the cornice of the Ionic, Corinthian and Composite orders.

MOORISH ARCH- A horseshoe-shaped arch, characteristic of Islamic architecture.

ORDERS- In classical architecture the various systems of proportioned, interdependent parts. Generally an order consists of the base of the column, the column shaft itself, the capital and the entablature. The ancient Greeks had

Roman Ionic

Corinthian

three orders: the Doric, characterized by columns without bases, simple flaring capitals and a frieze made up of alternating triglyphs and metopes; the Ionic, with its characteristic scroll-like or voluted capital and a continuous frieze, and the Corinthian, with its elaborate, bell-shaped capital decorated with acanthus leaf carving. To these three, the Romans added their own version of the Doric, with fluted column shafts and bases, the Tuscan, with unfluted shafts on bases supporting a Doric entablature, and the Composite, which is an amalgamation of the Ionic and Corinthian orders with acanthus-leaf, bell-shaped capitals with Ionic volutes at the corners of the top.

Palladian Window

Portico

PALLADIAN WINDOW- A three-part window, with the side light stopped by flat pieces of entablature and the central light capped by a round arch that springs from the entablature top of the side lights. Originally called a Serlian motif, after the 16th century Italian architect, Sebastiano Serlio, it was popularized by another Italian architect, Andrea Palladio.

PARAPET- A low, solid wall or similar barrier, placed as a protection where there is a sudden drop off, for example at the edge of a bridge or house top.

PEDIMENT- In classical architecture the low triangular space formed under the sloping planes of the roof. Also, a similar form used over doors, windows, porticos, etc., sometimes triangular and sometimes segmental.

PIAZZA- The Charleston term for a porch; generally located on the side of a house, but also sometimes found on the front.

Quoin

PILASTER- A shallow pier or rectangular columns projecting only slightly from a wall surface and treated like a column, with capital, shaft and base.

PORTICO- A porch with a roof supported by a colonnade.

QUOIN- The dressed stones, or, in Charleston, stucco treated as stone, at the corners of buildings, usually laid so that their faces are alternately large and small.

RIB- A projecting band on a ceiling or vault, separating and defining the cells of the vault. In Charleston architecture, ribs are exclusively decorative.

RUSTICATION- Roughly finished masonry, laid with deep joints, to give a rough-hewn, boldly textured effect.

SEGMENTAL ARCH- An arch that forms a curve that is less than half a circle.

STOA- In Greek architecture, a detached, roofed colonnade.

STRING COURSE- A narrow horizontal band on the face of building.

TENEMENT- A building built to be a rental. Originally not a pejorative term.

TRACERY- Decorative stonework set in window openings in Gothic architecture; similar ornamental patterns applied to other surfaces, particularly vaults.

TREFOIL- A Gothic ornamental figure of three lobes or foils.

Index

NATIONALLY IMPORTANT BUILDINGS

Charleston was the first community in the world with the wisdom to protect entire historic neighborhoods, recognizing that the tout ensemble matters more than isolated landmarks. However, within The Old and Historic District, there are individual buildings that were rated as Nationally Important in an inventory, published by the Carolina Art Association in 1944, entitled This is Charleston. This survey was a model for the National Register of Historic Places, established in 1968.

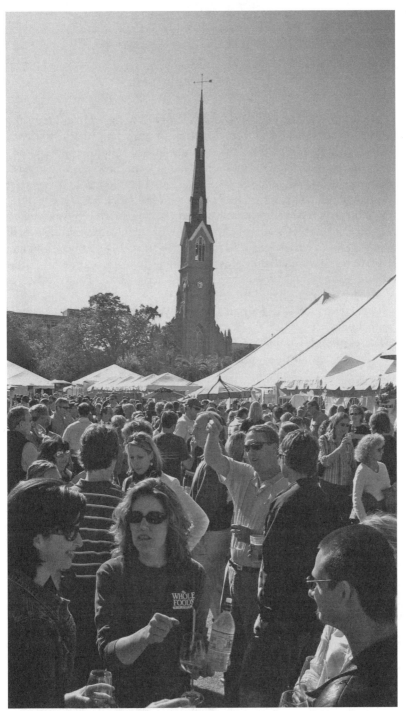

The Charleston Food and Wine Festival is a must for serious foodies. It is held in Marion Square. The 2007 Festival will be held March 1-4 and promises to be even more exciting. For more information, visit www.charlestonfoodandwine.com

Complete Charleston is the only guide to the whole of the Old and Historic District on peninsula Charleston with walking tours of all the neighborhoods and 400 photographs. It also includes tours of nearby plantations, Georgetown, Brookgreen Gardens, Beaufort and Savannah. *In Style* magazine called Complete Charleston "essential." Rachael Ray on the *Food Network* called it, "this cool little guidebook — it has all these self-guided walking tours." As Ray walked about Charleston, she referred to the newly expanded **Restaurant Guide** in Complete Charleston for her meals. *Southern Living* said Complete Charleston was filled with "fascinating anecdotes about the city" and would show you how to walk "everywhere." USA Today called it "excellent...goes beyond the usual spots."

The expanded **Restaurant Guide** is very up-to-the-minute. Many guidebooks are written a year or more before they reach the stores. The Moores publish *Complete Charleston* and are able to have the book on the shelves within three months of being updated.

About the Moores: Margaret Moore was a food

editor at *Glamour Magazine* in New York. She currently reviews restaurants in Charleston and France for the *Charleston Mercury*. She was a founding member of the Historic Districts Council, the Drive to Protect Ladies' Mile and The Committee to Save the City, three groups active in historic preservation in New York City. She studied architecture at Columbia University and researched the 400 buildings of Ladies' Mile (an area around the Flatiron Building in Manhattan), which was designated as an historic district in 1989. Her book, *End of the Road for Ladies' Mile?*, photo-